BATTLES
OF THE
AMERICAN
REVOLUTION

BATTLES
OF THE
AMERICAN
REVOLUTION
CURT JOHNSON

WASHINGTON FIRES THE FIRST SHOT
IN THE BOMBARDMENT OF YORKTOWN

RAND MCNALLY & COMPANY
NEW YORK CHICAGO SAN FRANCISCO

Copyright © Roxby Press Limited 1975
ISBN 0-528-81022-7
Library of Congress Catalog Card Number 75-18795
This edition is published by Rand McNally & Company
by arrangement with Roxby Press Limited
Made by Roxby Press Productions,
98 Clapham Common Northside,
London, SW4 9SG

Editor Michael Leitch
Art director David Pocknell
Designer Rose Verney
Picture research Susan Elwes

Figures and Terrain by Hinchliffe Models Ltd.
from the
collection of Peter Gilder

Printed and bound in Yugoslavia
by
Mladinska Knjiga, Ljubljana

CONTENTS

A
MILITARY
CHRONOLOGY

19 April 1775: Skirmishes at Lexington and Concord, Mass.

19 April 1775–17 March 1776: Siege of Boston.

10 May: Benedict Arnold and Ethan Allen take Fort Ticonderoga from British.

17 June: Battle of Bunker Hill.

28 August 1775–8 June 1776: American attempt on Canada.

30–31 December 1775: American assault on Quebec's Lower Town fails.

27 February 1776: Battle of Moore's Creek Bridge (near Wilmington, N.C.).

8 June: Battle of Trois Rivières.

4 July: Signing of Declaration of Independence.

27 August: Battle of Long Island.

16 September: Battle of Harlem Heights.

11–12 October: Battle of Valcour Island.

28–29 October: Battle of White Plains.

26 December: Battle of Trenton.

3 January 1777: Battle of Princeton.

13 June–8 November: Saratoga Campaign.

7 July: Battle of Hubbardton, Vt.

3–23 August: Siege of Fort Stanwix near Oriskany, N.Y.

6 August: Battle of Oriskany.

16 August: Battle of Bennington.

11 September: Battle of Brandywine Creek near Philadelphia.

19 September: First Battle of Freeman's Farm near Saratoga, N.Y.

4 October: Battle of Germantown.

17 October: Burgoyne surrenders to Gates at Saratoga.

May 1778–February 1779: George Rogers Clark campaigns in the Old North-West.

28 June 1778: Battle of Monmouth Court House.

29 August: Battle of Rhode Island.

June–October 1779: American expedition against the Six Nations.

8 September–9 October 1779: Siege of Savannah.

29 March–12 May 1780: Siege of Charleston.

16 August: Battle of Camden.

7 October: Battle of King's Mountain, S.C.

17 January 1781: Battle of Cowpens.

15 March: Battle of Guilford Court House.

25 April: Battle of Hobkirk's Hill, S.C.

22 May–19 June: Siege of Ninety Six, S.C.

8 September: Battle of Eutaw Springs, S.C.

28 September–19 October: Siege of Yorktown.

3 September 1783: Treaty of Paris signed.

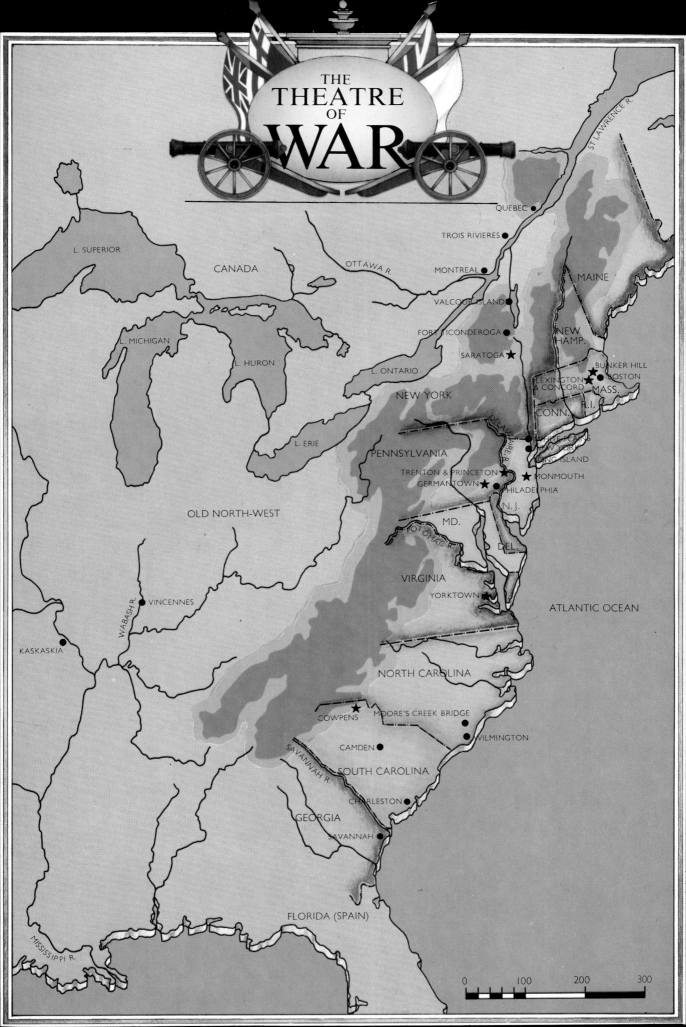

THE
THEATRE
OF
WAR

QUEBEC •

TROIS RIVIERES •

OTTAWA R.

MONTREAL •

CANADA

L. SUPERIOR

VALCOUR ISLAND •

FORT TICONDEROGA •

MAINE

SARATOGA ★

L. MICHIGAN

NEW HAMP.

L. HURON

L. ONTARIO

BUNKER HILL ★
LEXINGTON & CONCORD ★ BOSTON •
MASS.

NEW YORK

R.I.

CONN.

L. ERIE

DELAWARE R.

WHITE PLAINS
NEW YORK
LONG ISLAND

PENNSYLVANIA

TRENTON & PRINCETON ★ MONMOUTH ★
GERMANTOWN ★ PHILADELPHIA

OLD NORTH-WEST

N.J.

POTOMAC R.

MD.

DEL.

VIRGINIA

YORKTOWN ★

ATLANTIC OCEAN

VINCENNES •

WABASH R.

KASKASKIA •

NORTH CAROLINA

COWPENS ★ MOORE'S CREEK BRIDGE •

WILMINGTON •

CAMDEN •

SAVANNAH R.

SOUTH CAROLINA

CHARLESTON •

GEORGIA

SAVANNAH •

FLORIDA (SPAIN)

MISSISSIPPI R.

0   100   200   300

THE CAUSES OF THE WAR

The Peace of Paris (1763) ended the Seven Years' War and established Great Britain as the world's dominant colonial power. By the terms of the treaty France was forced to relinquish her vast colonial interests in North America and India to Britain.

For the American subjects of the King of England the successful resolution of the war brought an end to decades of intermittent warfare with the French in Canada. The defeat of Pontiac's Conspiracy in the same year (Pontiac relied considerably on French aid) substantially removed the Indian threat. These changes radically altered the relationship between the colonists and the mother country. As Josiah Tucker, the English churchman, put it, 'From the moment in which Canada came into the Possession of the English, an End was put to the Sovereignty of the Mother-Country over her Colonies'. In other words, the defeat of the French had made the colonists independent in all but the official sense of the word.

Nevertheless, political bonds cemented by a shared culture are difficult to break. It is conceivable that the Americans might have been content to continue as subjects within an imperial system modelled on that existing before the war. In that system the American colonies had been largely ignored by the London government. The only acts of the English Parliament which directly affected the colonists were the ancient Acts of Trade and Navigation; and these were generally given scant attention. The Americans were such consummate smugglers and the customs officers so lax in the enforcement of the laws that the customs service actually cost more to maintain than it collected in duties.

In 1763, however, the British government found itself preoccupied with a tremendous national debt of about £130 million. At least £70 million of that amount represented the cost of the war effort. Quite apart from the problem of reducing this debt, there was the added expense of garrisoning and administering the greatly expanded empire. Thus, to maintain the pre-war colonial system was by 1763 a manifest impossibility. Tax laws already in existence would have to be vigorously enforced, and new taxes would have to be levied.

The first clash came during the ministry of George Grenville, who became Prime Minister in 1763. Grenville's Sugar Act (1764) imposed new trade duties and attempted to check smuggling by means of an expanded and more alert customs service. The colonists, led by the New England merchants, protested. Later, in 1765, Parliament passed the infamous Stamp Act, a bill which sought to raise revenue by placing a stamp tax on legal documents, newspapers, and other public and private papers. The Stamp Act revenue was to be used specifically to defray just one-third of the annual £300,000 expense of maintaining British garrisons in America.

The imposition of the Stamp Act was met by widespread popular opposition in America. Mobs rioted in New York and Boston, and in Virginia Patrick Henry denounced the bill in the House of Burgesses, asserting that the British government had no right to tax Americans who were not represented in Parliament. The rallying cry of the radicals became, 'No taxation without representation'. In October, representatives from nine colonies met in New York for the Stamp Act Congress and voted to oppose the tax by boycotting English goods. The violence of American opposition and mounting criticism of the government's policy at home led to the repeal of the Stamp Act in 1766; but in the Declaratory Act, Parliament affirmed its right to tax the colonists.

Later, in 1767, the great taxation controversy was reopened when Parliament passed a comprehensive new revenue programme designed by 'Champagne Charley' Townshend, Chancellor of the Exchequer in the new Chatham Ministry. The Townshend Acts imposed new duties on sundry items such as glass, lead, paper, paints and tea. The administration, led by the brilliant Townshend, had argued persuasively that the Americans would accept the new taxes, since they had previously admitted the right of the English Parliament to regulate trade by imposing customs duties, which the Americans referred to as 'external' taxes. According to Townshend, who seriously misread the basis of American opposition to Parliament's taxing power,

BRITISH TROOPS LAND IN BOSTON IN 1768, SENT THERE TO HELP WITH THE ENFORCEMENT OF CUSTOMS DUTIES.

FIVE DIE IN THE 'BOSTON MASSACRE' OF MARCH 1770, SHOT BY A PARTY FROM THE 29TH REGIMENT GUARDING THE CUSTOMS HOUSE.

the objection to the Stamp Act had been based on the fact that it was an 'internal' tax, levied to produce revenue. Though many members of Parliament understandably failed to appreciate the distinction, the acts were passed.

The Townshend programme aroused a storm of opposition in America. The radicals attacked the measures, claiming that they were in fact revenue bills masquerading as bills to regulate trade. The boycott on English goods was revived, and in 1768 troops were sent to Boston.

The focal point of agitation against the Townshend Duties was Boston, where radical merchants like John Hancock led the opposition. The presence of the soldiers—the first garrison Boston had had since the French and Indian War (1754–63) —made the city an armed camp and excited the populace. Inevitably, there were incidents. In March 1770, troops guarding the Customs House

most famous being the Boston Tea Party.

This latest show of resistance outraged the British government, which responded by passing four Coercive Acts meant to punish the colony of Massachusetts. Under these acts, called 'Intolerable Acts' by the Provincials, the port of Boston was closed and Massachusetts was placed under the control of a military governor, General Thomas Gage, who was charged with enforcing the laws, and four additional regiments of infantry were dispatched to Boston.

The British, however, had underestimated the extent of colonial unity. The other colonies responded to Boston's plight by sending aid and convening the First Continental Congress, which adopted the Suffolk Resolves, a statement of principles declaring that Parliament had acted 'without the least color of right or justice' in imposing the Intolerable Acts. Gage reported that

THE FAMOUS TEA RIOT (OR PARTY) IN BOSTON HARBOUR, 1773.

fired on an unruly mob and killed five. This event profoundly disturbed public opinion, and propagandists such as Sam Adam labelled it the 'Boston Massacre'. However, the radicals had trouble convincing the majority of Americans that because of the new taxes their liberties were at stake, and when the English government substantially repealed the Townshend Duties in 1770, the problem faded into relative insignificance.

Nevertheless, the radicals kept up their attack, seeking an issue which would unite the colonies in opposition to England. In 1773, Parliament provided an opportunity by passing the Tea Act, which granted the East India Company a monopoly of the American tea market. The radicals pounced, and the first shipments were met by tea riots, the

'The Disease was believed to have been confined to the Town of Boston . . . But now it's so universal there is no knowing where to apply a Remedy'.

Gage's apprehension and indecision were understandable. The extent of the opposition stunned him. In October 1774, the people of Massachusetts defied the Intolerable Acts and created their own government. One of the first acts of the new government was to put the colony's militia—now called the Provincial Army—on a war footing. At this juncture, with both sides drifting inexorably toward war and the possibility of reconciliation fading, Gage abandoned his outposts along the coast and in the countryside and withdrew to Boston. As the British pulled back, so America advanced—to the threshold of revolution.

9

UNIFORMS

The beginnings of uniform dress can be discerned in the latter half of the 17th century. At first, the line troops of each nation wore clothing almost indistinguishable from civilian costume, but within a very short time military dress began to evolve along lines of its own, and the soldier's garb was soon quite distinctive.

The most obvious difference was in the cut and quality of the uniform coat. This garment was produced in quantity by contract tailors following government patterns. The material used was coarse, cheap woollen broadcloth. The few standard sizes produced by the contract tailors were further refined by regimental tailors so that most men had crudely fitted uniforms. Even so, the army coat, which was meant to last about two years, was inadequate to the exigencies of a campaign. Its raw, unhemmed outer edges quickly frayed, and patches, usually cut from the near-useless coattails, were commonly used to repair deteriorating garments, especially in remote campaigns like those of the Revolution.

Supply was often a problem during the Revolution. The British troops were better off than the Hessians, who went through many mutations of dress because no one seemed to want to assume the responsibility of supplying them. The dismounted Brunswick dragoon Regiment Prinz Ludwig was forced to stumble through the Saratoga campaign in stiff, knee-high jackboots because the firm contracted to supply them with shoes had shipped crates of ladies' shoes instead. Faced with critical deficiencies of supply, many German regiments improvised. The Brunswickers, for example, made new overalls from tent material.

The troops of each European nation could be readily identified by the colour of the uniform coat, which had been standardized for each country by the end of the 17th century. Generally, the uniform colour was based upon the dye most readily available. Thus, the British adopted a coat dyed madder red, and the German states (except Hapsburg Austria) chose indigo blue. The scarlet coats and sashes of British officers were dyed with cochineal, an insect dye.

There was a multitude of rank distinctions, not all of them evident to the modern eye. The most obvious were the epaulette, the sash, and the gorget—a vestigial remnant of the medieval knight's armour. Generally, too, officers wore finer lace than their men. The buttonhole lace of an officer's coat, for example, might be of silver in regiments where the ranker's lace was white cloth. Then, too, a man's rank might be recognized by the cut of his wig (as a rule, rankers did not wear wigs on campaign, their hair being left unpowdered and uncurled). Officers would affect 'the Major' or 'the Brigadier', both popular styles with the privileged classes. while the men wore the 'Temple Tye', a wig with a pigtail.

OFFICER OF GRENADIERS, ROYAL DEUX-PONTS REGIMENT

INFANTRYMAN, 3RD VIRGINIA REGIMENT

OFFICER, 23RD FOOT (ROYAL WELSH FUSILIERS)

LIGHT INFANTRYMAN, QUEEN'S RANGERS

INFANTRYMAN, REGIMENT VON DITTFURTH

In the 18th century about one-fifth of the French army was composed of foreigners, for the most part Swiss, Scots, Irishmen, Germans and Hungarians. These men served in separate foreign regiments and were considered to be among the élite troops of the army. As such they were privileged to wear distinctive uniforms. The Swiss and Irish regiments, for example, wore red coats, while German regiments, like the Royal Deux-Ponts, wore blue coats. French line regiments wore white coats. The colonels of the foreign regiments were in effect proprietors, who ran their regiments as business operations. They were more than usually concerned about the well-being of their men, who were paid on a higher scale than Frenchmen serving in French line regiments.

The men of the Royal Deux-Ponts Regiment were recruited from the Duchy of Deux-Ponts in the Bavarian Palatinate. This regiment was the largest of the seven regiments sent to America by the French. It was commanded by Count Christian des Deux-Ponts. His younger brother, Viscount Guillaume des Deux-Ponts, was second-in-command of the unit and led a picked 400-man assault column against the British advanced Redoubt No. 9 at Yorktown on the evening of 14 October 1781. This assault, which was launched simultaneously with the American attack on Redoubt No. 10, was brilliantly executed. The men selected for the assault column were the grenadier and chasseur (light infantry) companies of two regiments, the Royal Deux-Ponts and Gatinais. Guillaume des Deux-Ponts later rose to the rank of general under Napoleon. He was killed at the Battle of Leipzig in 1813.

The Continentals were the backbone of the American army. Without them, the war could not be carried on systematically. The militia had its uses but, as Washington noted, men 'unaccustomed to the din of arms' and sadly deficient in training and discipline 'might fly from their own shadows'. Only regular troops could reliably sustain an offensive, survive a setback and stand in line of battle. This was again emphasized by Washington when he stated that 'regular troops are alone equal to the exigencies of modern war, as well for defence as offence, and whenever a substitute is attempted it must prove illusory and ruinous'. The Continental establishment, though it was never very large (there were never more than 10,000 American regulars under arms at any given time), provided American commanders with professional troops equal to European regulars. Indeed, after von Steuben's drill was adopted, American regulars were noted for the rapidity with which they carried out the various battlefield evolutions.

The Third Virginia was one of many renowned Continental regiments. This unit, which was originally commanded by Hugh Mercer, joined Washington's army in time to participate in the battle of Harlem Heights, where its three rifle companies, commanded by Major Leitch, bore the brunt of the action. Subsequently, the regiment fought at Trenton, where it led the assault and captured the Rall guns, and at Brandywine and Germantown. At Brandywine the Third Virginia was badly hit covering the withdrawal of Sullivan's wing, and at Germantown, just a few weeks later, it was similarly employed, preventing a British pursuit of Greene's column. In both battles the unit distinguished itself by its tenacious and, at times, unsupported resistance against large sections of the British army. The remarkable career of this unit came to an end when it was surrendered as part of the garrison of Charleston on 12 May 1780.

The 23rd Foot or Royal Welsh Fusiliers is an old, distinguished regiment originally raised for service in the War of the English Succession (1689–97) as Lord Herbert's Welshmen. In 1702 the unit was designated a fusilier regiment and adopted the tall cloth mitre cap of the grenadiers as a badge of its new status. At that time fusiliers were selected men armed with fusils or flintlock muskets rather than the common matchlock musket. Their duties included guarding the army's train of artillery, and they were often called upon to make daring night assaults—tasks where the lighted slow match of the ordinary musketeer would be a hazard. A few years later all British infantry were armed with the flintlock. The fusiliers, however, retained their title and status as élite troops, and, of course, continued to wear the distinctive headdress of grenadiers. By the time of the American Revolution the old cloth mitre had been abandoned in favour of a black bearskin cap, which, for fusiliers, was slightly smaller than that of grenadiers.

During the American War the Royal Welsh Fusiliers participated in a number of battles and suffered very heavy casualties. The regiment played a heroic role at Guilford Court House and was a mainstay of the defence at Yorktown.

Among the many interesting anecdotes arising from the period of the 23rd's American service is the story that Billy, a goat with gilded horns which serves as the regimental mascot, accompanied the grenadier company of the regiment in the assault on Bunker Hill.

The Queen's Rangers, formed by Major Robert Rogers in 1776, was a Loyalist unit that inherited the name and reputation of Rogers's Rangers, the famous bush-fighters of the 'Old French War'. Rogers, who was by nature quarrelsome and something of a scoundrel, resigned the command of the Rangers early in 1777. Under his tutelage the recreated Rangers had not built an enviable reputation. He died in London a short time later, a penniless, embittered drunkard.

Later, under Major Wemyss, and, after Germantown, Major John Graves Simcoe, the Rangers achieved notoriety as the most effective of the Tory partisan corps. Simcoe, who commanded the unit until its internment at Yorktown, ranks with 'Light Horse Harry' Lee and Banastre Tarleton as a commander of legionary troops. He was a bright, innovative, no-nonsense leader who gained a reputation for swift, decisive action.

The Queen's Rangers operated mainly in the no man's land of Westchester County and northern Jersey—the contested territory surrounding British headquarters in New York City. Their mission was to forage for the army and patrol the approaches to the city. On campaign with the army they performed the regular duties of light troops.

The Von Dittfurth Regiment was one of the many Hessian units hired by the British government for service in America during the period 1776–83. Properly speaking, only troops from Hesse-Kassel and Hesse-Hanau were Hessians. Units from these principalities made up nearly two-thirds of the 29,875 German mercenaries sent to America; the rest were from four other small states: Brunswick, Anspach-Bayreuth, Waldeck and Anhalt-Zerbst. However, because the Hessians, especially Kasselers like the men of the Von Dittfurth Regiment, were so numerous, all the German auxiliaries in America were referred to as Hessians.

The Hessians were hired to fight because Britain's army was understrength and overextended in defence of the Empire. Moreover, recruiting was difficult in England, where soldiers were in general ranked with the lower classes of humanity, and, furthermore, the American War was unpopular. In Germany on the other hand, the petty princes were both able and willing to sell their subjects as mercenaries, using the 'blood money' to maintain themselves and their courts in splendid imitations of the French at Versailles. One of them, Landgrave Frederick of Hesse-Kassel, must have had a special need for extra income: 'Fat Freddy', as he was commonly known, was allegedly burdened with the care of one hundred bastard children.

The Hessians, who were excellent soldiers, were nevertheless freely reviled and belittled by their contemporaries. Thomas Jefferson made their hire one of the complaints of the Declaration of Independence. Frederick the Great of Prussia, an unabashed admirer of the young American republic, is said to have been so disgusted with the 'scandalous man traffic' that when Hessians marched through his kingdom, he ordered them to be assessed by the same toll as cattle, because they had been sold 'as one sells cattle to be dragged to the shambles'. This routine disparagement of the Hessians, combined with an inflated estimate of their battlefield prowess and absurd stories of their cruelty with the bayonet, seems to have reserved for them a position of contempt in the folklore of the Revolution. The record, however, tells a different story.

In 1779 an attempt was made to standardize American uniforms. As might be expected, the orders were honoured more in the breach than in the observance, and until 1782 the army presented a rather kaleidoscopic and shabby appearance in the field. Nonetheless, a few regiments did manage to achieve a unity of appearance, although others, notably in the South, achieved something of a new low in military costume by taking the field fully armed and accoutred but clothed with moss hanging from cord at the waist.

CONTINENTAL UNIFORMS (GENERAL ORDERS, 2 OCTOBER 1779)			
STATE	COAT	FACINGS, CUFF	LINING, COAT-TAILS, BUTTONS
MASS, NH, RI, CONN	BLUE	WHITE	WHITE (BUTTONS CLOTH-COVERED OR WHITE METAL, I.E. PEWTER)
NY, NJ	BLUE	BUFF	WHITE
DEL, PA, MD, VA	BLUE	RED	WHITE
GA SC, NC,	BLUE	BLUE	LINING AND COAT-TAILS WHITE, BUTTONS PEWTER, BUTTONHOLES EDGED WITH NARROW WHITE TAPE OR LACE

DETAILS OF MILITARY DRESS

The standardization of military dress grew during the 18th century to embrace not only the army coat but an entire range of secondary garments including shirts, breeches, vests or waistcoats, shoes, caps and wigs, some of which are shown on these pages. Military traditions founded in Britain, France and Germany had become fairly refined, in some cases highly so, by the time of the Revolutionary war. The following contemporary description of a Hessian grenadier conveys something of the degree of stylization that had taken root by the 1770s. The grenadier wore 'a towering brass-fronted cap; moustaches coloured with the same material that coloured his shoes, his hair plastered with tallow and flour, and tightly drawn into a long ap-pendage reaching from the back of the head to his waist; his blue uniform almost covered by the broad belts sustaining his cartouch box, his brass-hilted sword and his bayonet; a yellow waistcoat with flaps, and yellow breeches, were met at the knee by black gaiters; and thus heavily equipped he stood an automaton, and received the command or cane of the officer who inspected him.' The simple and varied turnout of American Provincial units at the beginning of the war makes a vivid contrast with that of the Hessian grenadier. By October 1779, however, as the table on page 13 demonstrates, the Continental army had been set, in theory at least, on the road to much greater uniformity of appearance.

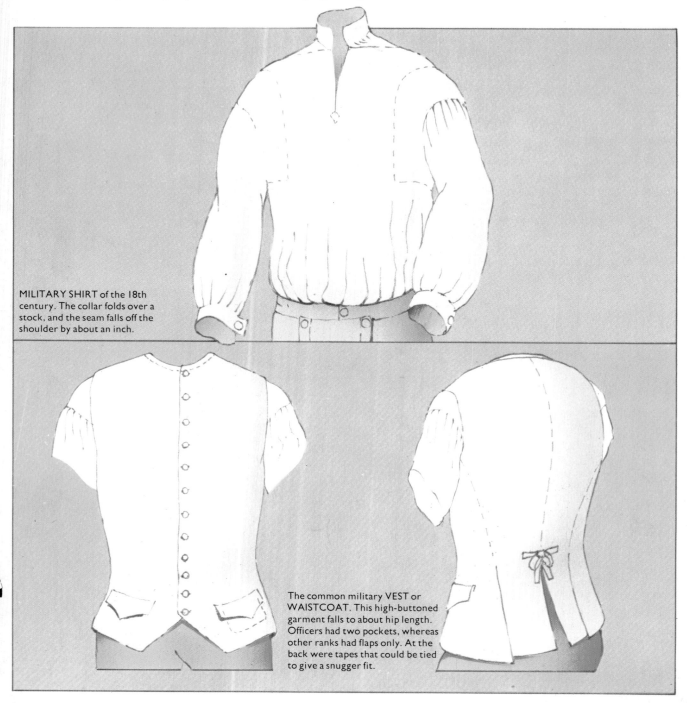

MILITARY SHIRT of the 18th century. The collar folds over a stock, and the seam falls off the shoulder by about an inch.

The common military VEST or WAISTCOAT. This high-buttoned garment falls to about hip length. Officers had two pockets, whereas other ranks had flaps only. At the back were tapes that could be tied to give a snugger fit.

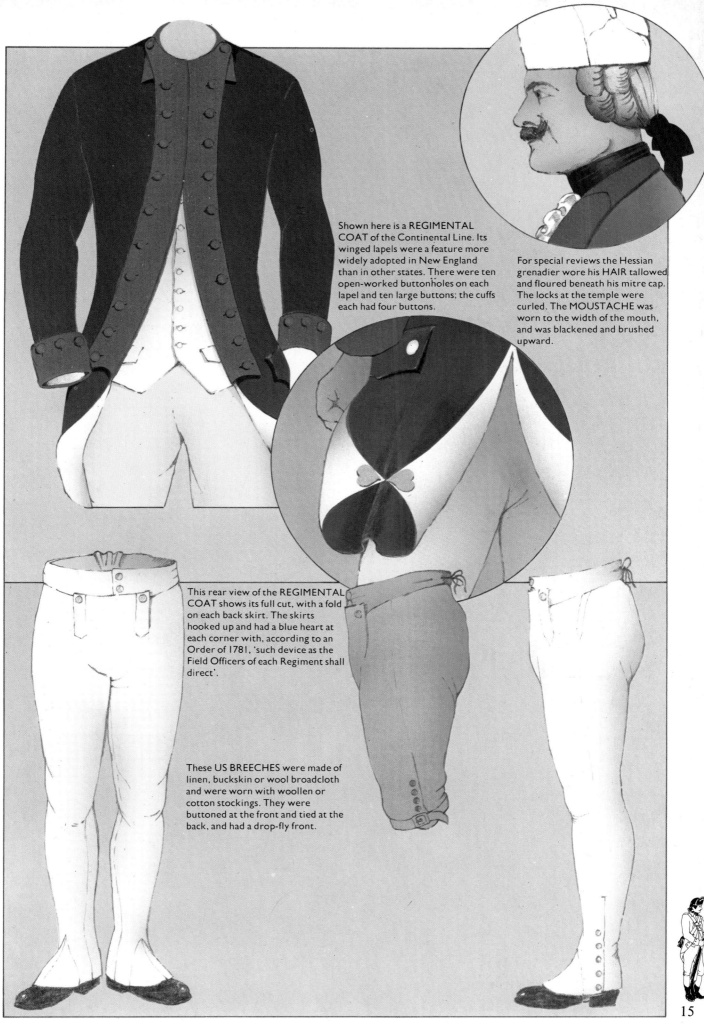

Shown here is a REGIMENTAL COAT of the Continental Line. Its winged lapels were a feature more widely adopted in New England than in other states. There were ten open-worked buttonholes on each lapel and ten large buttons; the cuffs each had four buttons.

For special reviews the Hessian grenadier wore his HAIR tallowed and floured beneath his mitre cap. The locks at the temple were curled. The MOUSTACHE was worn to the width of the mouth, and was blackened and brushed upward.

This rear view of the REGIMENTAL COAT shows its full cut, with a fold on each back skirt. The skirts hooked up and had a blue heart at each corner with, according to an Order of 1781, 'such device as the Field Officers of each Regiment shall direct'.

These US BREECHES were made of linen, buckskin or wool broadcloth and were worn with woollen or cotton stockings. They were buttoned at the front and tied at the back, and had a drop-fly front.

DRESS AND KIT OF THE AMERICAN RIFLEMAN

The American rifleman was regarded by most contemporary military men as the best light infantryman in the world. His battlefield instincts had been finely honed by years of service fighting Indians on the frontier in obscure quarrels such as Lord Dunmore's War. Contrary to popular mythology, he did not win the Revolutionary War, but his contribution was inestimable. On occasion riflemen won battles, as at King's Mountain; often, they contributed to victories won by regulars, as at Saratoga. But, regardless of the role they played when acting in concert with regular troops, they were always 'the mortal aversion of the red coat'.

THE HAT, which was called a 'round hat' or 'castor', was made of black felt. It had a 2–3-inch brim decorated in a variety of ways: with white or black tape or lace around the brim, a cockade, a buck's tail or, perhaps, a sprig of evergreen. The hat is shown sometimes with the brim turned up on the right or left side and also with the brim 'slouched' down all around.

THE POWDERHORN AND HUNTING BAG were characteristic of the rifleman. They were used because the rifle was loaded with a greased or wet patched ball which was not easily incorporated in a cartridge. Also, it was the practice of the rifleman to vary the powder charge with the range. This was a custom of the frontiersmen who regarded powder as a precious commodity. A small SHEATH KNIFE was frequently attached to the shoulder strap of the bag. This was used to cut the patch off level with the muzzle of the piece after the ball was 'started' in the barrel. A strip of linen patching material was sometimes pinned to the bag strap, and the pin doubled as a vent pick. The bag contained common items like a bullet mould, extra flints and patching material, and tow for cleaning the barrel. There were no pockets in the rifleman's dress.

THE RIFLE. At the time of the Revolution the Pennsylvania Rifle was still comparatively short. Its overall stubbiness and lack of elaborate ornamentation belies its ancestry. It is still similar in many respects to the German sporting rifle. This was a 'transition piece' linking the European Jaeger rifle to the slender Kentuckys of the 'Golden Age' of the American rifle in the early 19th century.

THE SHIRT was made of linen and was worn under the hunting shirt. In cold weather jackets were also worn under hunting shirts.

THE HUNTING SHIRT or rifle frock of the rifleman was a fairly common item of dress among American soldiers of the period. This was a loose-fitting coat, open down the front and lapped over and secured with a belt. It was made of linen, linsey-woolsey or 'tow cloth'. The material was left natural or dyed a variety of colours. The shirt had one or two capes and was frequently decorated with fringing of the same or contrasting colour.

THE 'SCALPING KNIFE' was a useful weapon with a long blade. It was crudely made by frontier blacksmiths. The rifleman carried no bayonet, so the 'scalping knife' was often used as a defensive weapon.

THE BELT was either a tie belt in leather of the contemporary Indian fashion or a leather belt with a buckle. Belts were sometimes black. When the belt was tied, it was always tied behind.

THE TOMAHAWK or small axe was carried in the belt or suspended from a case slung on a shoulder strap.

TROUSERS were made of buckskin or the same material as the hunting shirt. They were tailored with a drop fly in front, just as sailors' bell-bottoms are still made, and were sometimes ornamented with fringing to match the hunting shirt. Some riflemen copied Indian dress, wearing a breech clout and leggings of buckskin.
MOCASSINS of deerskin were commonly worn, though shoes are also mentioned. The most common form of mocassin was made of a single piece of hide with a gathered seam along the top. In winter the mocassins were stuffed with leaves or animal hair for warmth.

THE ARTILLERY AND ITS ROLE IN THE REVOLUTION

In the Revolution the infantry had nothing like the artillery support that it had already come to expect in Europe. There were two principal reasons for this: firstly, guns were in short supply in the war; secondly, gunners, as much as cavalrymen, depended on the horse for their motive power. And not only were horses in short supply, their use was hampered in America by broken terrain and thick woods, some of which were virtually impenetrable except on foot. Thus the cavalry, while a successful assault arm in Europe, had to be mainly restricted

HENRY KNOX AMERICAN CHIEF OF ARTILLERY

to the role of mounted infantry—scouting, foraging, and harassing the enemy. Shock actions were rare, and the classic cavalry pursuit of broken troops more uncommon still. Similarly, the movement of heavy ordnance off the few good roads (rivers were the highways of colonial America) presented extreme difficulties on many occasions. Even so, resourceful artillerists, notably the English General

William Phillips and Henry Knox, the American Chief of Artillery, managed time and again to drag their guns to decisive positions.

General Henry Knox (1750–1806) was the dominant figure in the Continental artillery effort. Of portly build, and by profession a bookseller in Boston, Knox was still a young man when Washington placed him in charge of the army's artillery. At that time he was one of a mere handful of Americans who understood the science of gunnery; under his tuition, however, the Continental artillery made rapid progress. After Monmouth, where Knox's guns smothered Clinton's army with a sustained crossfire, Washington claimed: 'No artillery could have been better served than ours'.

The guns used during the Revolutionary War were little different from their cumbersome ancestors of the 15th century. They were heavy, unwieldy weapons which threw a variety of missiles to a maximum effective range equivalent to that of the modern rifle. Precise gunnery, except at close range, was impossible.

Grapeshot, tarred lead balls held together by a net, and case or cannister, small shot packed into a tin can, were used defensively. The net or can broke apart on discharge and the balls scattered with a lethal shotgun effect up to a range of 300 yards. Round shot (ball) and crude shells—hollow spheres filled with bursting powder—were used at longer ranges.

The gunners of the Revolutionary War were not innovators, but tactically they used their guns to better effect than their predecessors. Whenever possible, the few guns available were massed to improve the effect of their fire. This was done with success at Trenton, Monmouth, and Saratoga, and marked a departure from the established 18th-century practice of scattering guns along the line to add weight to the infantryman's musketry. In this sense, therefore, the evolution of artillery to the independent, decisive role it played under Napoleon was advanced by the American experience.

17

SMALL ARMS

The average infantryman of the Revolution carried a smoothbore muzzle-loading musket of dubious efficiency and, sometimes, indeterminate manufacture. Without exception, these weapons were ponderous and inaccurate. The best of them was the French .69-calibre Charleville, named after its principal place of manufacture. This musket had first been produced in 1717 and had gone through successive mutations, new models being introduced in 1754, 1763 and 1777.

The first Charlevilles used in the Continental Army arrived in 1777. These were obsolete but serviceable M1763s shipped to the United States under the auspices of Caron de Beaumarchais' dummy French-Spanish export firm, known as Hortalez et Cie. Eventually, the M1763 Charleville came to predominate among the weapons of the Continental soldier, while French troops in America were generally armed with the 1777 model. The advantages of the Charleville over the standard British musket were that it was lighter and sturdier. Its distinguishing feature was its bright, banded barrel.

The .75-calibre 'Brown Bess' had, in one or another of its variations, been the standard British firelock since the time of Queen Anne. It was an especially graceful musket, with a pin-fixed barrel and brass fittings or 'furniture'.

The Brown Bess derived its name from the bright reddish-brown colour of its barrel and metal fittings. This colouring of the gun metal was produced chemically by a special browning solution.

FRENCH INFANTRY OF THE 1760'S AT DRILL PRACTICE

Several Brown Bess patterns were in use in America, including the venerable Long Land Model and the new Shorter Land Model. Light infantry, artillerymen and officers carried lighter, short-barrelled versions called fusils. The Brown Bess was the principal weapon of the Provincial and Continental armies until 1778. Most of these were older models left over from the French and Indian Wars. Provincial gunsmiths produced excellent copies of the Brown Bess called Committee of Safety muskets, but since few of these exist today, their manufacture may have been limited.

The Brown Bess remained in service with British regiments through the Napoleonic Wars and was still in general use in the Crimea, though by then it had been fitted with a percussion lock and was gradually being replaced by the new Minié rifle.

The German mercenaries arrived in America with a variety of weapons, mostly of indifferent Dutch or Prussian manufacture. These muskets were brass mounted and heavier than either the Charleville or Brown Bess. As the war progressed, the Hessians were resupplied with British weapons.

Rifles were used extensively in the war—perhaps to a greater extent than in any previous conflict. The American rifle, known commonly as the Pennsylvania rifle, was the singular creation of highly skilled German gunsmiths, most of whom pursued their trade in Pennsylvania and Maryland. It was a long, slender weapon which, in the hands of a marksman, could be fired accurately to ranges of 300 yards. This was an unheard-of range at the time, and the rifle understandably caused great concern and fear among the British, especially among the officers, since the 'epaulette men' were the most favoured targets.

The Ferguson rifle was the brain child of a Scots barrister and soldier, Major Patrick Ferguson of the 71st Highlanders. Impressed by exaggerated reports of the effectiveness of American riflemen in the early engagements of the Revolution, Major Ferguson set about designing 'various improvements upon firearms whereby they are loaded with more ease, safety, and expedition, fire with more certainty, and possess other advantages'. In the course of his work Ferguson invented three breech-loading mechanisms, and, in experimental tests conducted at Woolwich in June 1776, proved the effectiveness of his weapon under the most adverse weather conditions —heavy rain and high winds.

Following these experiments, Ferguson was permitted to form a corps of rifleman armed with a carbine incorporating his screw-plug breech action and sighted for 100–300 yards. This corps saw service at Brandywine, where Ferguson was wounded. During his absence, Sir William Howe, who seems to have been both 'father' and overseer of the British light infantry, disbanded the corps. Howe, it seems, was upset at not having been consulted over the formation of the corps. The rifles were stored.

Ferguson later led a force of Tories in the Southern Colonies and was defeated and killed at King's Mountain on 9 October 1780. His rifle died with him. When the British army finally adopted a rifle, it was the muzzle-loading Baker with an effective range of 150 yards. The Baker was first employed in the Napoleonic Wars.

The German jaeger corps were armed with stubby European huntsman's rifles, individually purchased and owned by the men of the various units. These were excellent weapons, though not capable of matching the Pennsylvania rifle in range.

18

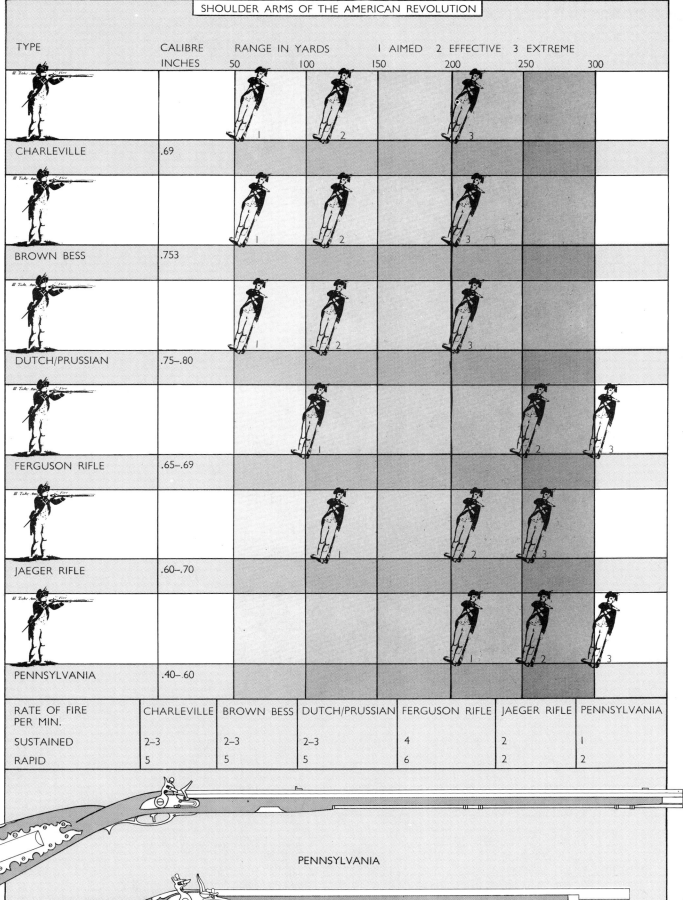

SHOULDER ARMS OF THE AMERICAN REVOLUTION

TYPE	CALIBRE INCHES	RANGE IN YARDS — 1 AIMED 2 EFFECTIVE 3 EXTREME					
		50	100	150	200	250	300
CHARLEVILLE	.69	1	2		3		
BROWN BESS	.753	1	2		3		
DUTCH/PRUSSIAN	.75–.80	1	2		3		
FERGUSON RIFLE	.65–.69		1			2	3
JAEGER RIFLE	.60–.70		1		2	3	
PENNSYLVANIA	.40–.60				1	2	3

RATE OF FIRE PER MIN.	CHARLEVILLE	BROWN BESS	DUTCH/PRUSSIAN	FERGUSON RIFLE	JAEGER RIFLE	PENNSYLVANIA
SUSTAINED	2–3	2–3	2–3	4	2	1
RAPID	5	5	5	6	2	2

PENNSYLVANIA

BROWN BESS

THE INFANTRY: ORGANIZATION AND TACTICS

The Revolutionary War was an infantryman's war. Nearly all the big set-piece battles, like Germantown or Monmouth, were decided by foot soldiers fighting stubbornly in linear formations. Only rarely did cavalry play a substantial role. Heavy cavalry, such as the cuirassiers of European armies, was not used at all. The artillery, a battlefield arm which had been on the ascendant in Europe, was rarely seen in America in anything resembling what the generals considered the proper proportion of guns to men. The use of both arms, cavalry and artillery, was limited by the nature of the terrain, and the widespread use of cavalry was further prohibited by a scarcity of proper mounts.

Eighteenth-century battles were won by manoeuvre, discipline and fire-power. Until 1778, when von Steuben's drill was introduced and adopted by the American army, the British, with their well-drilled and more experienced regiments, had a distinct battlefield advantage. Few Continental regiments could match any British unit in drill, manoeuvre or battlefield discipline. American units were clumsy and slow at manoeuvring, at handling a tactical offensive, and they could not stand up to a determined bayonet charge. Understandably, American commanders sought to place their men in strong defensive positions when giving battle. British commanders (Sir William Howe was a notable exception) generally abandoned any advantage they might have gained from their superiority at manoeuvring and, instead, threw their men directly at the American lines.

Von Steuben's drill, taught rigorously by the Prussian drillmaster in the miserable camp at Valley Forge during the early months of 1778, remedied certain battlefield failings of the American army. At Monmouth the Continentals stood their ground and contended on terms of equality with the best troops of England. Moreover, von Steuben had streamlined the Manual Exercise, and American troops were now quicker at manoeuvring than their English counterparts.

Additionally, because the Americans had always used aimed fire (the English troops levelled their muskets), they were just that much more effective in battle.

By 1780 the British were imitating the American drill—forming in lines two ranks deep (instead of the three ranks common in European armies) and delivering deadly, aimed platoon volleys in rapid succession. The 'thin red line', which Wellington used to perfection against Napoleon and his marshals, had been born.

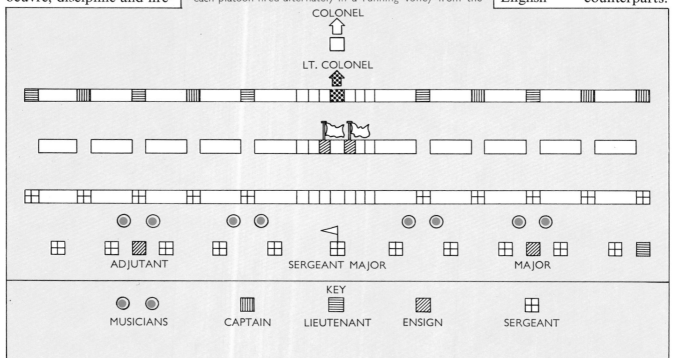

INFANTRY TACTICS

Here, and on page 22, some basic tactical formations and manoeuvres are discussed and demonstrated. In the first diagram, the five centre companies of a typical eight-company British regiment are shown as they appeared in line of battle. Note that the five companies are subdivided into ten platoons for firing (the lines closed toward the front when the regiment was to fire).

British regiments usually fired platoon volleys, that is, each platoon fired alternately in a running volley from the flanks of the regiment toward the centre. This allowed the junior officers to control the firing of their men and produced continual disruption in the enemy's line of battle. Other modes of alternate fire were by companies or by grand divisions (two companies made up a grand division).

Note also that many of the officers stood behind the third rank. They did so, as General James Wolfe wrote, 'to complete the files, to keep the men in their duty, and to supply the places of the officers or the sergeants that may be killed or dangerously wounded'.

COLONEL

LT. COLONEL

ADJUTANT SERGEANT MAJOR MAJOR

KEY

| MUSICIANS | CAPTAIN | LIEUTENANT | ENSIGN | SERGEANT |

During the Revolution the paper strength of a British infantry regiment was 477 men. On campaign, however, disease, desertion and battle casualties often reduced regiments to a fighting strength of about 300 men.

Each British regiment consisted of ten 38-man companies, eight of which were battalion or line companies, the other two being the light infantry and grenadier companies. Each regiment was organized as follows:

```
REGIMENTAL STAFF
Colonel
Lieutenant-Colonel
Chaplain
Adjutant
Surgeon
Surgeon's mate
COMPANY STAFF
Captain
2 Lieutenants
2 Sergeants
3 Corporals
1 Drummer
2 Fifers (in grenadier company only)
THE COMPANIES
10 × 38-man companies.
```

In addition, and not included in this system of organization, there was a Major, Ensigns, supernumerary officers and a Sergeant-Major.

An estimated 50,000 Loyalists or Tories served alongside their British cousins in Provincial corps: the great majority of these were infantry regiments, though some were legions or mixed units of cavalry and infantry. The organization of Provincial infantry units was not uniform. Generally, attempts were made to follow British practice, but most units seem to have been organized according to the whims of their commanders.

American infantry may be divided into three general categories—Continental Line, State Line and Militia. The Continental Line was the national standing army of the United States, consisting mostly of veteran regulars who had either enlisted or been 'draughted' into numbered units bearing the name of the state of origin. The Continental Army was created when Congress 'adopted' the Provincial Army besieging Boston in June 1775. Later, a light infantry corps of 'expert riflemen' was added, and the states were assigned quotas for furnishing troops.

Congress's first attempt to organize the new Continental infantry (in November 1775) was intended to impose some uniformity on the multitude of variously organized regiments then with Washington. Each regiment was to number 728 men in eight line companies and one headquarters company. This system seems to have died moments after its birth. Thus, when he joined the Continental Army at Valley Forge in February 1778, the Prussian Baron von Steuben observed that 'the words company, regiment, brigade, and division were so vague that they did not convey any idea upon which to form a calculation, either of a particular corps or of the army in general. They were so unequal in their numbers that it would have been impossible to execute any maneuver.'

Appalled by what he saw at Valley Forge, von Steuben set about re-modelling the Continental Army. One of the myriad fruits of his labours was the 27 May 1778 reorganization of the Continental infantry. Under this permanent organization each regiment was constituted as follows:

```
REGIMENTAL STAFF
Colonel
Lieutenant-Colonel
Major
Paymaster
Adjutant
Quartermaster
Surgeon
Surgeon's Mate
Sergeant-Major
Quartermaster Sergeant
COMPANY STAFF
Captain*
Lieutenant
Ensign
3 Sergeants
3 Corporals
MUSIC
Drum-Major
Fife-Major
18 Drummers and Fifers
THE COMPANIES
477 private soldiers in eight line and one light
company.
```

*There were six Captains. The Colonel, Lieutenant-Colonel and Major commanded a company each, but a Captain-Lieutenant was carried on the rolls to command the Colonel's Company. This expedient allowed the Colonel to direct the regiment as a whole in battle.

In 1781 the strength of Continental regiments was increased to 699 all ranks.

The State Lines were the regular troops of the various states, enlisted for service within the state but often directed to serve with Continentals for the duration of a campaign. The quality of state troops varied, but some, like the Virginia State Line, were the equal of Continental regulars.

REPRESENTATIVE ORGANIZATION OF STATE LINE REGIMENTS IN 1775			
STATE	COMPANIES	MEN PER COMPANY	TOTAL
Massachusetts	10	59	590
New Hampshire	10	59	590
Connecticut	10	70/100	700/1000
Rhode Island	8–10	60	480/600
Hampshire Grants (Vermont)	7	70	500
New York	10	75	750
North Carolina	10	50	500

Each state also had a militia organization composed of regiments formed locally in towns, counties and districts. These units were not intended for regular service but, rather, for home defence. This usually meant responding to local problems such as enemy raids or foraging expeditions. Nonetheless, the militia was often an important element in the plans of Continental generals, and militia contingents commonly constituted a large proportion of any Continental force, despite their unreliability and tendency to wander in and out of camp at will.

The upper diagram illustrates how a British regiment
formed into line of battle from a column of companies
(after the 1764 Manual Exercise). The whole manoeuvre
could be completed in a matter of minutes. Before the
introduction of von Steuben's drill in 1778 very few
American units could perform this manoeuvre.
Finally, an American regiment is seen going from a
double file route march into a line of battle two ranks deep.
This mode of march, known as marching 'Indian file',
took up much more road space than the usual four-abreast
marching column of other armies. When the regiment
went into line of battle, the men, who were unused to
sophisticated manoeuvres, simply ran after the lead platoon
and their officers, who pushed, kicked and cajoled them
into line at the proper place. The whole manoeuvre took
much longer than a textbook evolution and caused a
great deal of confusion in the ranks.

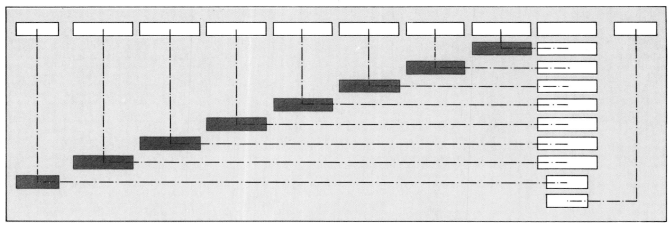

Grenadier companies had been formed in the line regiments of European armies in the late 17th century. The first British grenadier companies were raised in 1677. From the beginning the practice had been to brigade or mass the grenadier companies of several line battalions into special provisional battalions comparable to modern élite assault troops. Once constituted, provisional battalions of grenadiers were often used to form either the infantry reserve of an army or shock units for especially dangerous assault missions.

Similarly, the light infantry companies of line battalions were often brigaded to form provisional battalions of light troops. When the army was on campaign or in quarters, massed light infantry was often assigned to outpost duty or employed in gathering forage. When used in conjunction with what cavalry was available (or alone, as at Lexington and Concord) the light infantry screened and protected the column of march. In a set-piece battle these troops could be formed into assault battalions like the provisional battalions of grenadiers. In short, the light infantryman was the most versatile soldier in the Revolutionary War, and not

unnaturally was much prized by commanders.

The practice of brigading the flank companies of line regiments was generally successful, but there were some hazards connected with it. Some critics have contended that to 'skim' the flank companies from the line reduced overall effectiveness, but this was not a notable failing in the Revolution. The major problem was that the creation of provisional battalions played havoc with the command structure and increased the possibility of error among officers and men who all too often did not know one another before the battalion was assembled.

The answer to this problem, obviously enough, was the formation of entire regiments and corps of élite troops. Indeed, there was ample precedent for this in the British Army. Gage's Light Infantry (the 80th Foot) and the Royal American Regiment (the 60th Foot) were raised during the French and Indian War (1754–63) as standing light infantry regiments. But the precedent did not take hold until the Napoleonic Wars, when the French, by using whole divisions of light infantry, forced their opponents to adopt similar tactics and organization.

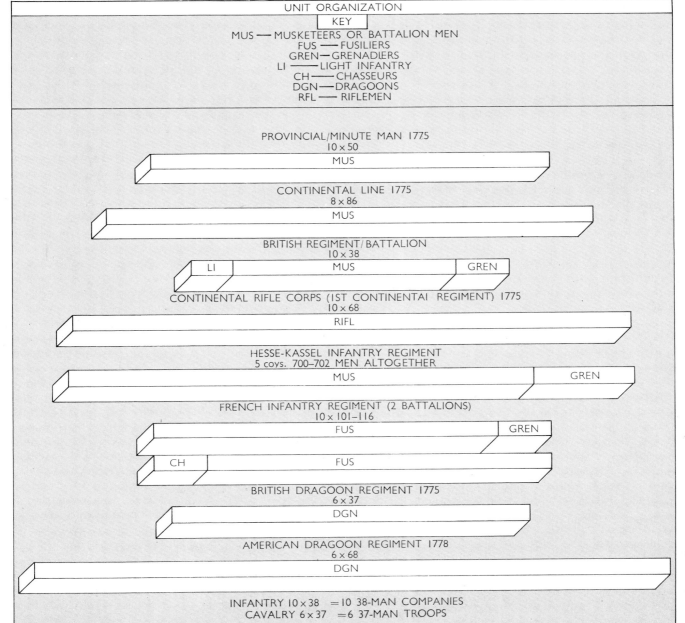

UNIT ORGANIZATION

KEY

MUS — MUSKETEERS OR BATTALION MEN
FUS —— FUSILIERS
GREN — GRENADIERS
LI ———— LIGHT INFANTRY
CH —— CHASSEURS
DGN — DRAGOONS
RFL —— RIFLEMEN

PROVINCIAL/MINUTE MAN 1775
10 × 50
MUS

CONTINENTAL LINE 1775
8 × 86
MUS

BRITISH REGIMENT/BATTALION
10 × 38
LI | MUS | GREN

CONTINENTAL RIFLE CORPS (1ST CONTINENTAL REGIMENT) 1775
10 × 68
RIFL

HESSE-KASSEL INFANTRY REGIMENT
5 coys. 700–702 MEN ALTOGETHER
MUS | GREN

FRENCH INFANTRY REGIMENT (2 BATTALIONS)
10 × 101–116
FUS | GREN
CH | FUS

BRITISH DRAGOON REGIMENT 1775
6 × 37
DGN

AMERICAN DRAGOON REGIMENT 1778
6 × 68
DGN

INFANTRY 10 × 38 = 10 38-MAN COMPANIES
CAVALRY 6 × 37 = 6 37-MAN TROOPS

THE COLOURS
OF THE REVOLUTION

Two square or rectangular flags, called colours, were carried by most infantry regiments during the Revolutionary War. One colour symbolized national or royal authority. This was known as the national flag by the United States army, the King's Colour by British forces, the Colonel's colour among the French, and the *Liebfahne* in the German regiments. The second colour (German regiments had several, usually one for each line company) was the symbol of the regiment. Generally, this was known as the regimental colour, but the French called it the *drapeau d'ordonnance*.

Cavalry and dragoons carried smaller, square flags called standards. Grenadiers, light infantry and artillery had no colours, but artillerymen valued their guns in much the same way that an infantryman regarded his regiment's colours. To lose a colour in battle would, of course, disgrace a unit.

These flags were entrusted to ensigns, young officers who had a variety of duties but whose chief responsibility in battle was the care and preservation of the regiment's colours. In British regiments the ensigns were escorted by picked men from each battalion company, led by a colour sergeant.

Quite apart from their symbolic value, flags were also functional. They were used to rally troops pressed back or forced to withdraw in battle, and were sometimes used to transmit orders. Colonel William Barrell of the 4th King's Own Regiment, for example, in 1707 devised a method of drilling a regiment in battle by beating drums and flourishing colours. This would be particularly valuable when verbal orders were drowned out by the din of battle. More importantly, general officers could recognize units manoeuvring at a distance by their colours.

American flags were never standardized or subject to regulation and presented the greatest variety. From the beginning, colonels, like the proprietary colonels of old, were allowed 'to fix upon any such [colour] as they could procure and might deem proper'. The result was a mind-boggling confusion of colours. Some, like the famous Bedford Flag, carried by the Bedford Company of Minutemen at Concord, had been made in England long before the war, but most were local products. The beautiful standard of Pulaski's Legion, for example, was made by the Moravian Single Sisters of Bethlehem, Pennsylvania, and the crude Eutaw Flag, carried by William Washington's dragoons at Cowpens and Eutaw Springs, was cut from crimson drapery and embroidered with a horseshoe-shaped wreath by one of Washington's admirers, Miss Jane Elliot of Charleston.

The first flag of the rebellious united colonies was the Great Union Flag. This flag was first displayed at the Siege of Boston on 1 January 1776, when it was hoisted to the top of a 76-foot mast on Prospect Hill in Cambridge. This flag was the old British Meteor Flag—the red ensign of the Royal Navy—with its red field charged in the canton with the combined crosses of the British Union but modified by the addition of six horizontal white stripes to the field. The new field thus had 13 horizontal stripes—seven red and six white—representing the 13 united colonies. The British model was used because at the time few American leaders were thinking of independence. Later, on 14 June 1777, Congress passed a Flag Resolution, modifying this design even further and creating the Stars and Stripes. The striped field of the Grand Union Flag was retained, but a new canton with thirteen white stars on a blue ground was substituted for the British crosses. The Stars and Stripes, however, was meant to be a naval ensign, not a military flag, and was probably never carried on a Revolutionary War battlefield.

Nevertheless, two flags closely resembling the Stars and Stripes were, apparently, used during the Revolution. One variant, said to have been the colour of the 3rd Maryland Regiment at Cowpens, measured three feet by five feet and had a canton with twelve stars arranged in a circle and one star in the centre of the circle. The other, a North Carolina militia colour carried at Guilford Court House, had seven blue and six red stripes and a long white canton with 13 blue eight-pointed stars. Claims made for other stars and stripe-type flags are less certain. The Fort Stanwix Flag, for example, created from a white shirt, a red petticoat and a blue officer's coat, was most probably the Grand Union Flag.

Each British line regiment carried a pair of colours. The Sovereign's Colour was the first Union Flag (in use 1606–1801), which was adopted during the reign of King James I. This flag, the familiar 'Union Jack', combined the cross of St. George and the saltire of St Andrew, representing England and Scotland respectively. The regimental colour had a field in the facing colour of the regiment with a small canton containing the Union crosses. Generally, too, the name or number of the regiment was centred on the field within a wreath.

French and German colours were more ancient in appearance. The Colonel's colour of French regiments was white within a plain white cross showing in a stitched outline. Regimental colours followed the same pattern, with a white cross dividing the flag into quarters of various colours long associated with each regiment. German colours included elements of heraldry identified with each state or principality furnishing troops. Some of these were the Lion of Hesse, the red Eagle of Anspach-Bayreuth, and the white Horse of Brunswick. These colours were also noteworthy in that they usually included the cypher (stylized initials) of the reigning monarch, for example 'F. L.' for Frederick, Landgraf of Hesse, and 'M. Z. B.' for the Markgraf zu Brandenburg.

A large number of German colours was captured during the war, but few have been preserved. What we know of these colours we have learned chiefly from contemporary paintings. One of the ten Anspach colours taken at Yorktown is on display at the Smithsonian Institute in Washington, DC. The colours of the Waldeck Regiment were taken by the Spanish at Pensacola, Florida, but these have disappeared and there is no known record of their appearance.

THREE AMERICAN FLAGS WITH CHARACTERISTIC MOTTOES:
ON THE LEFT IS THE NAVY ENSIGN OF
SOUTH CAROLINA, THE STATE IN WHICH THE POPULAR
RATTLESNAKE DEVICE ORIGINATED. IN THE CENTRE IS THE
TAUNTON FLAG, WITH THE MOTTO 'LIBERTY'.
AND ON THE RIGHT IS THE FLAG OF THE CULPEPPER
MINUTE MEN, A VIRGINIA MILITIA UNIT FORMED IN 1775
UNDER PATRICK HENRY, COLONEL OF THE FIRST
REGIMENT AND 'COMMANDER OF ALL THE FORCES RAISED AND
TO BE RAISED FOR THE DEFENSE OF THE COLONY'.
HENRY'S MEN ALSO DISPLAYED THE WORDS 'LIBERTY OR
DEATH', INSCRIBED IN LARGE WHITE LETTERS,
ON THE FRONT OF THEIR GREEN HUNTING SHIRTS.

THE HERALDRY
OF WAR

The selection of colours modelled below reflects the concern of the principal belligerents (British and American) to inspire their serving men either to win greater glory for their monarch, George III, or to be forever rid of him. Many of the American flags, with their bold mottoes proclaiming defiance and liberty, strike a fresh note that is itself at variance with the more staid, Establishment style displayed by their opponents. (Some specialist terms are of necessity used in the captions on these pages: the 'canton' or 'first canton' is the small, usually square division occupying the upper left corner of the flag, nearest the staff; the 'field' is the basic colour of a flag; for further explanation of terms, see page 24.)

King's Colour and regimental flag of the 63rd Foot (Manchester Regiment), which fought at Bunker Hill and later served in the New York campaign of 1776 and under Cornwallis in Georgia and the Carolinas. Typically, the number of the regiment (LXIII) is contained within the wreath on the field of the regimental colour.

King's Colour and regimental flag of the 27th Foot (Inniskillings), which took part in the New York campaign of 1776 and later fought in the Battles of Brandywine and Germantown. Note the absence in the Union Flag (King's Colour) of the red diagonal cross representing Ireland; this was added in 1801.

King's Colour and regimental flag of the 4th King's Own (Lancaster) Regiment. The King's cypher badge appears on the colours and the regimental number is indicated (IV) in the first canton of the regimental flag. The 4th King's Own fought at Lexington, Bunker Hill, New York and Germantown.

The flag of Butler's Rangers, a Loyalist corps raised in New York in 1777. The Rangers wore dark green coats faced with red, hence the red field of the flag (which traditionally followed the facing colour). At the end of the war, members of Butler's Rangers withdrew to Canada and founded a settlement at Niagara.

King's Colour and regimental flag of the 42nd Royal Highland Regiment (Black Watch). This famous regiment arrived in New York in July 1776 and fought at Long Island, New York, in the New Jersey campaigns of 1776-77, and at Monmouth and Charleston. In 1778 the Black Watch was sent to Florida.

King's Colour and regimental flag of the 17th Foot (Royal Leicestershires). The regiment arrived in Boston in December 1775 and fought in the New York and New Jersey campaigns of 1776-77 and at Brandywine, Germantown and Monmouth. At Stony Point, in 1779, the 17th was captured and lost its colours; later exchanged, it again suffered defeat at Yorktown.

Next to the plain lettering on the flag of Sherburne's Continental Regiment is the bright, intricate design that distinguished the 3rd New York Regiment. This flag was made in the period 1778-79 and features a modified version of the State Arms; it was carried at the Siege of Yorktown, by which time the 3rd had been consolidated with the 2nd New York Regiment.

These minuteman colours are representative of the many used by Patriot militia companies throughout the colonies. The rattlesnake, either coiled or straight, was widely adopted, as were the mottoes 'Liberty' and 'Don't Tread On Me' According to Benson J. Lossing, author of *The Pictorial Fieldbook of the Revolution*, the latter motto could be made to sound 'supplicating' or 'menacing', depending on whether the spoken emphasis was placed on the first word or the last.

Another unit to adopt the 'Liberty' motto was the 2nd Canadian (Congress's Own), a regiment raised in 1776 and consisting mainly of men from Pennsylvania and Canada. The figures are shown wearing the early version of the uniform, when facings were white; in 1779 these were changed to red.

One of the two colours of the 2nd New Hampshire Regiment of the Continental Line, raised in May 1775. This colour, known as the 'Blue Flag' (the other, shown below, was called the 'Buff Flag'), features a red shield in the centre and the motto 'The Glory Not The Prey'. In the first canton two red and gold crosses are superimposed. Both regimental colours were taken by the British during the Saratoga campaign.

The Buff Flag of the 2nd New Hampshire Regiment, at the centre of which is a golden sun bearing the motto 'We Are One'; from it 13 lines radiate towards an encircling band of 13 linked rings, each containing the name of a colony. In the first canton two white crosses separate alternating triangles of red and blue.

Flag of the 1st Pennsylvania (Continental) Line Regiment. Its green field has a central red patch, whose size is here exaggerated to show the two figures of a hunter and a lion. The motto 'Domari Nolo' means 'I Refuse To Be Subjugated'.

Regimental colour of the 1st Maryland which was raised early in 1776 and served with Washington's Continental army in the New York region. This flag was carried at the Battle of White Plains. The design features a crossed sword and pole bearing a red 'liberty cap'.

This Rhode Island flag displays elements of the colours of the 1st and 2nd Regiments, which were consolidated in 1778. The word 'Hope' is associated with the 1st Rhode Islanders, the blue scroll and its lettering 'R. Island Reg't' with the 2nd; the white field is common to both. The flags of the individual regiments both had a blue canton containing 13 white stars.

Regimental colour of the Queen's Rangers, a Loyalist corps raised in 1776 by Robert Rogers. The flag has a blue field with a red shield (here enlarged) that carries the words 'Queen's Rangers 1st Amern.' in gold. Above the shield is a gold and crimson crown, and flanking it are two sprigs of greenery.

Flag of the 1st New York Regiment. Like that of the 3rd New York shown in the upper row, the design is based on the State Arms. Under Colonel Alexander McDougall, the 1st fought at Trenton, Saratoga and Yorktown.

THE ACTION AT NORTH BRIDGE, OUTSIDE CONCORD: CAPTAIN LAURIE REDCOATS ARE CONFRONTED BY COLONEL BARRETT'S ADVANCING MILITIAMEN.

19 April 1775
The long-threatened war flares on
Lexington Green when British light infantrymen
press too close to the local militia: orders are
ignored, shots are fired. Later in the day the British column
narrowly avoids annihilation at the hands of a gathering
swarm of angry and determined Provincials. From then on
General Gage, the British military governor, finds
himself and his troops under siege in Boston.

LEXINGTON & CONCORD

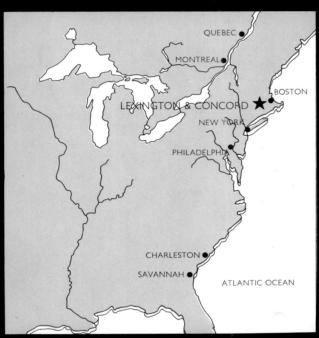

THE BACKGROUND TO THE BATTLES

By the end of 1774 there were two Massachusetts. One was ruled, with an increasing lack of conviction, by the British military governor, General Thomas Gage; the other had been set up in October by militant Americans in defiance of the Coercive Acts. The latter, introduced as a punitive measure following the tea riots, had been roundly condemned not only by the people of Massachusetts but also by the First Continental Congress, which spoke for the Patriot cause throughout the American colonies.

As further proof of their determination to succeed, the Americans in Massachusetts had wasted no time in preparing their Provincial Army, as it was called, for action. From the official British point of view, the situation was fast deteriorating, and General Gage wrote to London from his headquarters in Boston in search of guidance. Tentatively, he proposed a suspension of the Coercive Acts. However, when King George III heard this idea he called it the 'most absurd that can be suggested' and declared that 'We must either master them [the Americans] or totally leave them to themselves and treat them as Aliens'.

For his part, Gage had little wish to bring on hostilities; rather, if his notions had been followed, the army would have been withdrawn and a naval blockade imposed. In the face of such regal bombast, though, there was little he could do but try to prevent the Provincials from growing strong enough to make an attempt on Boston. In response to London, Gage planned to seize the Patriots' powder and cannon, which, incredibly, were stored in makeshift magazines within easy march of Boston. The Patriots were nonetheless aware of the vulnerability of their supplies, and created an elaborate alarm system, labouring all that winter to perfect it. Gage countered by marching his men about the countryside in harmless excursions partly intended, it seems, to convince the Provincials that the sight of British regiments marching from Boston was no cause for alarm. Both sides relied extensively on spies and informers to keep abreast of each other's actions.

The war of nerves continued until February 1775, when Gage ordered Colonel Alexander Leslie and his 64th Regiment to seize the Patriot ordnance depot at Salem. Leslie's men descended on Salem by sea and marched into the town unopposed, but alert Patriots raised a drawbridge and prevented them from reaching their objective. As militia gathered nearby, Leslie parleyed with the town's leaders and agreed to leave if the drawbridge were lowered and his men allowed to march across and then return, thereby symbolically complying with his orders. This was done, and Leslie returned to Boston empty-handed.

The outcome of Leslie's almost vaudevillian raid on Salem did not discourage Gage. He soon learned from spies that the Patriots were stockpiling a considerable amount of military stores at Concord and Worcester, and he determined that these must be seized or destroyed.

During March and early April Gage dispatched several parties of disguised officers into the countryside to scout the roads and obtain more information. From the reports of these officers Gage decided that Concord was the more practicable objective, since it was closer—just 18 miles from Boston —and because the road to the town offered few opportunities for ambush. To throw the Patriots off balance, more diversionary marches into the countryside were planned and executed.

Finally, on 18 April, Gage issued orders for the march. Lieutenant-Colonel Francis Smith, the ponderous but capable commander of the 10th Regiment, was selected to lead the column, which was to consist of 21 companies of grenadiers and light infantry—the army's best troops. Major Pitcairn of the Marines was assigned to the column as second-in-command. Smith's orders, put simply, were to march to Concord, destroy the Patriots' military stores (especially their cannon) and return to Boston. There were probably also orders to arrest the Patriot leaders John Hancock and Samuel Adams, who were known to be in the vicinity. The troops were to leave Boston by ships' boats, crossing Back Bay to Cambridge, where they would begin their march.

Colonel Smith's march was the worst-kept secret in Boston that night. Despite elaborate security precautions, the preparations for the march were evident to anyone who cared to look in the direction of Boston Common. The Patriots knew the British were marching, and they knew the objective of the march. The only remaining question was, which route would the column take? If the troops marched by way of Boston Neck, they could be easily stopped by the destruction of the Great Bridge over the Charles River. On the other hand, if they went 'by sea', that is, across Back Bay, only the militia would stand between them and their objective. In order that Patriots across the bay in Cambridge should have advance warning Paul Revere, a Boston silversmith, arranged for signal lamps to be hung in the steeple of Old North Church. The signal was to be, 'One if by land, two if by sea'.

The British troops began to embark from the foot of the Common at about 10.30 pm. Almost immediately, the signal, two lamps, was hung in the church steeple. Revere and another man, William Dawes, then set off on horseback by different routes to spread the alarm. The two met again at Lexington, where they informed the men of Captain John Parker's minuteman company that the British were approaching. Then they set off for Concord, but were shortly captured by a British patrol led by Major Edward Mitchell. Dawes managed to escape, but Revere was held. Some while later, as Mitchell's patrol neared Lexington with its bag of prisoners (four others had been taken before Revere), some militiamen exercising on the Green fired a volley, and Major Mitchell, thoroughly frightened by the sound of shots fired in the dead of night, released his prisoners and galloped off. Revere made his way into Lexington, where he met Hancock and Adams and, with some difficulty, persuaded them to escape to a place out of harm's way.

It was then about 2 am. Back in Cambridge, Colonel Smith's men had finished their crossing of Back Bay and were ready to begin their fateful march for Concord.

THE COMMANDERS

Unlike every other significant encounter in the war, the minutemen and militia who fought at Lexington and Concord were not directed by an army commander. Instead, they were commanded by local men who had been elected to positions of responsibility within the various companies and regiments of the Provincial Army. Few of these Patriot commanders managed to exercise effective control over more than a handful of men at any point in the day's action. Colonel Barrett and Major Buttrick at Concord and, later in the day, General William Heath at Menotomy and Cambridge were the principal exceptions to this rule.

Despite the fact that the Provincial Army lacked an effective command structure, it did manage to respond to the British 'surprise' march with con-

Lieutenant-General Thomas Gage (1721–87), the British Commander-in-chief in America and governor of the Province of Massachusetts, was a handsome, genial man, but an indifferent leader.

Gage entered the army in 1741, rising to high rank through purchase and preferment despite a poor record. He was prominent in the two major British disasters of the French and Indian War (1754–63)—Braddock's defeat and Abercromby's ill-fated attack on Montcalm's lines at Fort Ticonderoga. In 1759 he bungled his first independent command so badly that Sir Jeffery Amherst, who succeeded Abercromby as Commander-in-chief in America, swore that he 'may not have such an opportunity [again] as long as he lives'. But Gage somehow managed to weather the storm of criticism,

RIGHT: 'THEY USED TO DRILL EVERY EVENING': AN AMERICAN MILITIA COMPANY, DEPICTED BY HOWARD PYLE.

ABOVE: GENERAL GAGE.

certed action. This response was not spontaneous (as many latterday historians have seen it). It was, in fact, part of a carefully orchestrated plan of operations worked out in advance by Patriot leaders and rehearsed on numerous occasions when the British garrison in Boston made forays into the countryside. At the very heart of this plan were the minutemen—ordinary militiamen directed to hold themselves in readiness to march at a minute's warning. To their presence was joined a finely organized system for sounding the alarm: this had been developed originally as a means of responding to Indian raids on the frontier.

and when Amherst was removed from command in 1763, he was appointed Commander-in-chief.

Once installed in his new post, he put down Pontiac's Uprising (1763) and came to be much admired by the colonists despite the fact that he advocated a hard line toward American extremists. During a brief sojourn in London (1773–74) he urged the King to crush the incipient rebellion in Massachusetts with a military force large enough to compel obedience to the Coercive Acts. But he, like the King and the administration, misjudged the determination and unity of the American rebels and blundered into war.

THE BATTLE

Between three and four o'clock on the morning of 19 April Smith's column passed Alewife Brook, which marked the boundary line between the towns of Menotomy and Cambridge. Here the column left the tidal plain and entered a more picturesque rural district. A bright full moon guided the march of the regulars along the Lexington Road; ahead, on rising ground, was Menotomy, a pleasant market town. To the right and left of the road were the plain, tidy farms of the Provincials.

Before Colonel Smith's column reached Menotomy, at about 4 am, Smith detached Major Pitcairn and six companies of light infantry to push ahead of the main column and secure the two bridges at Concord. Pitcairn, in turn, detailed a platoon to scout ahead of his 'flying column'.

this active little party overtook Lieutenant William Grant of the Royal Artillery, who was proceeding to Concord in a small cart loaded with hammers, spikes and other tools to be used in rendering the Patriot artillery useless. Grant reported hearing gunshots in the night and said he thought the countryside might be alarmed. Shortly, Major Mitchell's patrol rode up from Lexington. Mitchell confirmed Grant's observation and added that he and his men 'had galloped for their lives'.

Lieutenant Sutherland, who had taken command of the scouting party, rode ahead to investigate these reports. At Foot of the Rocks, about a mile from Menotomy, he stopped a man in a carriage who reported that 600 men had gathered at Lexington, just a few miles ahead, to oppose the British

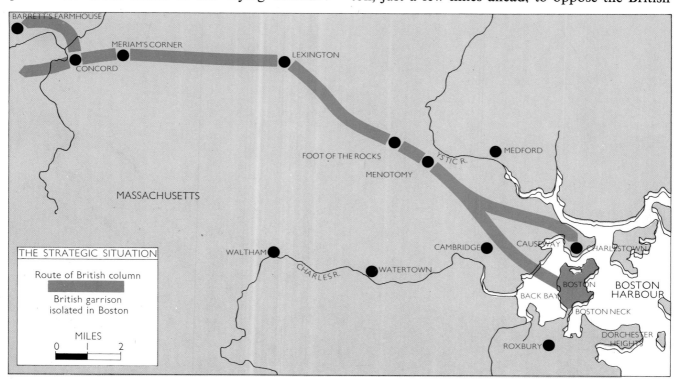

THE STRATEGIC SITUATION

Route of British column

British garrison isolated in Boston

MILES
0   1   2

BARRETT'S FARMHOUSE · MERIAM'S CORNER · CONCORD · LEXINGTON · FOOT OF THE ROCKS · MENOTOMY · MYSTIC R. · MEDFORD · MASSACHUSETTS · WALTHAM · CHARLES R. · WATERTOWN · CAMBRIDGE · CAUSEWAY · CHARLESTOWN · BOSTON · BACK BAY · BOSTON HARBOUR · BOSTON NECK · DORCHESTER HEIGHTS · ROXBURY

Accompanying this platoon were three adventurous young officers who, strictly, had no business to be with a scouting party—Lieutenant William Sutherland of the 38th Foot, Lieutenant Adair of the Marines and Surgeon's Mate Sims of the 43rd Regiment. Sutherland should not have been with Smith's column at all; he had, it seems, 'tagged along', looking for excitement.

As Pitcairn's light infantry set off at the double from the main column, Smith was still confident that his night march had not been discovered by the Patriots. But, before he had a chance to congratulate himself, alarm bells began to peel in Menotomy and the hollow pop-pop of signal guns could be heard from the surrounding hills. Smith was enough of a realist to know that now, with the countryside alarmed and his men still hours from their objective, he might need some help. Immediately, he sent a dispatch rider back to Boston with a request for reinforcements.

In the meantime, in the centre of Menotomy, Pitcairn's scouts arrested two American farmers on suspicion of being alarm riders. Moments later,

march. Thoroughly alarmed, Sutherland rode to the top of a hill near the road to gain a better view of the country toward Lexington. There he saw (or thought he saw) 'a vast number of the country militia going over the hill with their arms to Lexington'. Minutes later, he reported his findings to Pitcairn (who had already heard Mitchell's somewhat wild account).

Pitcairn was no light infantry officer, but he had heard enough to know that his fast-moving column might run into trouble at any moment, so he put out flanking parties and reinforced Lieutenant Sutherland's vanguard. Shortly, in the grey light before dawn, there were more shots from the fields near the road. Sutherland and his scouts saw the shots fired but ignored them. The young Lieutenant had, by that time, become thoroughly acquainted with the alarm guns of the American minutemen.

A few hundred yards ahead of Major Pitcairn's advancing column, Captain Parker's Lexington militia company mustered on the village green. Parker and his men were well aware of the Redcoats' approach, and they had already decided among

themselves 'not to be discovered, nor meddle, or make with said regular troops unless they should insult or molest us'. Sergeant William Munroe, Parker's orderly, counted 77 men on the Green—too few to offer resistance to Pitcairn's column. Nonetheless, as Pitcairn's leading companies jogged into view, Parker gave a momentous order: 'Stand your ground. Don't fire unless fired upon. But if they mean to have a war let it begin here!'

At that point, Pitcairn judiciously ordered a halt, the confusion and terror of the rapid night march having produced no small amount of disorder in the ranks. Just ahead, the sound of a drum beating 'To Arms!' could be heard. Pitcairn ordered his men to prime and load and then gave the command to proceed into Lexington.

What happened next has never been satisfactorily explained. The question of who fired first has consistently intrigued historians, and for a time, about

infantry filed around the meeting-house at the fork in the road and formed directly in front of the Lexington company. Parker ordered his men 'to disperse and not to fire'; but still the British came 'rushing furiously on'. Most of the company obeyed Parker's order, but others, like Jonas Parker, Captain Parker's cousin, stood their ground. Jonas Parker had resolved 'never to run from before British troops'; and now, true to his word, he stood facing the onslaught.

The next few moments were utterly confused. Major Pitcairn, who had temporarily dropped back as the British moved round the meeting-house, rode on to the Green and yelled, 'Disperse, you rebels!' Then, turning to the light infantry, he cautioned: 'Soldiers, don't fire, keep your ranks, form and surround them'. In the excitement of the moment, Pitcairn's orders, the best under the circumstances, were ignored. The light infantry con-

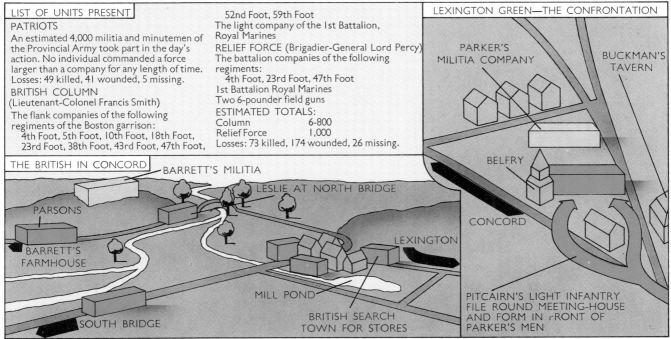

LIST OF UNITS PRESENT

PATRIOTS
An estimated 4,000 militia and minutemen of the Provincial Army took part in the day's action. No individual commanded a force larger than a company for any length of time. Losses: 49 killed, 41 wounded, 5 missing.

BRITISH COLUMN
(Lieutenant-Colonel Francis Smith)
The flank companies of the following regiments of the Boston garrison:
4th Foot, 5th Foot, 10th Foot, 18th Foot, 23rd Foot, 38th Foot, 43rd Foot, 47th Foot,

52nd Foot, 59th Foot
The light company of the 1st Battalion, Royal Marines
RELIEF FORCE (Brigadier-General Lord Percy)
The battalion companies of the following regiments:
4th Foot, 23rd Foot, 47th Foot
1st Battalion Royal Marines
Two 6-pounder field guns
ESTIMATED TOTALS:
Column   6–800
Relief Force   1,000
Losses: 73 killed, 174 wounded, 26 missing.

LEXINGTON GREEN—THE CONFRONTATION

PARKER'S MILITIA COMPANY

BUCKMAN'S TAVERN

BELFRY

CONCORD

THE BRITISH IN CONCORD — BARRETT'S MILITIA

LESLIE AT NORTH BRIDGE

PARSONS

BARRETT'S FARMHOUSE

LEXINGTON

MILL POND

SOUTH BRIDGE

BRITISH SEARCH TOWN FOR STORES

PITCAIRN'S LIGHT INFANTRY FILE ROUND MEETING-HOUSE AND FORM IN rRONT OF PARKER'S MEN

a century and a half ago, the towns of Lexington and Concord were embroiled in a bitter local controversy over the question of whose militia had offered the first organized, forcible resistance to the Redcoats. These arguments have never been resolved, but one by-product of the debate has been a great accumulation of documentary evidence, most of it in the form of participants' and onlookers' first-hand recollections; as a result, Lexington and Concord is the best-documented encounter of the Revolution.

In reconstructing the events on the Green that morning, it is helpful to remember that Pitcairn's men were light infantry, in other words bright, agile men, used to acting independently and trained to take the initiative in battlefield situations. The moment Pitcairn, a Marine, ordered them into Lexington at a trot he had, in effect, relinquished control over their actions. Pitcairn, who was used to commanding 'battalion men', probably did not realize his error until it was too late to retrieve the situation.

The rapidity and determination of the British advance astonished Parker; instead of keeping to the road and passing on toward Concord, the light

tinued to press the attack, shouting and huzzaing.

Suddenly, there was a shot. Pitcairn remembered seeing 'a Gun in a peasant's hand . . . flash in the pan without going off: and instantly or very soon 2 or 3 Guns went off by which he found his horse wounded and also a man near him wounded'. Other witnesses recalled seeing British officers discharge 'a pistol or two on the Lexington company'. Amid the confusion, there were shouted commands. A British officer pointed his sword in the direction of Parker's company and yelled to his men, 'Fire! Fire! Damn you, fire!' His command was echoed by others, and the Redcoats fired two volleys at the militiamen. The first volley was high, but the second hit with deadly effect. Captain Parker's command, which was still dispersing, was devastated by this fire. Several men fell, including Jonas Parker, who was bayonetted as he writhed on the ground.

Pitcairn had by now completely lost control of his men. The regulars began to run amok on the Green; according to one militiaman, they 'kept up the fire, in all directions, as long as they could see a man of our company in arms'. Lieutenant John Barker of the 10th Regiment later stated that the light infantry 'were so wild they could hear no orders'. During

33

this time Pitcairn and other officers tried vainly to restore order by moving among the men on horseback and ordering them to cease fire. Finally, Lieutenant-Colonel Smith rode up from the main column, found a drummer and ordered him to beat 'To Arms!' At this signal the Redcoats stopped pursuing the rebels and returned to the Green.

The light infantry had gained a cheap victory. At a cost of just one man slightly wounded they had routed a company of the Patriot militia. Still drunk with excitement, 'they drew up and formed in a body on the common, fired a volley and gave three huzzas, by way of triumph. . . .' Parker's Lexington company had not been so lucky. The brief stand on the Green had cost the militiamen eight killed and nine wounded. The war that Captain John Parker had suspected the British of wanting had begun with a massacre.

Pitcairn's troops continued to mill about on the Green for a time, but eventually the junior officers regained control and persuaded the men to return to the ranks. A short distance away, Pitcairn, Smith and several other officers conferred. Smith reportedly reproached Pitcairn on the conduct of the light infantry, who, he said, were 'not attending to their officers and keeping their ranks'. There were, however, other, more pressing matters to be discussed. The whole affair at Lexington had consumed about half an hour; now Smith wanted to push on to Concord and fulfil his mission without delay. Some of the officers baulked at the idea of continuing the march, pointing out 'the certainty of the country being alarmed and assembling'. Smith, however, was unimpressed by these arguments and impatiently ordered the march to resume.

The seven-mile march to Concord passed almost uneventfully. Nevertheless, there were unmistakeable signs that the countryside was, indeed, assembling. Parties of Americans could be seen shadowing the British line of march, and at Meriam's Corner, about a mile from Concord, a strong body of militia was glimpsed briefly on a hill commanding the road. These men, however, disappeared when Smith's flankers approached their position. Later, as the British column neared the town, the strangest incident of the day occurred. A company of Concord militia, accompanied by its regimental music, was observed drawn up across the road as if to block the British march. But, as Smith's men drew closer, the militia wheeled about and began to march toward the town. The militia band struck up a tune (probably *Yankee Doodle*, which was popular with the British troops), and the British musicians joined in the catchy melody. Militiaman Amos Barrett, who marched in the strange parade, later recalled: 'We had grand music'.

The Concord men were not engaging in an aimless charade. They were well aware of the skirmish at Lexington, and their commander, Colonel Barrett, was playing for time. Although he considered he did not have enough men to prevent the British troops from entering the town, he knew that most of the Provincial Army stores, which the British sought, had been hidden or removed to places of safety. Moreover, Barrett knew, an intensive search would occupy the British for several hours. In the meantime, his own strength was growing by the hour. If the British tarried long in Concord, he would soon be in a position to attack them with a numerical advantage. So, as the British troops filed into Concord, he ordered his militia regiment to retreat over the North Bridge, which spanned the Concord River at the west end of town. After crossing the river, the militia were instructed to form on Punkatasset Hill, a low ridge about 1,000 yards north of the bridge.

Barrett's new position was well-chosen. The ridge offered a commanding view of the town and the surrounding countryside and, besides, served as a convenient rallying place for the various militia and minuteman companies marching toward the town.

As Barrett's men withdrew over the river, they were followed closely by six light infantry companies under Captain Moses Parsons of the 10th Regiment. Parsons's men moved so quickly and deliberately that some of the Patriot militia thought they were about to be attacked. Instead, Parsons stopped at the bridge, where he divided his command, leaving three companies under Captain Walter Laurie to guard the river crossing and taking the remaining three companies with him toward Barrett's Farm, where, it was rumoured, a large portion of the Provincials' military stores was hidden. As Parsons's contingent marched out of sight toward the Barrett Farm, the militia on Punkatasset Hill abruptly shifted their position to the Buttrick field, which was closer to the bridge.

The sight of Barrett's 500 militiamen forming just a few hundred yards from his 100 light infantrymen put Laurie in a temporary panic; after consulting with the ubiquitous Lieutenant Sutherland, he requested a reinforcement of grenadiers from Colonel Smith.

Meanwhile, in the town, Smith and Pitcairn were directing the search for military stores. Although almost every building in the town was stuffed with supplies, surprisingly little of importance was found and destroyed. (Another detachment pursued the search beyond South Bridge, with similarly poor results.) The grenadiers, who for the most part were involved in the search in the centre of the town, were tired and hungry. They were not used to operating at speed, as the light infantry were, and already several of their number had fallen behind and been made prisoner on the road from Lexington; nor had Smith allowed them a chance to eat breakfast. As a result, many of them spent the morning trying to buy food from the townspeople. In the meantime, however, contraband goods were found, and they were piled in the road and burned. By 10.30 am there were several columns of smoke rising from the town and its environs.

The appearance of the smoke threw Barrett's men into a rage. Even before it had been spotted, Major John Buttrick and several company officers had been trying to convince Barrett to launch an attack. Now the militiamen were certain their homes were being destroyed. When Barrett hesitated, Adjutant Joseph Hosmer bluntly said: 'Will you let them burn the town down?' Hosmer's words settled the matter. Captain Isaac Davis's Acton company was selected to lead the attack because Davis's men were equipped with bayonets, and, according to patriot Amos Baker, 'It was not certain whether the British would fire, or whether they would charge bayonets without firing'. A few minutes later the militia formed a compact column and advanced down to the bridge. A drum and fife played *The*

White Cockade, an appropriately rebellious tune.

The sudden advance of the Patriots caught the British off-guard, and Laurie and Sutherland had to throw themselves rapidly into the task of getting the light infantry back across the bridge and formed to receive the Americans. As the last of Laurie's men clattered over the bridge Sutherland made an attempt to pull up the planks, hoping to deny passage to the militia. The Americans were now so close that Buttrick could be heard bellowing orders and calling on Sutherland to leave the planks alone. Laurie, in the meantime, tried to form his men for the 'street fighting' manoeuvre but, as Lieutenant Barker relates, 'The rebels were got so near him that his people were obliged to form the best way they could as soon as they were over the bridge'. A few moments later some of Laurie's men opened a scattered fire (probably against orders). These shots were followed by a volley. The British fire was inaccurate, and only six militiamen were hit, including Captain Davis, who was killed. (The Concord men spoke of receiving a 'dropping shot', and one marvelled that more men were not killed, stating that the British 'fired too high'. British musketry was notoriously ineffective throughout the war. Partly this was due to lack of training, although the American cavalryman 'Light Horse Harry' Lee advanced the novel theory that the British soldier 'always overshot' because he used 'too much powder for the lead' in making his cartridge.)

Almost immediately Buttrick ordered his men to return the fire. Because the militia column approached the bridge at an angle and parallel to the river, most of the Patriots in the column could see, and fire at, the light infantry. So, the first militia volley rippled from one end of the column to the other. Laurie's formation was torn to pieces by this musketry. Sutherland and three other officers fell, and despite Laurie's pleas the Redcoats turned and ran 'with the greatest precipitance' back to Concord. Corporal Baker, who was among the first of the Americans to cross the bridge in the wake of the British retreat, recalled that, 'There was two lay dead and another almost dead. We did not follow them. There was eight or ten that was wounded and arunning and hobbling about looking back to see if we was after them.'

On the way they ran into Colonel Smith leading two companies of grenadiers to their support. The grenadiers opened ranks to allow the light infantry to pass and made a tentative advance on the detachment of militia that had crossed the bridge. Then, satisfied that the Americans did not intend to follow up their success, Smith ordered his men to

CAPTAIN PARKER'S MEN FIRE ON THE BRITISH ADVANCING ACROSS LEXINGTON GREEN; FROM A VIEW BY HOWARD PYLE.

regroup back in the centre of the town.

The brief action at the North Bridge brought an abrupt halt to the activities of the troops in Concord. Now Smith's main concern was to get his men out of town, and he bent every effort to collecting his scattered units. This took longer than expected because Parsons's men, who had had to make a four-mile round trip to Barrett's Farm, could not be sent for. Finally, at about 11.30 am, Parsons's detachment was sighted. Bold in their ignorance of the events of the previous hour, these men marched unmolested right past Barrett's force. However, when they got to the bridge and realized what had happened, they, too, ran as fast as they could to rejoin the main column.

Smith completed preparations for the return march about noon, and shortly thereafter the column set out for Boston. The light infantry once again covered the flanks and rear of the column, while the grenadiers marched in a compact body on the road.

The mile or so to Meriam's Corner was covered without incident. Large bodies of militia moved parallel to the road through fields and woods on either side but stayed clear of the light infantry who shielded the road column from interference. At Meriam's Corner, however, everyone — British grenadiers and light infantry and American militia — crowded toward the small bridge which crossed the Mill Brook. Smith's flankers crossed the bridge and then, sensing that the militia had drawn too close to the column, wheeled and delivered a volley at the nearest Americans.

This volley acted like a catalyst on the collective will of the militia units surrounding the column. Where before there had been doubt and indecision, now the militia acted as if animated by the same avenging spirit. Every man had but one object—to get within range of the Redcoat column and deliver his fire. Ensign Jeremy Lister of the 10th Regiment was so surprised by the prompt, heavy return fire that he swore the Patriots opened the battle at Meriam's Corner. He said:

'As we descended the hill into the Road the Rebels begun a brisk fire but at so great a distance it was without effect, but as they kept marching nearer when the Grenadiers found them within shot they returned their fire just about that time I recd a shot through my Right Elbow joint which effectively disabled my Arme, it then became a general firing upon us from all quarters, from behind hedges and walls.'

The fight at Meriam's Corner was just the beginning of what was to become a long running battle without interruption all the way to Charles-

town. The militia, who now numbered about 2,000 men, abandoned their old tactic of standing in line of battle and volleying with the British and, instead, began to fight 'Indian style'. Reverend Ebenezer Foster, who fought with the Reading militia, recalled: 'Each one sought his own place and opportunity to attack and annoy the enemy from behind trees, rocks, fences, and buildings, as seemed most convenient.' The British considered this new style of fighting cowardly, but, had General Gage been with his troops, he would have instantly recognized it as the same tactic that had destroyed Braddock's expedition to the forks of the Ohio in 1755.

The battle increased in fury as the Redcoats drew nearer to Lexington. In Lincoln township, where the road curved sharply through a dense tangle of woods and underbrush, hundreds of Provincials waited in ambush at the very edge of the road. As Smith's column pushed through this area it was lashed by a deadly fire from both sides. Farther on, scores of militiamen, including the remnants of Captain Parker's Lexington company, fired diagonally down the length of the British column from a hill near a bend in the road.

The shock of this last attack was more than the Redcoats could bear. Up until this point the light infantry had managed to fend off all but the worst of the attacks, but now they too had become fatigued and abandoned the flanks for the relative security of the column. Many of the men gave up the fight altogether and sat down numbly beside the road. Others began to run, and the retreat became a rout; all the while, the rebels kept up a deadly fire.

By the time Smith's troops had reached Lexington, the column had degenerated into a panic-stricken mob, and its destruction seemed imminent. The wounded had been abandoned on Fiske Hill nearby; then in Lexington, as British Ensign John DeBerniere related, 'The officers got to the front and presented their bayonets, and told the men if they advanced they should die; upon this they began to form under a very heavy fire.' Suddenly, however, Smith's men began to shout and leap for joy. Ahead, to the south-east, straddling the road to Menotomy, was a long line of British soldiers. These men, about 1,000 in all, were the reinforcements Smith had requested earlier in the day.

The relief force, which was commanded by the capable and personable Brigadier-General Lord Percy, had arrived just in time. Providentially, Percy had brought two 6-pounders with him, and when the Provincials pressed too close to the British lines the artillerymen opened fire. The militia, who

LORD PERCY, COMMANDER OF THE BRITISH RELIEF FORCE.

apparently had little respect for British musketry, were overawed by their first experience of cannon. Although the cannonade was ineffectual, they fell back to Lexington Green, and for the first time in two hours of steady fighting the British troops enjoyed a nervous rest. Their ordeal was, however, far from ended. The militia, as they had been doing all day, began to run across country to new positions; and when the British started back from Lexington at 3 pm, the militia were once more ahead, waiting with cocked muskets.

Percy's march began, as had Smith's from Concord, in relative quiet. Then, at Foot of the Rocks, near Menotomy, the firing began again. This was the heaviest fire of the day. Percy described it as being 'like a moving circle'. Even worse, the Patriots had occupied many of the buildings along the road (the built-up area of Menotomy extended for about half a mile) and were firing point-blank into the column. The fighting grew particularly vicious as the column moved toward the centre of the town, and the regulars were forced to set fire to houses and mêlée with bands of militia occupying them.

The fighting in Menotomy was the worst of the day, since most of it was fought savagely at close-quarters. Eventually, though, the British cleared Menotomy and entered Cambridge, where the firing started again but with less vigour, numbers of the Patriots having moved up to the Great Bridge over the Charles River, thinking that Percy would return to Boston by the way he had come. Percy, however, anticipated this ambush and chose the shorter, safer route through Charlestown. The militia of Charlestown, threatened by Gage with bombardment, did not attempt to contest his march.

Percy's column marched across Charlestown Neck at dusk and took up a position on Bunker Hill, overlooking the Neck and the road to Charlestown. Later in the evening Smith's battered light infantry and grenadiers were ferried to Boston in ships' boats, and Percy's force, manning the defence line on Bunker Hill, was strengthened by General Robert Pigot's 2nd Brigade. The Patriots, for the most part, did not return to their homes but stayed on, blockading the Redcoats on Charlestown peninsula and in Boston. Within a few days the Provincial Army was reinforced and Gage was under siege.

The march to Concord and back cost the British 273 men, of whom 73 were killed, while the Patriots lost 95 men altogether. Lexington and Concord began the war and showed the British, as Washington said, that 'the Americans will fight for their liberties and property, however pusillanimous . . . they may appear in other respects'.

17 June 1775
In one of the bloodiest fights of
the 18th century, General Howe's force
from the besieged British garrison in Boston is
twice repelled with grievous casualties
before finally driving the American
Patriots from their defences on the
Charlestown peninsula.

BUNKER HILL

THE BACKGROUND TO THE BATTLE

The news of the fighting at Lexington and Concord, though not entirely unexpected, was greeted with a mixture of surprise, doubt and outrage on both sides of the Atlantic. In the colonies, where there was still no thought of separation from England and where devotion to the King was a common sentiment, the events of 19 April provoked a sharp reaction. Throughout New England men shouldered muskets, bade goodbye to their families, and rushed to join units assembling on village greens in response to the news from Massachusetts. By the end of April, the Provincial army besieging General Gage's 'Ministerial Army' in Boston had been joined by contingents from Connecticut and Rhode Island (New Hampshire's two regiments reported later), and the number of men manning the extensive siege lines swelled to over 10,000. Gage, with less than 5,000 regulars in his command, abandoned his last remaining mainland outpost on Charlestown peninsula on 26 April and concentrated his army on Boston peninsula, where it would be secure from attack.

From a military point of view, Gage's decision to abandon Charlestown peninsula and retreat to Boston was a blunder. The city of Boston, which straddled a peninsula connected to the Massachusetts mainland and Roxbury by a narrow isthmus, was easily defended from attack but was dominated by high ground to the north and southeast. The heights to the north, known locally as Charlestown Heights or Bunker Hill, lay just half a mile across the estuary of the Charles River from Copp's Hill, at the tip of Boston peninsula. The hilly ground to the south-east, Dorchester Heights, adjoined the harbour opposite Boston Neck. These heights were important because artillery emplaced on them could bombard the Boston garrison and possibly batter it into submission.

The Provincial army besieging Boston was a motley rabble of undisciplined farmers and artisans. Its organization and command system were rudimentary even by 18th-century standards. The commander was Artemas Ward, a thorough patriot, but now regrettably too sick to exercise effective control over the heterogeneous host which had answered the alarm and rallied to the aid of Massachusetts. Ward's dispositions, such as they were, were subject to the approval of the Provincial Committee of Safety, a civilian *junta* controlled by the brilliant, charismatic Dr Joseph Warren.

Throughout late April and May, Ward's chief concern was with keeping his army intact. He was playing for time, maintaining a sham siege, while attempting to accumulate ammunition and cannon. Attacking Boston, even applying pressure on the British by seizing the heights, was the last thing he wanted to do. Gage, of course, was of a similar mind. He was waiting for reinforcements before moving to break the noose about Boston.

The strange, uneventful Siege of Boston might have dragged on interminably despite the proximity of the armies had Gage managed to retain control of the decision-making process in his army. However, it has always been a major criticism of Gage's conduct of American affairs that he was too timid—a

do-nothing general who had lost the initiative to a rabble in arms. In order to prod him into action the British government had dispatched three of the army's best and brightest major-generals to Boston in April. The three were, in order of seniority: Sir William Howe, an accomplished soldier who had served in America during the French and Indian War and who numbered himself among America's friends in Parliament; Henry Clinton, a shy, retiring intellectual who had served as an aide-de-camp to the Duke of Brunswick in Germany; and 'Gentleman Johnny' Burgoyne, an ambitious, flamboyant *bon-viveur*, whose military experience included service as a commander of light dragoons in Portugal. This 'triumvirate of reputation', as Burgoyne described the trio, sailed from Portsmouth on the frigate *Cerberus* on 20 April (the day after Lexington and Concord) and arrived at Boston on 25 May after a remarkably swift passage. As the *Cerberus* neared its dock at the Long Wharf, Burgoyne, the most enthusiastic of the three, is said to have exclaimed, 'What! Ten thousand peasants keep five thousand King's troops shut up? Well, let us get in, and we'll soon find elbow room!'

Burgoyne's remark set the tone for what followed. With an industriousness that must have appalled Gage, who was sensible of the weakness of the garrison, Howe, Clinton and Burgoyne set about formulating plans to create 'elbow room'. Gage was shunted aside, and Howe virtually assumed command. On 12 June, martial law was declared by a florid proclamation which could only have been written by Burgoyne. Clinton, for his part, inspected the defences and discovered that the heights at Dorchester and Charlestown had been ignored by both armies.

Clinton's trained eye recognized at once that these heights were the key to the British army's position at Boston. Dorchester Heights, especially, were essential to the safety of the garrison, because they overlooked and commanded the inner harbour. Clinton communicated his apprehensions to his colleagues, and a council of war was held to discuss a plan of operations to correct the oversight. The council adopted Clinton's plan for a landing on Dorchester Neck and set 18 June as the date for the operation.

The Americans, too, had given much thought to occupying the heights, but General Ward and the Committee of Safety were reluctant to bring on a confrontation with the British while the Provincial army was disorganized and almost destitute of the means to make war. Moreover, there were no heavy cannon in the army, and skilled artillerists were as rare as barrels of powder in the Cambridge camp.

When a spy brought word of the British plan, however, the American command was forced to reconsider its policy of non-aggression. At a council of war held on 13 June, Major-General Israel Putnam and Colonel William Prescott persuaded Ward and Dr Warren to commit men to the defence of the heights at Dorchester and Charlestown. General Ward was probably opposed to the plan from the beginning, but his actions were dictated by the Committee of Safety, which, as we have seen, was controlled by Dr Warren.

THE COMMANDERS

At the time of Bunker Hill the Provincial Army was still suffering from the disorganizing and debilitating effects of its decentralized command system. General Artemas Ward, who opposed the seizure of Charlestown peninsula, was the nominal commander, but his authority was limited. He was responsible to the Provincial Committee of Safety, a group of civilians who made broad military policy. Further confusion arose because no one had bothered to define the extent of the Committee's power or Ward's place in the power structure. Dr Joseph Warren, who controlled the Committee, was not a military man, but the Provincial Congress elected him to the rank of major-general just three days before the battle.

ISRAEL PUTNAM.

JOHN STARK.

General Israel Putnam, a hard-bitten veteran of the 'Old French War' who commanded the Connecticut troops in the Cambridge sector of the American lines, had suggested that Charlestown peninsula be seized and fortified against the British in early May. 'Old Put' was obsessed by the idea of bringing the British to battle on ground where the Americans would have the advantage of position. His arguments, however, impressed neither Ward nor the Committee.

Later, when word of the planned British move against the heights was received, Putnam repeated his plea for pre-emptive action. This time he won Warren's support, and a weak force was detailed to seize the heights. The plan of operations was Putnam's, but his role in the battle has been the subject of debate. No one American officer directed the battle. Putnam spent most of his time on Bunker Hill acting the part of a staff officer. He went to Cambridge for reinforcements and tried to coax or

cajole frightened regiments forward, but he did not exercise command.

Colonel William Prescott, in the redoubt, and Colonel John Stark, at the rail fence, directed and inspired the defence. To them belongs much of the credit for the prolonged resistance of the tired, thirsty soldiers in the firing line. But even these officers operated independently of one another. Nevertheless the defence, haphazard as it was, won the admiration of the British officers.

The British decision to mount an immediate assault on the Breed's Hill redoubt was conceived at a council of war held in Province House in Boston at dawn on 17 June 1776. All of the major participants in the planning session—Gage, Howe, Clinton and Burgoyne—are profiled elsewhere in this volume.

The plan of attack seems to have been dictated by Gage, though he was probably strongly seconded by Howe. Clinton, who proposed a landing in the rear of the American position near the Neck, noted later that 'Mr. Gage thought himself so well informed that he would not take any opinion of others, particularly of a man bred up in the German school, which that of America affects to despise'.

The plan of battle envisioned a frontal attack on the American redoubt. Howe, who was of the 'American school', that is, officers who had served their military apprenticeship in America, was designated to lead the assault. Clinton was given command of the reserve, and Burgoyne was, in his own words, 'left . . . almost a useless spectator'.

Gage has been severely criticized for choosing to make a direct attack on the American lines, but none of the officers at the council of war knew the strength of the American position. Moreover, the waters surrounding Charlestown peninsula had not been charted. Extensive mud flats would have prevented an amphibious landing at any spot other than the eastern tip of the peninsula at high tide. The choice of the landing place, in effect, dictated the mode of attack.

In further mitigation of the British plan, it can be said that the British had every reason to feel confident in the superiority of their troops—a view shared, incidentally, by the Provincial General Ward, who was by no means sure that his farmboys would stand against British regulars outside the comparative security of the siege lines.

THE BATTLE

On 15 June the Provincial Committee of Safety issued orders to occupy the strategic heights around Boston in the form of the following resolution:

'Whereas it appears of importance to the Safety of this Colony that possession of the hill called Bunker's Hill in Charlestown be securely kept and defended; and also some one hill or hills on Dorchester be likewise secured. Therefore resolved unanimously that it be recommended to the Council of War that the above mentioned Bunker's Hill be maintained by sufficient force being posted there and as the particular situation of Dorchester Neck is unknown to this Committee they advise that the Council of War take and pursue such steps respective to same, as to them shall appear to be for the security of this colony.'

Nevertheless, when the Provincial Council of War attempted to work out the details of this two-pronged operation, it ran into difficulties. General John Thomas, who commanded the Roxbury sector of the American lines, refused to co-operate in the venture, pleading that he could not spare the men. When General Ward acquiesced in this piece of insubordination, the Dorchester end of the operation was cancelled. At the same time, Ward cut the number of men in Putnam's Bunker Hill force by half and failed to make arrangements for relieving or reinforcing the men after they had spent the better part of a night marching to Charlestown and fortifying the peninsula. Still, despite the embarrassing weakness of the force, Putnam was determined to proceed, and orders were issued for the men to assemble on Cambridge Common at 6 pm on the afternoon of 16 June.

At the appointed time just over 1,000 men gathered together under the elms of the Common. Most of them were from Massachusetts, and because Putnam held his commission as a general from Connecticut, Colonel Prescott shared the command. In addition to 300 men from Prescott's regiment, there were 250 each from the regiments of Colonel Ebenezer Bridge and Colonel James Fryes, plus a contingent of 200 Connecticut troops from Putnam's regiment under Captain Thomas Knowlton and Captain Samuel Gridley's 4-gun artillery battery. At dusk the men formed to hear Reverend Samuel Langdon, the president of Harvard College, pray for the success of the expedition. Later, at about 9 pm, the column set out for Charlestown.

To guard against discovery, the men were ordered to keep strict silence on the march, and the way was lit by masked lanterns. Prescott led the march, guiding the troops through the camp of the Connecticut men at Lechmere Point and past the advanced pickets of the army in Charlestown. When the column reached Charlestown Neck, there was a halt, and patrols were sent forward to scout the forbidding 'no man's land' of the peninsula. Then the column proceeded to Bunker Hill, the first of two prominent hills, where a second halt was ordered, and the officers discussed their instructions.

No record remains of this discussion, nor even of who was present, but it seems likely that Putnam,

Prescott, and Colonel Richard Gridley, the army's chief engineer and chief of artillery, were involved. It seems likely, too, that these men were debating whether to fortify Bunker Hill, where they stood, or Breed's Hill, a more suitable position, closer to the tip of the peninsula. Bunker Hill, which had been named in the orders, was 110 feet high and closer to the mainland, but Breed's Hill, which was 62 feet high at its summit, commanded the water approaches to the peninsula and was the best position from which to resist the expected British attack. Finally, Breed's Hill was selected as the site for the fortifications, and Prescott led his men down the slope of Bunker Hill and over the intervening saddle of high ground to the new position. Colonel Gridley, an experienced engineer who had served at the Siege of Louisbourg in 1758, laid out the lines of a square redoubt about 50 yards on each side, and at midnight Prescott ordered his men to the laborious task of digging the parapet, ditch and firing platform.

Most of the men toiling on Gridley's redoubt that night were used to hard work, and the parapet began to take shape rapidly. Still, Prescott worried constantly that the British would discover the presence of his force. Standing on Breed's Hill, he could make out the silhouettes of British warships riding placidly in the brackish waters of the Charles River not a quarter of a mile away; just beyond were the lights of Boston. His men were working under the guns of the British fleet and Boston's Copp's Hill battery. It seemed incredible that they had not been discovered.

Prescott's fears were not unfounded. General Clinton had been on the prowl that evening, and he had seen or heard enough to convince himself that the Americans had beaten the British to the heights. But, when he informed General Gage of his reconnaissance, the Commander-in-chief discounted the report and deferred further action until morning.

Shortly before dawn, the night was shattered by the unmistakeable bellowing of a ship's broadside battery. A sentry on the sloop *Lively* (20 guns) had spotted the nearly completed redoubt and given the alarm. Within moments, *Lively*'s vigorous cannonade was joined by the fire of the big guns on Copp's Hill.

The unexpected bombardment roused the Boston garrison from its slumber. All over the city soldiers and officers tumbled from their billets; drums beat, and regiments formed. Admiral Samuel Graves was one of those whose sleep was rudely interrupted. Like Gage, he refused to credit reports that the Americans had built a redoubt overnight on Charlestown Heights. His first orders were for the *Lively* to cease fire. Minutes later, when he saw the redoubt, he realized his mistake and dispatched orders for all the warships of his fleet to 'commence firing immediately'.

In the meantime, the British command huddled in Province House, Gage's headquarters. A sense of urgency pervaded the meeting, for the unexpected appearance of the Breed's Hill redoubt had radically altered the situation of the Boston garrison. Guns emplaced in the redoubt, even light field guns (the

Americans had no siege artillery), could bombard the city half a mile away. The Americans had to be driven from the peninsula, and it had to be done quickly, before they completed their defences. All the officers present understood this; the only question was, how were they to do it?

Clinton proposed a landing at the narrow neck of the peninsula behind the American redoubt. Once landed, the British troops would seize Bunker Hill, a move designed to prevent both the escape and the reinforcement or relief of the Americans on Breed's Hill. Prescott's command would be 'shut . . . up in the Peninsula as in a bag', as a British officer later put it.

Clinton's plan was defective, however, and Gage dismissed it out of hand. He was reluctant to place a division of the army between two hostile forces. Moreover, Charlestown peninsula was surrounded by mud flats and shallows. An amphibious landing was practicable only at high tide. Gage did not want his men struggling ashore against the kind of musketry they had faced on the return march from Concord. This ruled out a landing from the Charles River, since the men would have to fight their way through the town or over a causeway and through a mill pond—terrain where they might be butchered by Americans firing from cover. A landing from the relatively open Mystic River flank was, likewise, out of the question because Admiral Graves would not risk his ships in the treacherous shallows of the estuary. The only safe landing place was on the eastern shore of the peninsula. This, of course, meant that the regulars would have to storm the redoubt along its face, but Gage was certain that the Provincials could not stand against a determined attack. The Commander-in-chief's plan, though fraught with hazards, was enthusiastically approved by most of the officers present.

Howe, the senior field officer, was given the honour of leading the attack. His strike force of 1,550 men included the brigaded light infantry and grenadier companies of the army, plus the 5th, 38th, 43rd, and 52nd Regiments. A second division of 700 men, consisting of the 47th Regiment, part of the 63rd, and two battalions of Marines, formed the reserve.

As the British generals perfected their plans, Prescott's men strengthened the redoubt. Work on the parapet and ditch continued at a furious pace, despite the spectacular naval bombardment. Fortunately for the Provincials, the storm of shot and shell was proving largely ineffectual: this was because the naval guns, which were direct-fire weapons, could not be elevated sufficiently to bear on the redoubt. Most of the balls hit the hill below the redoubt and tore furrows in the earth or bounded and scudded up the slope in unpredictable trajectories.

Nevertheless Prescott's men were green troops, and the sound and fury of the bombardment un-

nerved many of them. Quite early in the morning a chance shot entered the redoubt and decapitated Private Asa Pollard of Bridge's regiment. Pollard was the first American casualty of the battle, and many of his comrades abandoned their work to stare horror-stricken at his gruesome corpse. Others dropped their tools and began to slip away toward Bunker Hill. Within moments, a preacher had come forward to pray over the remains. Prescott looked around and discovered that the men were milling about all along the line. He ordered them back to their work, but no one obeyed—some looked away disconsolately while others stared dumbly back at him.

At this juncture, with his command in danger of falling apart under the pressure of the cannonade, Prescott climbed to the top of the parapet and boldly strode its length, proving by his example that the intense bombardment was not to be feared. Other officers joined him, and presently the men shook off the trauma of Pollard's death and returned to the task of completing their fort.

This strangely silent near-mutiny was but the first of many crises Prescott faced as the morning wore on. His men were tired, hungry and thirsty, yet there was still work to be done. The redoubt, by itself, was not sufficient to cover the approaches to the neck, so men were detailed to erect a breastwork at right-angles to the north-east face of the fort. This breastwork and, behind it and to the left, three *flèches* (arrowhead-shaped earthworks) completed the defences of Breed's Hill. Captain Knowlton's men fortified a rail fence 600 feet to the left and rear of the *flèches* to extend the line almost to the Mystic River. Although these last few defensive arrangements were improvised, Prescott was certain he could hold a British attack if he could obtain reinforcements. So far, not one regiment had been sent to relieve the dog-tired men of the fatigue party. Earlier in the morning Major John Brooks had been sent to army headquarters with an urgent request for reinforcements but, hours later, nothing had been heard from him. Unbeknown to Prescott, Putnam had also hastened to Cambridge to plead with General Ward for more men. Time was running short. Across the river, clearly visible through the haze of smoke from the warships' guns, the British were collecting barges and small boats in readiness for the crossing.

Howe's regulars paraded on Boston Common at 9 am, but various delays ensued and the men did not begin to enter the boats and barges until past noon. At 1.30 pm the two dozen boats available were fully loaded and ready. As they set off, the fleet and the Copp's Hill battery redoubled their fire to protect the landing. About a quarter of an hour later, the first boats nosed up to the shore at Morton's Point, and scores of light infantrymen splashed ashore, filing to the right and left and deploying in open order to cover the landing of their comrades.

BRINGING THE POWDER TO BUNKER HILL; AS SEEN BY HOWARD PYLE.

PATRIOTS
Major-General Israel Putnam
Colonel William Prescott

MASSACHUSETTS REGIMENTS OF: 1,500
Prescott, Frye, Bridge, Brewer, Nixon,
Woodbridge, Little, Ephraim Doolittle

CONNECTICUT REGIMENTS OF: 500
Putnam, Gerrish

NEW HAMPSHIRE REGIMENTS OF: 1,200
Stark, Reed

ARTILLERY
6 field guns from the companies of
Gridley, Trevett, Callender

ESTIMATED TOTAL 3,200

Losses: 145 killed, 304 wounded, 30 captured.

BRITISH
Major-General Sir William Howe;
second-in-command
Brigadier-General Sir Robert Pigot

ASSAULT FORCE 1,550
11 companies of light infantry
11 companies of grenadiers
5th Foot, 38th Foot, 43rd Foot, 52nd Foot

RESERVE 700
47th Foot, light infantry and grenadiers
of the 2nd Battalion Royal Marines, 63rd
Foot, and 1st Battalion Royal Marines

ADDITIONAL TROOPS 400
63rd Foot, 2nd Battalion Royal Marines

2,650

Losses: 226 killed, 828 wounded.

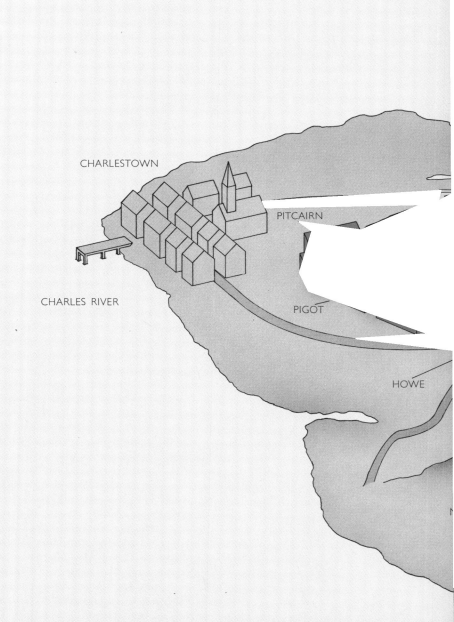

CHARLESTOWN

PITCAIRN

CHARLES RIVER

PIGOT

HOWE

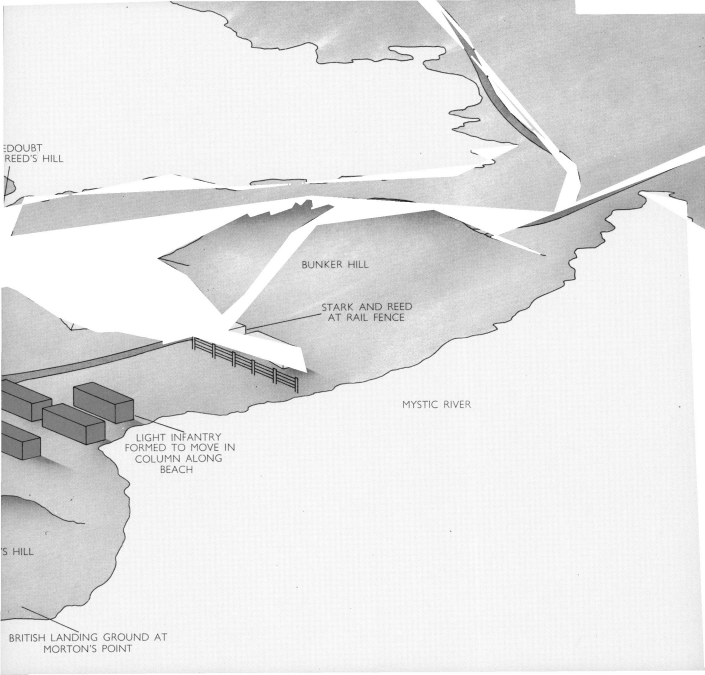

REDOUBT
ON REED'S HILL

BUNKER HILL

STARK AND REED
AT RAIL FENCE

MYSTIC RIVER

LIGHT INFANTRY
FORMED TO MOVE IN
COLUMN ALONG
BEACH

'S HILL

BRITISH LANDING GROUND AT
MORTON'S POINT

General Howe and a detachment of artillery arrived with the second wave. Once ashore, Howe formed his men on Morton's Hill and pushed his guns as far forward as possible. Then, accompanied by Brigadier-General Robert Pigot, his second-in-command, he walked to a vantage point to study the American line and formulate his tactical plan.

What Howe saw must have unsettled him somewhat. Even as he and Pigot exchanged observations, a column of fresh troops marched down the slope of Bunker Hill and then ran toward Knowlton's undermanned position at the rail fence. A portion of these men broke away from the main body and crowded onto the narrow beach by the Mystic River, where they began to pile stones together to extend Knowlton's line right to the water's edge.

The American line was stronger than any of the British generals had suspected it would be. Howe decided to delay the attack until later in the after-

As it turned out, though, Stark's contingent was the last substantial reinforcement to arrive on Breed's Hill. The Provincial army's woefully confused command system broke down again, and most of the regiments spent the afternoon marching and countermarching about the countryside. Those that did arrive at Charlestown Neck were disorganized and frightened by the fire of British gunboats. Some companies—even regiments—refused to cross the shot-swept isthmus. Men sought cover wherever they could find it, while many officers pleaded indisposition and simply walked away from the field. The tangle at the Neck became even greater and more shameful when scores of deserters pushed across in the opposite direction. Among the first to leave the redoubt was Colonel Gridley, who claimed to be sick, but he was followed shortly by his son's artillery company, which had abandoned the fort when the British cannonade became more

THE DRUMS BEAT, AND THE BRITISH LINE AGAIN ADVANCES UP
BREED'S HILL; FROM A PAINTING BY HOWARD PYLE.

noon, and he sent back to Boston for the reserve brigade.

The troops that Howe spotted on his reconnaissance of the American position were 1,200 men of John Stark's and James Reed's New Hampshire regiments. These men were the vanguard of a reinforcement that General Ward had reluctantly ordered to the front during the forenoon and early afternoon. Throughout the morning Ward's headquarters had been besieged by officers imploring him to release regiments from their duties on the siege lines for the impending battle on the peninsula. But Ward feared an amphibious attack on Cambridge as much, if not more, than an attack on Charlestown. He had to think first about defending the army's meagre but all-important magazine in Cambridge. However, when the British design became apparent, he ordered the New Hampshire regiments forward and later added several Massachusetts regiments and a company of artillery to the reinforcements.

intense, and correspondingly more fearsome.

Israel Putnam rode into this mass of cowed, shaken men like a whirlwind. Shouting orders, cursing, and pleading with them to push forward, he finally resorted to flailing at them with the flat of his sword, but even this desperate measure failed. In the end he was forced to admit bitterly that he 'could not drive the dogs'.

A few hundred men did shoulder their way through the mob near the Neck, however, and these men Putnam put to work fortifying Bunker Hill. Other men, singly and in small groups, decided to join the troops in the redoubt. Among them were two volunteers, Seth Pomeroy and Dr Joseph Warren. Pomeroy, who was 70 years old, was a familiar figure to many of them. A local gunsmith, he had served at the Siege of Louisbourg in 1745 and ten years later it was reputedly he who had shot down Baron Dieskau in the desperate fight at Fort William Henry in 1755. Dr Warren, like Pomeroy, had come to serve in the ranks. When Prescott

offered him the command, he refused, saying, 'I came as a volunteer with my musket to serve under you'.

By 3 o'clock the British reserves had landed, and Howe was ready to attack. His plan called for 11 companies of light infantry to move in column down the beach by the Mystic River, overrun Stark's barricade on the extreme left of the American line, and then turn and attack Knowlton's line at the rail fence from the rear. As this attack went in, Howe himself would lead the massed grenadiers and the 5th and 52nd Regiments directly against the rail fence. On the left, Pigot was to lead the 38th and 43rd Regiments, plus a small contingent of flankers, against the redoubt from the south. Major Pitcairn, with the Marines and the 47th Regiment, was detailed to protect the flank of Pigot's attack from the numerous American snipers in Charlestown. If the plan worked, Howe's wing would join Pigot's men in the redoubt, and the Provincials would be trapped and forced to surrender.

Just before the attack was launched, Howe addressed his soldiers. In booming tones, he reminded them that failure would be disastrous. But, he reassured them, 'I shall not desire any one of you to go a step further than where I go myself at your head'. Then, as the light infantry doubled away to the beach, he walked to the right of the line of grenadiers and waved them forward.

Howe's advance was magnificent. Two lines, each three ranks deep, moved in perfect order down the slopes of Morton's Hill toward the rail fence some 800 yards distant. Pigot's men kept pace on the left, skirting the back lots of Charlestown in their advance on the redoubt. Then, suddenly, there was trouble. One after another, the 6-pounder field guns supporting the attack ceased firing. The gunners had used up all the roundshot in the side-boxes and then discovered that ammunition chests sent over from Boston contained only 12-pound shot. The error was reported to Howe, who ordered the cannon to be moved to a new position closer to the American lines, from which they could fire grapeshot. However, when the guns were moved, they became stuck up to their axles in marshy ground near the bottom of Morton's Hill. The artillerymen fired their grapeshot from that position, but the guns were too far from Prescott's breastwork to damage anything.

Howe's infantry had to negotiate the same swampy ground and, in addition, a number of low walls and fences partly hidden by high grass. In consequence, their advance was slow, and there were frequent stops to reorder the ranks.

The light infantry contingent, however, faced no such obstacles. They trotted down the beach led by the company of the 23rd Royal Welsh Fusiliers, General Howe's own regiment. Just behind were the men of another famous regiment, the 4th King's Own. There were 11 companies altogether, and, one behind the other in dense columns, they moved briskly and confidently toward a nondescript pile of stones and fence rails far ahead on the narrow, sandy strand.

Behind that barricade lay John Stark and, perhaps, 200 of his men. These New Hampshire frontiersmen were the best shots in the army; even so, to make certain, Stark had earlier hammered a stake into the sand some forty yards in front of the barricade. He warned his men not to fire until the front rank of the British column passed the stake. As a further precaution, he had arranged his men in several ranks and instructed them to fire successive volleys into the attackers' faces.

The British were closer now. Stark waited patiently until the first glittering bayonets passed the stake, then he rose to his feet and shouted, 'Fire!' The barricade erupted in smoke and flame, and the leading company of light infantry was torn to pieces. The men who weren't killed outright stumbled around blindly or fell writhing to the sand.

The men of the 4th Regiment pushed determinedly past the wreckage of the Royal Welsh, but they, in turn, were devastated by a volley from the barricade. Others behind them crowded forward to fill the places of the casualties, but again and again the barricade spat fire. The bodies of the slain began to pile up on the beach near the stake, haphazardly defining the limit of the British advance. Finally, when they could take no more, the light infantry bolted for the rear. The first phase of Howe's attack had failed, smashed in a welter of blood and broken bodies. Ninety-six dead lay on the beach in front of the barricade. Later, John Stark recalled, 'I never saw sheep lie as thick in the fold'.

Pigot's men, meanwhile, were having trouble deploying for their attack on the redoubt. Scores of militiamen fired into them from the buildings of Charlestown as they attempted to form in the cramped area between the town and the lower slope of Breed's Hill. This fire was so severe that Pitcairn's Marines were staggered by it and forced to quit the town in disorder. Pigot's distress was relieved when the fleet, at Howe's request, bombarded the town with red-hot shot (cannon balls heated in furnaces before firing) and set it ablaze. Most of the Provincials were driven from the town by the conflagration, but a stubborn handful remained and continued to gall Pigot's men with their fire throughout the afternoon.

Finally (just minutes after the repulse of the light infantry on the beach), Pigot's ranks were ordered, and he began his ascent of Breed's Hill. Almost simultaneously, Howe's men closed on the rail fence. Burgoyne, watching the spectacle of the attack from Copp's Hill in Boston, was almost overcome by emotion. He described the assault as 'one of the greatest scenes of war that can be conceived. . . . A picture and a complication of horror and importance beyond anything that ever came to my lot to be witness to'

The Americans had had ample time to prepare for both attacks. Prescott, in the redoubt, cautioned his nervous men to reserve their fire until he gave the order. Some of them nevertheless fired impulsively at Pigot's perfectly dressed lines, and Prescott was forced to walk the length of the parapet kicking aside levelled muskets. Again, he repeated his instructions: 'Wait for the word, every man, steady!' Down at the rail fence Putnam studied the near-silent, awesomely steady advance of the grenadiers and yelled to his men: 'Don't fire until you see the whites of their eyes! Then, fire low'. All along the American line hammers clicked as men anticipating the order to fire pulled the cocks of their muskets to the full-cock position.

Howe's grenadiers were doomed men. They numbered 400 in all, officers and men, yet they were marching straight at well over 1,000 militiamen, who

were securely posted behind a stone wall and rail fence. Nevertheless, they pushed bravely on, loosing a volley at the Provincials from about eighty yards. Then, bringing their muskets to the 'charge bayonets' position, they broke into a trot. They covered about thirty yards more before they were rocked backward by a blast of musketry from the fence. Men fell in heaps and windrows, and survivors swore that the earth seemed to buckle with the first crash of gunfire. The line of grenadiers was shattered, but the officers courageously pulled the remnants together, reformed the line, and attempted to renew the advance. A second volley lashed this line, and it, too, broke up and floundered like a wounded animal.

Howe was shocked by this carnage but not deterred. The line of the 5th and 52nd regiments was fed into the inferno, but these units, too, were mauled by the storm of fire from the fence. Next Howe tried desperately to retrieve the situation by ordering some of the reformed light infantry companies forward to sustain the line. But it was too late. Soon bunches of sullen, disorganized men began to trail back in the direction of Morton's Hill.

In the meantime, Pigot's men were undergoing a similar experience. Their advance, too, was deliberate and awe-inspiring, but when they closed on the redoubt they were swept by a deadly fire and forced to retire in confusion. Looking on from Boston, General Clinton was shocked: 'General Burgoyne and I saw appearances on the left of the army engaged which made us shudder—in short, it gave way'. The sight of the army in retreat was too much for Clinton to bear. He deserted his post at the Copp's Hill battery and made his way to the North Wharf where he gathered together the remainder of the reserve and collected longboats for the crossing.

From Howe's point of view the situation was not quite as bad as it might have appeared to onlookers. Within fifteen minutes he had reformed his men, conferred with Pigot, and settled on a new plan of action. The next attack was to be launched all along the line. Pigot's axis of advance on the redoubt was shifted a few hundred yards to the

right in order to link with Howe's contingent and avoid the fire from Charlestown. Howe would assault the breastwork from the front, while the remnants of the grenadiers and light infantry were to storm the rail fence.

Presently, drums beat and fifes squealed, and the splendidly dressed ranks of red and white marched forward to the attack. Once again, the Provincials allowed the British to advance to within a few dozen yards of their works. Then the muskets thundered. A blinding flash, accompanied by a tremendous roar, ran the length of the defensive line. Hundreds of the attackers crumpled and tumbled under the impact of the volley. Regimental formations ceased to exist. The clumps of men remaining were savaged by an incessant stream of fire. On the left, Major Pitcairn of the Marines was mortally wounded and toppled into the arms of his wounded son, who screamed, 'I have lost my father!' Some of

48 THE DEFENCE OF THE HEIGHTS — VIEWED FROM BEHIND THE PATRIOT LINES.

the Marines nearby tried to console the young officer, while others, overcome with emotion, moaned, 'We have lost our father!'

Everywhere the broken bits of regiments and companies struggled to continue the advance, but the impetus of the attack had been smashed, and within moments a panic seized the survivors, who ran pell-mell down toward the landing place. Casualties were appalling. One officer who fought at the rail fence remembered: 'Most of our Grenadiers and Light-infantry, the moment of presenting themselves, lost three-fourths, and many nine-tenths, of their men. Some had only eight or nine men a company left; some only three, four, and five.' Howe was dazed by the carnage and wrote later that he felt 'a moment that I never felt before'.

As the second British attack receded Prescott and his men scavenged about the redoubt looking for powder. Most of the Provincials entered the fight with about fifteen cartridges apiece, and the men were now desperately short of powder and ball. Even after breaking open a few artillery cartridges and ransacking the pouches of the dead, the defenders were still able to share out only a few more rounds apiece. This was the crisis of the battle. Prescott and every man in the redoubt knew that they could not hope to stop another charge. Only one question remained: would the British try again?

In the meantime, Sir William Howe was reforming his decimated regiments and preparing to renew the assault. Several officers protested but to no avail. Howe was determined to conquer the hill. Clinton had arrived, bringing with him 400 fresh troops of the 63rd Regiment and the 2nd Battalion of Marines. These men, along with some of the walking wounded, helped to flesh out the lines. New orders went out. All the troops but the light infantry were to converge on the redoubt and the breastwork. The light infantrymen, what few remained, were to skirmish with the troops at the rail fence and, hopefully, prevent them from aiding their comrades in the redoubt. At about 5.30 pm all the preparations for the attack were complete, and for the third time the British lines tramped up the slope of Breed's Hill.

Prescott, keenly aware of his deficiency in ammunition, allowed the British to close to within twenty yards of the redoubt; then he gave the command, 'Fire!' The British lines were fairly enveloped in the smoke and flame of the discharge, but above the screams of the scores of wounded, there was a new cry, 'Push on! Push on!' The regulars had come too far and suffered too much to be deterred from their goal. Breaking from the shambles of their ranks, they surged forward, led by their officers. At this point, according to Lord Rawdon, 'The rebels . . . rose up and poured in so heavy a fire upon us that the oldest officers say they never saw a sharper action'. But this volley was the defenders' last. There were only a few scattered shots as the British troops, led by the 47th Regiment and two companies of Marines, scrambled over the parapet and into the redoubt[1].

The mêlée inside the redoubt was brief but bloody. Adjutant Waller of the Marines, who was among the first over the parapet, recalled: 'Nothing could be more shocking than the carnage that followed the storming of this work. We tumbled over the dead to get at the living.' Prescott saw that there was little

his men could do against British bayonets and ordered a retreat. Dr Warren gathered a few men together to act as a rearguard, and he and his little band fought on briefly by the sally port while the rest withdrew. Finally, as Warren turned to make good his escape, he was shot through the base of the skull and killed instantly.

The capture of the redoubt did not end the battle. Most of the American casualties were suffered in the stubborn rearguard fighting by the rail fence and on the slopes of Bunker Hill. The British pursuit, however, ended at Bunker Hill. The Redcoats were spent—completely done in by the day's exertions. On the American side, Putnam, who had tried desperately to organize a last-ditch defence on Bunker Hill, led the remnants of his force down the road to Cambridge, where, presently, the Provincials fortified Prospect Hill. The British had captured Charlestown peninsula, but the siege lines of the militia just beyond the isthmus prevented any further advance. 'We have got a little elbow-room,' commented one English wag. 'But I think we have paid too dearly for it.'

The cost was indeed high. Bunker Hill proved to be the war's bloodiest single day of battle. Howe's force of 2,650 men suffered 1,054 casualties, including 226 killed. Among the British officers, 89 were killed or wounded. The Americans had about 3,200 men in the vicinity of the field, but no more than 1,800 saw action. This force had 145 killed and 304 wounded.

Bunker Hill was a British victory, but it was an empty triumph. The British army was as much besieged after the battle as it had been before, but there was no further talk of a breakout or of 'elbow room' or even of improving the army's position. The staggering casualty list of the battle and the spectre of more Bunker Hills served as a warning against any further offensive operations.

In the American camp, morale was high. Bunker Hill ended the shambattle aspect of the war and destroyed the myth of the British army's invincibility. America's confidence in her ability to wage war, and wage war successfully, soared to a new high. After all, so the conventional argument went, hadn't untrained militia stood their ground and repelled regulars?

Strangely enough, Dorchester Heights remained unoccupied by either army until March 1776. Then George Washington, the new American commander, who arrived in Cambridge shortly after Bunker Hill, ordered a fort to be erected there. Washington's Dorchester operation closely resembled Putnam's Bunker Hill move. The Americans built their fort overnight and emplaced in it heavy guns stolen from Fort Ticonderoga. Howe, who replaced Gage as Commander-in-chief in September, evacuated the city shortly thereafter. The British were never again to occupy Boston as a colonial power.

---

[1] One of the officers wounded here was Captain George Harris, the commander of the 5th Regiment's grenadiers, who was shot in the head. He tumbled into the arms of Lord Rawdon, who had him taken from the field. Harris's skull was trepanned (an operation he watched with a mirror), and he survived. Later, he defeated Tippoo Sultan at Seringapatam and became Baron Harris. Rawdon, likewise, figured prominently in the conquest of India. As the First Marquis of Hastings, he was Governor-general and Commander-in-chief in India.

26 December 1776 – 3 January 1777
Washington's retreat across the Delaware to
Pennsylvania is the low-key prelude
to two brilliant counterstrokes at Trenton and Princeton.
These last thrusts in the winter campaign
revive American hopes and keep the
Continental army in a state to continue a
war it has come close to losing.

TRENTON & PRINCETON

THE BACKGROUND
TO THE BATTLES

The first phase of the Revolutionary War ended when Sir William Howe evacuated Boston (March 1776). During this period the infant American nation (Congress adopted the Declaration of Independence on 4 July 1776) had somehow managed to defend itself and had even launched a bold invasion of Canada. But these halcyon days of the young American republic were near an end. Independence had to be won by force of arms, and the full might of the British Empire was about to be brought to bear on the colonists.

In June 1776, an armada of 500 ships under Admiral Lord Howe assembled at Halifax, Nova Scotia, to transport Sir William Howe's army of

PART OF THE BATTLEGROUND AT TRENTON, 1776.

32,000 men to New York. This was the largest army the British Crown had ever put together for a foreign expedition. The statesmen in Whitehall meant to end the war that year.

On 30 June, the British fleet entered New York Bay. Sir William Howe made his camp on Staten Island; and then, inexplicably, did nothing. In the meantime Washington had marched from Boston with the largest army he would ever command—almost 25,000 men. Although few of his men were regulars and fewer still had training or combat experience, Washington was compelled by political necessity to defend New York City. So, while Howe's men marked time on Staten Island, the Continental army fortified Brooklyn Heights on Long Island and prepared for the imminent assault.

The Howe brothers preferred the indirect approach. Admiral Howe, probably mindful of the drubbing Sir Peter Parker's fleet had taken from Fort Moultrie at Charleston, would not run his 'liners' into the East River until Sir William had silenced the American batteries commanding the harbour.

Finally on 27 August, Sir William attacked the Americans on Long Island. The British battle plan was nearly perfect. Washington's over-extended front crumbled when it was hit by a cleverly orchestrated flank attack. Had he pressed his advantage, Howe might have ended the Revolution that

day. However, when the Americans fell back to a prepared line on Brooklyn Heights, he demurred. There was no pursuit, and during the night Colonel John Glover's famous 'amphibious regiment' of Marblehead mariners ferried the American army across the East River to Manhattan.

In the weeks following the Battle of Long Island, the Howe brothers gradually made themselves masters of New York City and the surrounding district. Washington was driven repeatedly from defensive positions on Manhattan and in Westchester County. In November, the American army crossed the Hudson into New Jersey.

On 1 December, Washington's army numbered only 4,300 men. The British, albeit in a sluggish manner, were following the American retreat across the Jerseys, and Washington realized that his best chance of saving the army and defending Philadelphia lay in putting the Delaware River between his army and the enemy's. The last American troops crossed to the south shore at Trenton on 8 December. When the crossing was completed, the boats were either destroyed or moored on the Pennsylvania shore under the protection of the army. Howe, finding that he had no means of crossing the river, called off the pursuit and went into winter quarters in New Jersey and New York.

Even before the American army slipped across the Delaware, Washington had sought an opportunity to strike the British forces in New Jersey. He was embarrassed by the succession of defeats after Long Island, and he desperately sought a means of reversing the tide of misfortune which seemed to be sweeping the dwindling American army and the cause of independence toward oblivion. Moreover, on 31 December, the enlistments of all but a handful of his troops would expire, and the army, already sadly reduced by the fighting in New York and the long retreat across New Jersey, would virtually cease to exist. 'The game,' Washington later admitted, 'was pretty nearly up.'

But the opportunity for the counterstroke Washington contemplated was not long in coming. By 22 December he had been reinforced by Sullivan's division from New Jersey and troops from the northern army under Horatio Gates. His army now numbered 10,106—even though only 4,707 of them were fit for duty. In addition to the regulars there were nearly 2,000 Pennsylvania militia under General John Cadwalader guarding the Delaware between Trenton and Philadelphia. With this army Washington prepared to attack the Hessian garrison at Trenton.

THE COMMANDERS

George Washington (1732–99), the commander of the American forces, was 44 years old at the time of the Trenton-Princeton campaign. Washington was the son of a Virginia gentleman and was a great landowner and entrepreneur in his own right. His military record, organizational and administrative abilities and noble appearance won the respect and confidence of the delegates to the Second Continental Congress, and he was elected Commander-in-chief of the American Army on 15 June 1775.

Washington's contribution to the war effort was immense. He was the soul of resistance. The army he fought with, though but one of several American armies, was *the* Continental army—America's main field force and a nursery of regiments and leaders. So long as this army, which was dominated by Washington's majestic will, maintained the field, the cause of independence flourished. Had Washington's army been shattered in battle or destroyed piecemeal by a combination of circumstances, or had the commander's will to persevere and continue the fight broken down in the face of persistent adversity and against overwhelming odds, then a British victory must surely have followed.

As a military leader Washington was a remarkably gifted strategist. He had a keen grasp of the operational aspects of warfare. He was also skilled at using the meagre resources at his command to maximum advantage. His effectiveness was marred, though, by an indifferent appreciation of the tactical capabilities of his army. Too often he demanded—and didn't get—the kind of parade-ground manoeuvring and precise execution that European commanders expected of their troops. His tactical plans were sometimes complex and far-fetched. In his defence it must however be said that in 1775 no American had experience in moving large bodies of men about a battlefield, much less organizing them and caring for their needs, and if the Congress had to find a man to learn the trade while working at it, then Washington was the obvious best choice.

Following the Trenton-Princeton campaign Washington retained the military leadership until after the capitulation of Cornwallis's army that virtually assured the Americans of victory. In due course, as the new nation's greatest hero, he became in 1789 the first president of the United States of America.

Colonel Johann Gottlieb Rall (1726–76) was the ambitious and exceptionally brave senior officer of the Hessian brigade at Trenton. He was mortally wounded in the battle, and this moment is the subject of the illustration on page 55. Rall was born an *enfant de troupe*—the 18th century's equivalent of an 'army brat'. His father, Joachim Georg Rall, was an officer in the Hessian infantry regiment von Loewenstein, the unit in which young Johann began his military career in 1740. Johann Rall's rise through the ranks was meteoric by 18th-century standards, more especially so since he was not of the nobility but, rather, of the class of officers the French referred to as *roturiers*—men of comparatively humble origin.

By 1771 Rall had attained the rank of colonel and commanded his own regiment. The Rall regiment was sent to America in the first batch of Hessians and formed part of the brigade of Major-General Werner von Mirbach. When von Mirbach suffered an attack of apoplexy Rall assumed command of the brigade, leading it with distinction at White Plains, where the Hessians turned the American flank on Chatterton's Hill (28 October 1776), and at Fort Washington (16 November 1776), where the German troops bore the brunt of the fighting and suffered severe losses. Rall was subsequently confirmed in the command of the old von Mirbach brigade, which he led into New Jersey on 28 November 1776.

Although little has been written about Rall's character, the principal image is of a bluff, boisterous man, something of a bully and an unreluctant drinker, overly keen on martial music and monotonous drill and inspections; at Trenton, safe from the gaze of superior officers, he was apt to rise late after a night's carousing and then keep the guard waiting in the snow while he finished his bath. Such minor inadequacies usually mask greater ones, and perhaps Rall's major flaw lay in his succumbing to the conventional wisdom that the Americans were a starving, ragged mob, unlikely to cause much trouble for his fine brigade despite its exposed position. He was, in short, a brave soldier but otherwise no more than a mediocrity—not unlike many of his contemporaries in both armies.

GEORGE WASHINGTON.

THE BATTLE OF TRENTON

The Hessians, about 1,600 strong, occupied the most exposed post in General Howe's extended line of detachments which stretched from Burlington, New Jersey, in the south, to the Hackensack River near New York—a distance of 77 miles. The nearest friendly troops were at Princeton and Bordentown, each roughly a half-day's march from Trenton. The American army, which was based at Newtown in Bucks County, Pennsylvania, was closer to the Hessians at Trenton than any friendly troops; even so Colonel Rall, the commander of the Hessian brigade, had failed to improve his post either by erecting earthworks or by sending patrols beyond the outskirts of the town.

By the 23rd, Washington's plans for the strike at

Ferry $7\frac{1}{2}$ miles above Trenton and advance on the town from the north and west in two columns. At the town, the columns would envelop the enemy position and drive them toward the Asunpink.

On Christmas Day Washington's army marched to McKonkey's Ferry and awaited nightfall for the crossing.

In the meantime Colonel Rall's Trenton garrison was celebrating the Yule season with all the rowdy excess characteristic of German soldiers of the period. The Colonel himself spent Christmas Day as he had most days since his brigade occupied Trenton on the 14th. He was up at 9 am to view the morning parade and superintend what one of his junior officers later described as the 'noisy occupation around his headquarters'. Rall, very much a parade soldier, delighted in the military bearing and appearance of his men. 'Service,' the same young officer recalled, 'was extraordinary. Guard duty, commands, picket posts without end.' But, in fact, none of the smart platoons busily engaged in marching and countermarching about the town that morning and afternoon was involved in anything more serious than occupational duties meant to take the edge off the boredom of garrison life.

Rall's own regiment had the guard that night, but most of the grenadiers seem to have preferred the warmth and revelry of their quarters to the windswept chill of the picket line. In reality, the only guard the town had that Christmas night was two isolated, under-manned picket houses, each situated about half a mile from the town. One guarded the approach to the town from the north-

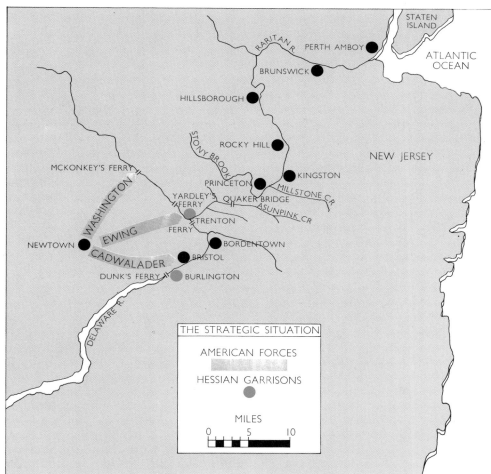

THE STRATEGIC SITUATION

AMERICAN FORCES

HESSIAN GARRISONS

MILES

0   5   10

Trenton had matured, and on Christmas Eve a council of war was held at General Greene's headquarters where the plan was outlined as follows:

1. Cadwalader's militia (which included Hitchcock's Rhode Islanders) was to cross the river at Bristol and demonstrate against the Hessian brigade at Burlington commanded by Colonel von Donop.

2. General Ewing's brigade (about 1,000 men) was to cross at Trenton Ferry and seize the bridge over Asunpink Creek south of Trenton. Ewing's mission was to block the escape of the Trenton garrison and prevent any reinforcements sent by von Donop from reaching the town.

3. Washington, with the main army of 2,400 men and 18 guns, would cross the river at McKonkey's

west along the River Road, and the other watched the Pennington Road, which entered the town from the north.

In the early evening Colonel Rall went to the home of a Trenton Tory to attend a Christmas party. There he stayed until the small hours of the morning, playing cards, drinking countless toasts and enjoying the company. Before the evening was fairly advanced there was a commotion at the door of the home. An American farmer begged to see the Colonel, but was turned away by a staff officer. Before he left, the farmer scribbled a message on a piece of paper and handed it to one of Rall's aides. This note contained a plain warning that the American army was crossing the Delaware in force.

53

When the note was brought to Rall he tucked it away in his coat without reading it. No doubt he thought it was a petition or a complaint. At any rate he couldn't read English, and seems to have decided that such business could well wait.

In contrast to the warmth and good cheer pervading the Hessian quarters at Trenton, the scene up-river at McKonkey's Ferry was altogether more grim. Glover's Marbleheaders, who had saved the army at Long Island, were assigned to ferry the troops across the Delaware. Once more, the skills of these Yankee fishermen were put to the test. The river was filled with block ice caused by a recent thaw, and the weather was terrible. The boats used in the crossing were mostly sturdy, flat-bottomed Durham boats, shallow-draft scows about 60 feet long which were used to carry iron ore down the Delaware to Philadelphia. The crossings, which began at dusk, were uneventful until about 11 pm when a furious storm descended on the area.

By 3 am the last of the infantrymen was across, and an hour later all 18 of Henry Knox's guns had been landed. The storm had spoiled the timing of the operation, but Glover's amphibians had accomplished the impossible: not one man, horse or gun had been lost to the river.

At 4 am the army was formed up and marched toward Bear Tavern and the River Road. At Bear Tavern the army swung off in the direction of Birmingham, some 3½ miles away. The storm had abated somewhat, but still the men were slipping and sliding along the rutted, icy road, walking half-bent into windlashed curtains of sleet. General John Sullivan reported that the muskets in his division were drenched and useless. Washington replied, 'Use the bayonet. I am determined to take Trenton.' No one was inclined to remind Washington that in all the army there was but one bayonet among five men. At Birmingham the army split. Sullivan, with three brigades and four batteries, continued along the River Road, while Nathanael Greene's division of four brigades and three batteries set out across the fields on the left to gain the Pennington Road above Trenton.

At 7.30 am, well past dawn, Greene's division

drew near the Hessian picket on the Pennington Road. The town lay just ahead but could not be seen through the snow flurries. The Americans fanned into the sparse woods and fields near the picket house and approached at the run or 'long trot', as one of them later described it. Captain Andreas Wiederhold, the commander of the picket, ordered his guard of 17 men into line. The Americans fired three volleys from a distance and charged the picket. Wiederhold's men answered with a volley, but then the Hessian captain noticed that the Americans were ignoring his men and rushing past the post toward the town. Now Wiederhold feared that his men would be surrounded, and he ordered a retreat. As the picket ran toward the town, the men yelled, 'Der Feind! Heraus! Heraus! (The enemy! Turn out! Turn out!).'

On the high ground near the junction of King and

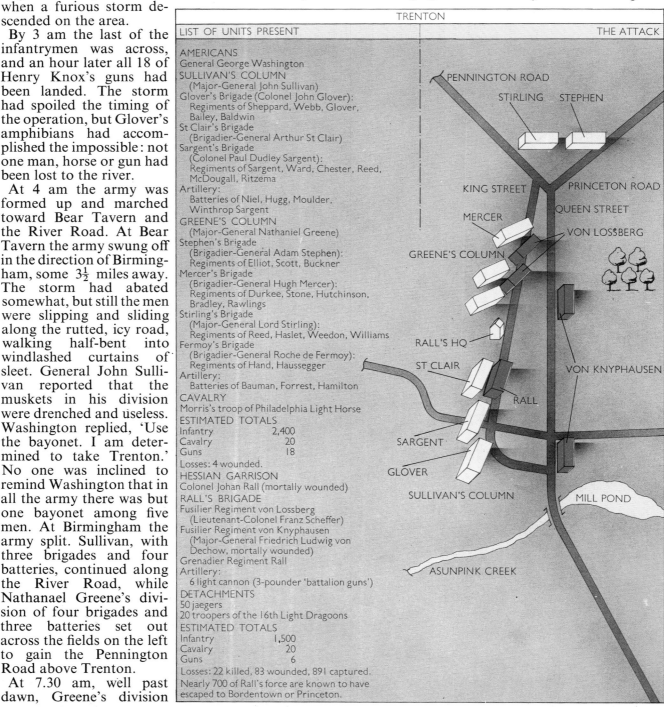

TRENTON

LIST OF UNITS PRESENT

THE ATTACK

AMERICANS
General George Washington
SULLIVAN'S COLUMN
  (Major-General John Sullivan)
Glover's Brigade (Colonel John Glover):
  Regiments of Sheppard, Webb, Glover,
  Bailey, Baldwin
St Clair's Brigade
  (Brigadier-General Arthur St Clair)
Sargent's Brigade
  (Colonel Paul Dudley Sargent):
  Regiments of Sargent, Ward, Chester, Reed,
  McDougall, Ritzema
Artillery:
  Batteries of Niel, Hugg, Moulder,
  Winthrop Sargent
GREENE'S COLUMN
  (Major-General Nathaniel Greene)
Stephen's Brigade
  (Brigadier-General Adam Stephen):
  Regiments of Elliot, Scott, Buckner
Mercer's Brigade
  (Brigadier-General Hugh Mercer):
  Regiments of Durkee, Stone, Hutchinson,
  Bradley, Rawlings
Stirling's Brigade
  (Major-General Lord Stirling):
  Regiments of Reed, Haslet, Weedon, Williams
Fermoy's Brigade
  (Brigadier-General Roche de Fermoy):
  Regiments of Hand, Haussegger
Artillery:
  Batteries of Bauman, Forrest, Hamilton
CAVALRY
Morris's troop of Philadelphia Light Horse
ESTIMATED TOTALS
Infantry   2,400
Cavalry   20
Guns   18
Losses: 4 wounded.
HESSIAN GARRISON
Colonel Johan Rall (mortally wounded)
RALL'S BRIGADE
Fusilier Regiment von Lossberg
  (Lieutenant-Colonel Franz Scheffer)
Fusilier Regiment von Knyphausen
  (Major-General Friedrich Ludwig von
  Dechow, mortally wounded)
Grenadier Regiment Rall
Artillery:
  6 light cannon (3-pounder 'battalion guns')
DETACHMENTS
50 jaegers
20 troopers of the 16th Light Dragoons
ESTIMATED TOTALS
Infantry   1,500
Cavalry   20
Guns   6
Losses: 22 killed, 83 wounded, 891 captured.
Nearly 700 of Rall's force are known to have
escaped to Bordentown or Princeton.

PENNINGTON ROAD

STIRLING   STEPHEN

KING STREET   PRINCETON ROAD

                     QUEEN STREET

MERCER   VON LOSSBERG

GREENE'S COLUMN

RALL'S HQ

ST CLAIR   VON KNYPHAUSEN

                RALL

SARGENT

GLOVER

SULLIVAN'S COLUMN   MILL POND

ASUNPINK CREEK

DURING THE BATTLE OF PRINCETON,
WASHINGTON INSPIRES HIS FALTERING RANKS TO RALLY
BY RIDING BETWEEN THE OPPOSING ARMIES.

Queen Streets, in the upper part of the town, Captain von Altenbockum's company of the Alt von Lossberg Regiment turned out to support Wiederhold's men, but the Americans pressed on, spreading out to the right and left, forming long lines that threatened to surround the town. The Hessians attempted to charge but were beaten back.

To the south, in the lower part of town, Sullivan's attack hit almost simultaneously with that of Greene to the north. Again, the advanced pickets were brushed aside, and the Americans rushed toward their objectives. Glover's brigade led this attack, veering to the south-east and the bridge over the Asunpink in order to cut off the Hessian retreat.

In the meantime the town of Trenton was fairly seething with activity. Rall, awakened, set about collecting his grenadiers for an advance to the high ground at the upper part of town, where Knox's American artillery was going into battery at the spot vacated minutes before by von Altenbockum's men. Other Hessians tried to break out of the trap on the Princeton Road, but they were turned back by Hand's Pennsylvania Riflemen. Away to the south the Von Knyphausen Regiment's fusiliers formed for battle in the open ground east of Queen Street.

Rall's grenadiers formed company columns and advanced on Knox's guns, but their dense formation was savaged and torn by round shot, and the men sought safety in the fields and orchards east of town where they joined the Von Lossberg Regiment. By this time Lord Stirling's brigade, led by 'Joe Gourd' Weedon's 3rd Virginia Regiment, had infiltrated much of the town from the west, and the Hessians who hadn't escaped to open ground beyond the town were taking fire from several directions.

The Americans were now masters of the town. Leaderless Hessians took refuge in cellars and lofts or scrambled down King and Queen Streets toward the Asunpink. Nearly 400 escaped over the Asunpink bridge before Glover's men seized it. Ewing's militia, which should have been in position to prevent escape by this route, had been unable to cross the river at Trenton Ferry. Away to the south, Cadwalader's contingent had likewise failed in its mission.

The Hessians captured in the town were hustled away, but the regiments reforming east of the town still remained to be dealt with. The Rall and Von Lossberg Regiments milled about in confusion for a time in the apple orchard where they had sought shelter from Washington's artillery. Eventually, Rall and other officers brought some order out of the chaos and started the men toward the Princeton Road, as if to attempt a breakout. For some reason, possibly, as Wiederhold later wrote, to recover the baggage left in town. Rall then had the two regiments turn back and form to charge the town. When everyone was in place, Rall stood in his stirrups, waved his sword and shouted, 'Alle was meine Grenatir seyn, vorwerds! (All my grenadiers, forward!).' This charge, which was to end in disaster, began boldly. Lieutenant Ernst Schwabe of the Von Lossberg Regiment recalled that the Hessians 'advanced on the town with drums beating and had marched into the place obliquely opposite Rall's quarters . . . There they fired on the enemy who were hidden in the houses, cellars and behind fences . . . .' The Americans were everywhere and nowhere.

Wraith-like figures in the open fired and receded before the Hessians' bayonets, while the fire from the houses and the artillery was incessant. In the storm the Hessians were almost defenceless. Schwabe reported that the charge took place in 'a continual snowfall and heavy rain' and that 'the men's guns would not in some instances fire off any longer'. Rall, a conspicuous figure on his charger, was wounded in the hip. Seconds later a musket ball slapped into his shoulder. Stunned, he toppled from his saddle. A few of his grenadiers picked him up and carried him to a nearby church where they placed him on a pew.

When Rall went down the Hessians wavered. From the north and east, closing toward their foe, a long, steady line of American infantry advanced on the desperate crowd of Hessians. No shots were fired, but periodically American officers would call on the Germans to surrender. Few of the Hessians understood what was being said to them, but the gesture was clearly comprehended, and scarcely an hour after the first shots fired at the picket house, two of Rall's three regiments surrendered.

Half a mile south of the orchard the Von Knyphausen Regiment fought on for a few minutes more. This regiment had been shunted out of town by Sullivan's attack and retreated eastward in the direction of the Mill Pond (a wide, shallow portion of the Asunpink). After Glover's men seized the Asunpink bridge, they raced eastward on the south bank of the creek, nearly keeping pace with the Von Knyphausen Regiment on the north bank. Some of the Von Knyphausen fusiliers escaped by fording the Mill Pond, but Glover's brigade cut off the retreat of the others. About this time Glover's artillery opened up from the high ground south of the Asunpink; their fire sealed the issue.

The Battle of Trenton lasted little more than an hour. Washington lost only four men wounded, but the Hessian garrison had been literally wiped out as a cohesive fighting force. Of Rall's entire brigade, which had numbered some 1,500 men at the start of the action, 22 had been killed and 83 wounded. There were nearly 900 prisoners. The six brass battalion guns of the Hessian brigade, its band and all its baggage had also been taken. Only 700 escaped before the trap closed.

But Washington could not afford to loiter in Trenton. His little army was vulnerable to a counterstroke from Princeton and Bordentown, and furthermore the men would need to return the way they had come before recrossing the Delaware to the safety of their camps in Pennsylvania.

The march back to McKonkey's Ferry was as brutal as the approach had been. Two men froze to death, but for the most part the victors managed to forget their cares and laughed and joked about what they had accomplished.

The recrossing was completed early in the morning of the 27th, and the American army settled down to a few days of well-deserved rest. In New Jersey, von Donop abandoned his exposed position in the Burlington area and fell back on Brigadier-General Alexander Leslie's force at Princeton. General Howe, who could scarcely believe the news from Trenton, was determined not to abandon New Jersey. He recalled Lord Cornwallis, who was in New York City preparing to return to England on leave, and gave him the command in New Jersey.

THE PRINCETON CAMPAIGN

Washington was planning another attack on the British in New Jersey even as the last of the Trenton strike force trailed into camp from the ferry. The plan for a second attack might have been prompted in part by news that Cadwalader's militiamen, who had failed in their attempt to cross the river on the 26th, had succeeded on the 27th. Washington might have recalled Cadwalader, but his intelligence service and patrols reported that the British had quit the countryside adjacent to the river and that the militia were not in danger. The American commander may then have realized that if he could return to New Jersey with all the forces at his disposal, he had 'a fair Opportunity . . . of driving the Enemy entirely from, or at least to, the extremity of the province of Jersey'. He informed Cadwalader that he would cross the river on the 29th and march to Trenton, which was fixed as the rendezvous for American forces in the area.

But before this second stroke at the British could be made, the vexatious problem of enlistments had to be resolved. In the last week of December the year-long enlistment period of the Continental troops was expiring. If the Continentals could not be induced to re-enlist, the American army would effectively cease to exist. Congress helped the situation somewhat by empowering Washington to offer the regulars a bounty on re-enlistment. Even so, most of the best troops went home, and the force Washington took to Trenton included just over 3,000 regulars.

The second crossing took three days (29–31 December) because although the river was iced over at McKonkey's Ferry, where Sullivan's division was to cross, the ice was not thick enough for the men to cross safely on it. Four miles downstream, at Yardley's Ferry, the ice was thicker, and most of General Greene's division crossed there during the evening of the 29th. Greene's division entered Trenton at 10 am on the 30th, and a few hours later the first elements of Sullivan's division arrived.

Once in Trenton, Washington realized that he knew little about the disposition of British forces in Jersey, and also that in creating another opportunity for his army, he might well have provided the British with a chance to gain revenge. To guard against a British surprise, strong detachments were thrown out along the Trenton-Princeton Road as far as Maidenhead, and patrols scoured the area for intelligence of the enemy's strength and intentions. Cadwalader's force was ordered to march to Trenton post-haste so that the army would be at full strength when the time came to move on the British.

In the meantime Lord Cornwallis hastened to Jersey to assume command of the British and Hessian forces in the province. There were nearly 14,000 British and Allied troops in Jersey, and allowing for garrisons along the over-extended line of communications and supply with New York, Cornwallis could bring almost 8,000 of them into action against Washington. During the night of 1–2 January Cornwallis arrived at Princeton. He had ridden 50 miles without pause in severe weather to join the troops concentrated there by General Grant. Tireless, active and spoiling for a fight, he immediately convoked a council of war and declared that the army would march on Trenton in the morning.

The next day, 2 January, the British army advanced down the road covered by Washington's delaying force, and ran into trouble almost immediately. The Americans, commanded by Colonel Edward Hand, contested almost every mile of their advance and made firm stands at each creek and defile intersecting the British advance. In the intervening time Washington had the main army at Trenton take up a defensive position to the south of the Asunpink.

At dusk Colonel Hand's men were driven into Trenton, and two battalions of British light infantry, followed by two battalions of Hessian grenadiers and a handful of jaegers, pressed into the town. Colonel Daniel Hitchcock's Rhode Islanders crossed the Asunpink to cover Hand's withdrawal and ran foul of the light infantry and grenadiers. There was a brief but bloody skirmish among the buildings of the town before Hitchcock's men were forced back by fast-moving flanking parties from the light infantry. The withdrawal of the Rhode Islanders was covered by powerful concentrations of artillery on hills behind the creek. Stung by this fire, the British halted and brought up their own guns. The 'Second Battle of Trenton' ended in a prolonged cannonade across the Asunpink. Finally, after a few tentative jabs at various points along the American line, the British bivouacked for the night.

There were those among the British that night who pressed Cornwallis to continue the attack. Among them was General Sir William Erskine, who counselled that, 'If Washington is the general I take him to be, he will not be found there in the morning'. But Cornwallis demurred. He was tired, and the men were worn-out by the day's march. The 'old fox' was trapped, he reassured Erskine.

On the American side of the Asunpink Washington held a council of war with his generals. None of them needed to be reminded of the desperate plight of the army. There were not enough boats at Trenton to ferry the army across the Delaware, so retreat by that route was out of the question. Moreover, any retreat was certain to demoralize the army and negate the effect of the victory at Trenton. As the generals mulled over the alternatives, it was possibly General Arthur St Clair who suggested an attack on the British post at Princeton. (It may also be that Washington had such an attack in mind all along, and held the council of war to discuss the plan with his general officers.) However it surfaced, the idea of a march on Princeton was breathtakingly simple and brilliant: it allowed the Americans a chance to save themselves from immediate danger and still retain the initiative.

The army stole away from its camps along the Asunpink at about midnight. Five hundred militia were left behind to stoke the camp-fires and 'amuse the enemy'—a ruse that Washington hoped would mask the movement of his men.

THE BATTLE OF PRINCETON

By dawn the vanguard of the army was at Stony Brook about three miles below Princeton. The night march—the army's third in the space of ten days—had been especially gruelling, and the men, many of whom had no proper footwear, had left a bloody trail to mark their progress. Some of them had actually fallen asleep standing up during pauses in the march, but discipline was firm and no one was allowed to lag far behind.

In Princeton, meanwhile, Lieutenant-Colonel Charles Mawhood prepared two of the three regiments in his brigade, the 17th and 55th Foot, for a march to join Cornwallis above Trenton. These regiments and a handful of light dragoons were to provide an escort for some supplies the British commander had requested. The remaining regiment, the 40th Foot, was to be left behind in Princeton to guard the army's magazines there.

Mawhood's detachment paraded before dawn and marched from Princeton well before Washington's van crossed Stony Brook below the town. By 8 am, Mawhood's column, led by the 17th Foot, was crossing Stony Brook by the bridge at Worth's Mill on

THE BRITISH 17TH FOOT RESORT FOR A SECOND TIME TO THEIR BAYONETS AS THEY ATTEMPT TO BREAK OUT.

the Trenton Road. One mile directly south of the British and marching straight for the Mill was Hugh Mercer's brigade of Washington's army. Neither party, for the time being, was aware of the presence of the other.

Mercer's brigade was the lead element in a column Washington had detached and pushed north along the Quaker Road to 'break down the Bridge and post a party at the mill on the main road, to oppose the enemy's main army if they should pursue'. Following Mercer and completing the column was Cadwalader's Pennsylvania militia brigade. The bulk of the army, under Sullivan, left the Quaker Road about a quarter of a mile north of the Stony Brook crossing and swung away to the north-east toward Princeton along the Saw Mill Road.

Colonel Mawhood's energetic light dragoon detachment spotted Mercer's column some moments before Mercer had knowledge of Mawhood's presence. After the sighting Mawhood ordered the 17th to double back across the brook toward a hill just south of the main road. As the British raced toward the hill, Mercer received a message from Washington

THE ACTION AT PRINCETON, PORTRAYED BY WILLIAM MERCER, SON OF THE AMERICAN GENERAL WHO LIES MORTALLY WOUNDED BESIDE HIS HORSE IN THE CENTRE. THE MOUNTED FIGURE WITH SWORD TO THE LEFT IS GENERALLY TAKEN TO BE WASHINGTON.

stating that British infantry had been observed to his front and ordering him to engage. Until this moment Mercer was unaware that the British were nearby in force, though he had seen flanking parties. He too appreciated the tactical value of the hill that the 17th was now rapidly approaching, and he set his men in motion for it. Mercer's infantry had a shorter distance to go and reached the hill first. There, behind a rail fence which marked the boundary of one William Clark's property, they went into line of battle in the ragged, ungainly 'Indian file' fashion affected by the Continental soldier before von Steuben's drill, introduced early in 1778, improved the field evolutions of the army.

The brigade that Mercer led into battle that morning was, in fact, little larger than the 400-strong British regiment opposing it. Moreover, the Americans were at a disadvantage, as few of them had bayonets. Most of Mercer's men were riflemen whose weapons would not take the bayonet. A portion of the brigade—probably no more than a hundred—carried muskets and bayonets. These men were the remnants of the famous Virginia, Maryland and Delaware Continental regiments. They were steady, veteran soldiers, but there were too few of them to contend man-for-man with the 17th in a bayonet duel.

Mercer's riflemen were already firing on the 17th when the Continentals fell into line next to them. The British halted and fired a volley, but it passed harmlessly over the heads of the Americans. Captain John Fleming, commanding the 1st Virginia, ordered his regiment to dress ranks before delivering a volley, and the British soldiers yelled back, 'Damn you, we will dress you!' But when Fleming's men fired into them, the British reportedly 'screamed as if so many devils got hold of them'. A moment later the 17th charged forward over the hundred or so feet of snow-covered ground separating the two forces and pitched into the American line with the bayonet. The riflemen ran, and the full fury of the British onslaught was concentrated against the outnumbered Continentals. Cheering and huzzaing, Mawhood's men burst over the rail fence and swarmed among the little band of men in William Clark's orchard. The Continentals gave ground and then broke and ran. General Mercer tried to rally the fugitives a little farther back, but he was clubbed to the ground and bayonetted repeatedly. Colonel Haslet, the commander of the Delaware regiment, was shot nearby, and Captain

Fleming fell mortally wounded. The mêlée lasted just a few minutes, but Mawhood's men were in a blood-lust and Mercer's brigade was fearfully cut up. Mercifully, the 17th did not pursue them beyond the bottom of the hill.

As Mercer's men trailed back from this encounter, Cadwalader's militia brigade, which had taken position on a second, smaller hill opposite the William Clark property, charged forward against the 17th. But Cadwalader's bold effort went for naught. As soon as the Americans came within range, the 17th's line flamed and rippled with musketry, and the militia, unused to such rough treatment, recoiled in confusion.

About this time Washington rode up and surveyed the field. The American commander had been with Sullivan's column on the Saw Mill Road and had not, at first, given much thought to the action taking place among the hills and fields away to the

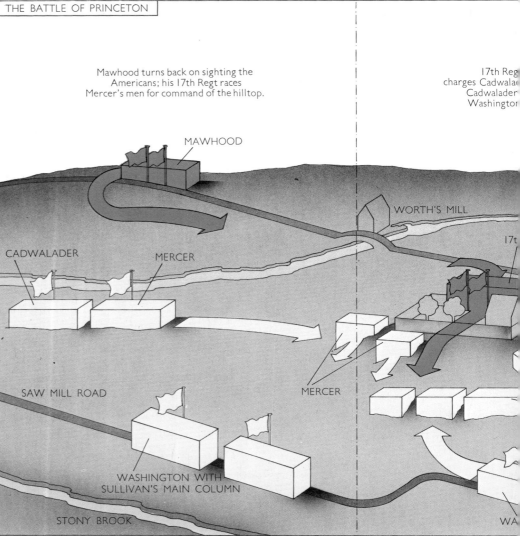

THE BATTLE OF PRINCETON

Mawhood turns back on sighting the Americans; his 17th Regt races Mercer's men for command of the hilltop.

17th Reg[t] charges Cadwala[der] Cadwalader[...] Washington[...]

MAWHOOD

WORTH'S MILL

17t[h]

CADWALADER   MERCER

MERCER

SAW MILL ROAD

WASHINGTON WITH SULLIVAN'S MAIN COLUMN

STONY BROOK

WA[...]

left and rear of the main army. The rising volume of musketry, however, soon convinced him that what he thought was a skirmish had, in fact, become a battle. Taking Hitchcock's Rhode Islanders and the Philadelphia Light Horse with him, he rode toward Cadwalader's position and arrived at the moment the militia were routed by the 17th's fire. What Washington saw must have dismayed him. Mercer's men were reforming but were obviously demoralized. Cadwalader's brigade had panicked, and though some maintained a line, others were drifting

away from the battle. Only Captain Joseph Moulder's 2-gun battery kept the British from capitalizing on their success.

Almost by instinct, Washington realized that the panic gripping these men might spread to his entire army. Immediately, he rode between the lines, exposing himself recklessly to the fire of both sides in a desperate effort to rally the militia. Again, the 17th volleyed. Its fire was answered by some of Cadwalader's men, and Washington was enveloped by smoke. Colonel John Fitzgerald of Washington's staff hid his eyes. He was certain Washington had been killed. Seconds later the commander emerged from the smoke unhurt. Fitzgerald cried for joy at the sight of Washington as he now rode about the field urging resistance.

Spurred by Washington's example, Cadwalader's shaky line stiffened. Other militiamen worked around Mawhood's right flank, and by their fire

Cadwalader's men, who were closest to the 17th, drew back and filed through the ranks of Hitchcock's Continentals, but Major Israel Angell's 1st Rhode Island Regiment continued to advance on the British. Mawhood's men fired one more volley and then ran, tossing muskets and accoutrements aside in their gathering panic.

Washington led the pursuit of Mawhood's men in person. Dozens of British soldiers were captured along Stony Brook in what the American commander described as 'a fine fox chase'. Mawhood himself rode toward Princeton with a handful of infantrymen and 'a pair of springing spaniels playing before him', but he was forced to turn back and flee when two of his party were shot by Sullivan's men.

Sullivan's column had an easy time with the two remaining regiments of Mawhood's brigade. These regiments, the 40th and the 55th, made a brief stand at Frog Hollow (see diagram) and then retreated to

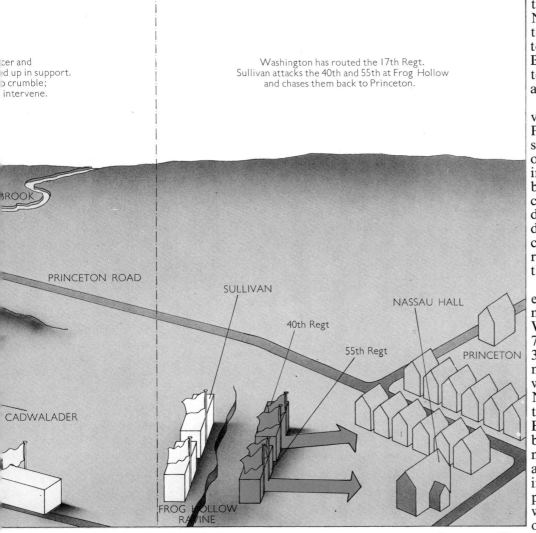

cer and
d up in support.
o crumble;
intervene.

Washington has routed the 17th Regt.
Sullivan attacks the 40th and 55th at Frog Hollow
and chases them back to Princeton.

BROOK

PRINCETON ROAD

SULLIVAN

40th Regt

55th Regt

NASSAU HALL

PRINCETON

CADWALADER

FROG HOLLOW RAVINE

prepared positions within the town near the College of New Jersey (today Princeton University). Once in the town, however, most of the British surrendered or attempted to escape through adjoining fields.

The only resistance Sullivan's men encountered in Princeton came from a few score infantrymen who had occupied Nassau Hall, an imposing stone dormitory building belonging to the college. These men surrendered after the Americans dragged a cannon into the college yard and sent a few rounds of ball crashing into the structure.

The Battle of Princeton ended with the short cannonade at Nassau Hall. Washington had lost '6 or 7 Officers and about 25 or 30 Privates' killed. The number of American wounded was not reported. No Americans were captured or missing. On the British side, Mawhood's brigade had been decimated. British casualties approached 300 altogether, including, as officially reported, 18 killed, 58 wounded and 187 captured or missing. This cannot be

caused the British to withdraw a short distance to their right. Just then Hitchcock's men appeared, driving in column directly at the 17th. It was only then, perhaps, that Mawhood appreciated the seriousness of his situation. The 17th was in imminent danger of being overwhelmed. There was only one hope. If those terrible bayonets could be made to work their battlefield magic once more, the Americans might be thrown off balance long enough to allow the 17th to retreat unmolested across Stony Brook. So, once more, the British pushed forward.

accurate, however, for on 4 January 21 British were buried in one mass grave alone.

After the battle Washington led his men into winter quarters at Morristown. A short while later, General Howe abandoned New Jersey to the Americans. In effect, though, the Trenton-Princeton campaign did more than prevent the British from capturing Philadelphia and overrunning the Jerseys. It preserved the Continental army from a winter's decay following a season of defeat, and in so doing kept the cause of American independence alive.

61

4 October 1777
Stripped of their capital, Philadelphia,
and swept aside at Brandywine,
Washington's Continentals effect a surprise
comeback that restores international faith
in the Americans' conduct of the war.

GERMANTOWN

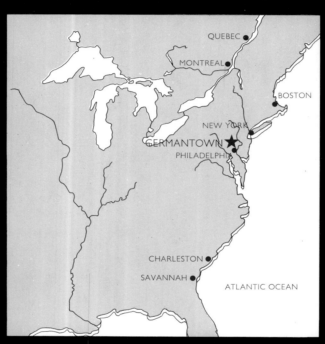

THE BACKGROUND TO THE BATTLE

The Battle of Germantown brought to an end the puzzling Philadelphia Campaign of 1777. This had begun—to the astonishment of Washington—when Sir William Howe abruptly turned his back on Burgoyne, his comrade-in-arms to the north, and embarked on a seaborne invasion of the Chesapeake with Philadelphia, the American capital, as his ultimate aim.

Howe had decided that Philadelphia should be his strategic objective early in 1777, but he did not decide how to proceed there until the late spring. Two routes were available to him. On the one hand he could move across New Jersey and ford the Delaware above Philadelphia. For this plan to succeed, however, Washington's army would first have to be destroyed in a pitched battle or manoeuvred across the Delaware; the simple reason for this was that the American army could not be left straddling extensive lines of communication and supply across the Jerseys. The alternative plan involved transporting the entire army by sea to the Delaware or the Chesapeake, landing and approaching Philadelphia from the south. This plan was hazardous, too, but if everything fell into place, it would be preferable to the first. Characteristically, Howe wasted a great deal of time making up his mind which plan to pursue.

As the springtime wore on, Howe dilly-dallied in New York City, and his army had little martial amusement aside from hit-and-run raids in New Jersey and Connecticut. In the meantime, Washington's army, which had survived a terrible winter at Morristown, doubled in size.

Unable to fathom Howe's intentions, Washington assumed a secure defensive position in the Watchung Mountains parallel to the New Brunswick–Philadelphia road. From this position Washington could move to defend the Highlands if Howe proceeded north, or, if the British commander chose to move overland across the Jerseys and toward the Delaware, the American army was admirably poised to strike across the axis of his advance.

Still more time passed. In June, after a lame attempt to manoeuvre the American army from its stronghold, Howe withdrew his troops from their advance posts to Brunswick and then to Amboy. Washington followed this withdrawal at a safe distance, but one American division under Lord Stirling drew too close to Amboy, and on the 26th the British made a

SQUIRE CHEYNEY, A LOCAL MAN, RIDES UP TO WARN WASHINGTON OF CORNWALLIS'S OUTFLANKING MOVEMENT BEFORE THE BATTLE OF BRANDYWINE.

sortie from their post, brushed with Stirling and advanced to Westfield. For a moment it seemed that the British had resumed the offensive. Washington extricated Stirling and fell back to his prepared position in the foothills. Unable to lure Washington into battle in the open, Howe resolved to gain Philadelphia by sea. By 31 June the British had evacuated their posts in New Jersey, and earnest preparations were under way for the amphibious move south.

As for Burgoyne, at this time laying siege to Fort Ticonderoga some 200 miles to the north, Howe had no intention of aiding him directly by thrusting up the Hudson, nor did he plan to co-ordinate his operations with those of the Canadian army. It would be sufficient, in his mind, to draw Washington away from the Hudson to defend Philadelphia. Burgoyne's army was to be left to shift for itself. No doubt, too, both commanders preferred to operate under the assumption that each was conducting a separate campaign against separate forces. The risk attending such a policy seems to have been completely overlooked at the time, despite the fact that the American armies occupied the strategic centre and, by moving on interior lines, could easily dispose to meet widely divergent British thrusts in the Hudson and Delaware valleys, maintain unbroken communications and reinforce one another at will.

On 23 July the British fleet sailed from Sandy Hook, New Jersey. A week later the armada was off the Delaware. Howe had originally planned to proceed up the Delaware and land below Philadelphia, but reports of natural and man-made obstructions forced a change in plans; instead, the fleet set sail for the Chesapeake. Howe's movements were causing Washington a great deal of trouble. He had an intimation that Philadelphia was Howe's ultimate objective, but when the British fleet beat to sea again after appearing off the Delaware, he could not be quite so certain. The British objective could now be Charleston, Philadelphia, the Hudson or New England. The American army was poised at Coryell's Ferry on the Delaware River, ready to move north or south as the occasion warranted. Finally, on 22 August, intelligence of Howe's appearance in the Chesapeake was communicated to Washington, and the American army was put in

motion toward the district below Philadelphia. On 25 August the British army began to disembark at Head of Elk (Elkton), Maryland, about 50 miles south of Philadelphia. Washington was too far away to oppose the landing, but he did detach a corps of riflemen under General 'Scotch Willie' Maxwell to harass the British advance. Maxwell ran into Howe's large advance corps of jaegers and light infantry and fought several skirmishes but was forced back upon the main army.

On 8 September Washington decided to make a stand below Philadelphia, and the next day his army fell back to a strong defensive position on the east bank of Brandywine Creek. The Brandywine position, which covered a front of about six miles, blocked the most direct route to Philadelphia. The Continental army, then about 11,000 strong, occupied an advantageous position. On the far left Armstrong's Pennsylvania militia watched Pyle's

mile stretch between Chadd's Ford, which was two miles above Pyle's Ford, and Wistar's Ford, below the point where the Brandywine forked into the North Branch and the West Branch. Greene's wing held the left centre and centre, and Sullivan's wing guarded the right flank. Maxwell's light corps held an advanced position on the right bank opposite Chadd's Ford.

Howe, with 18,000 men, camped near Kennett Square, seven miles from the Brandywine, on the 10th. The British commander's plan of attack for the next day was proper and predictable—his mode of operation had not changed since the Battles of Long Island and White Plains in the previous year. One wing of his army under General von Knyphausen was to demonstrate against Greene at Chadd's Ford, while the other wing, under Lord Cornwallis, marched north beyond the American right, crossed the Brandywine (North Branch) at an unprotected

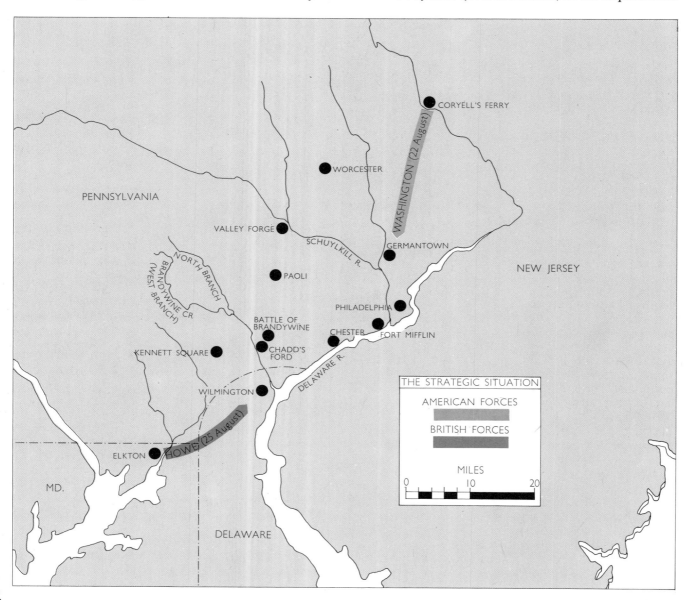

Ford, the first of numerous fords on the Brandywine above its junction with Christiana Creek, which emptied into the Delaware. The countryside around Pyle's Ford was rocky and difficult to negotiate, and Howe's attack was not expected there. The two wings of the regular army under Generals Greene and Sullivan watched the Brandywine on the four-

upper ford and descended on Sullivan from the right and rear.

On the next day, 11 September, Howe's plan was carried out with admirable regularity and precision. Von Knyphausen drove Maxwell across the creek, brought up his artillery and exchanged cannon fire with Proctor's Continental artillery on the east bank.

Cornwallis's wide outflanking movement was detected but was not continuously observed. Washington's own plan for a tactical counter-offensive against von Knyphausen's wing was suspended when Cornwallis appeared on the American right and rear at Birmingham Meeting House, and Sullivan had to shift from front to flank to meet his attack. As Cornwallis's attack developed, von Knyphausen ended his charade at Chadd's Ford and pushed a column led by General Grant across the creek. By this time one of the divisions guarding the ford (Greene's) had been detached to stabilize Sullivan's hard-pressed line, and the defence of the ford had been left to Maxwell's riflemen and Wayne's Pennsylvania division. Von Knyphausen nevertheless found the going rough until one of Cornwallis's columns moved over from the battle against Sullivan and struck Wayne's division on its right flank. This was a decisive blow.

The American army was now everywhere in retreat. Greene's division fought a sharp rearguard action to cover Sullivan's withdrawal toward Chester through Dilworthtown, while Wayne's men retired in good order to the south-east. At dusk the British pursuit ended, and Washington collected his army together in Chester. The battle had cost the American army about 800 men, while the British had lost 600.

The Battle of Brandywine was followed by two weeks of manoeuvre. During this period Washington contemplated giving battle—indeed, at one point only a sudden, intense storm prevented the two armies from clashing. But then the American army was out-manoeuvred and, on 26 September, a British column under Cornwallis marched into the American capital unopposed.

The defeat at Brandywine and the distressing occupation of the capital—next to London the second largest city in the English-speaking world—gave many Americans cause for despair. For his part Washington knew that the occupation of the capital was, militarily speaking, a relatively inconsequential matter; but at the same time it had great symbolic and propaganda value. The defeat at Brandywine was galling, and Washington burned for revenge. He now sought battle as the best way to restore the delicate political and propaganda balance wrecked by the late campaign. He would fight, as he put it, 'to repair the consequences of our late ill success'.

In the meantime, General Howe had established his headquarters at Germantown, a rambling village six miles north of Philadelphia. Germantown was then a tidy, substantial settlement. It had been founded as a refuge for Palatinate Germans in 1683. Many of the dwellings were constructed of dark grey stone, and most had been built on or near the

MAJOR-GENERAL GREY, WHO ON THE NIGHT OF 20-21 SEPTEMBER LED A DEVASTATING SURPRISE ATTACK ON GENERAL WAYNE'S TROOPS BIVOUACKED NEAR PAOLI.

Main Street or Skippack Road, which entered the town from the north-west at Chestnut Hill and continued through the town itself to Philadelphia. The British camp was laid out at right angles to the Main Street, extending to the west along the Schoolhouse Lane and to the east along the Mill Road. The terrain about the town was hilly and intersected by creeks: it had been cleared, though it was by no means open ground and was broken up by numerous fences and walls marking off town lots and garden plots.

Picket guards and patrols ensured the safety of the 9,000 men in Howe's camp at Germantown, but there were no fortifications (except for a small redoubt on the right at Luken's Mill) because, oddly, Howe believed that to fortify the camp would be an admission of weakness! Moreover, he did not expect Washington to attack, and in the few days that elapsed before he was proved wrong, he seriously weakened his army with detachments.

In fact, Washington was biding his time, awaiting reinforcements. Nonetheless, during the period 29 September–2 October, the American army drew closer to the British camp. On 1 October, Washington was reinforced, and the Continentals and militia advanced to Worcester Township, just 16 miles north-west of Germantown. Two days later a council of war was held in a farmhouse. By then Washington had received information of Howe's detachments, and the generals concluded unanimously in favour of attack. Washington's plan of battle for the next day envisioned a broad pincer movement by four columns converging on the British camp at Germantown. As a plan it was probably too complicated to succeed. Also, too much depended on the uncertain fighting qualities of the militia, who were to constitute two of the columns. One of these columns—composed of Armstrong's Pennsylvanians—was to strike the British left near the Schuylkill River. The other column, which consisted of Maryland and New Jersey militia under Smallwood and Forman, was to move by the York Road and attack the right rear of the British camp. In the event, these columns played no significant role in the battle, the burden of the fight the next day being borne by the Continentals. These regulars were still organized in 'wings' (in effect, corps) as they had been at Brandywine. Sullivan, whose inadequacy had been only too apparent at Brandywine, commanded the centre column, which was to advance directly down the Main Street toward the British centre at the Market Square. The other column, under Greene's command, was to attack the British right at Luken's Mill and drive down the Mill Road to link with Sullivan at the Market Square. The army was to march at 7 pm on the evening of the 3rd, to be in position to attack before dawn.

THE COMMANDERS

Sir William Howe (1729–1814) was the youngest of three sons born to the second Viscount Howe and his wife Maria Sophia. Howe was a physically imposing man, about six feet tall and not unlike Washington in appearance, though the deeply set eyes, dark complexion and prominent nose and lips of the Englishman suggested more the aspect of a saturnine melancholic than of a member of the nobility. This sullen demeanour, shared by all the Howe brothers, earned for one, Richard Lord Howe, the nickname 'Black Dick'.

Howe's military career included periods spent overseas in Flanders (1747–48) and in America, France and Cuba (1758–62). Despite this diversity of service—and the fact that he became a champion of the revolutionary system of light drill for the army following the French and Indian War (1754–63)—he remained at heart a conservative, his military philosophy rooted in the neo-classical tradition of 18th-century warfare.

As Commander-in-chief in America following Gage's recall in September 1775, Howe used his army, then the largest England had yet fielded, in a manner that might have redounded to the credit of a Saxe or a Luxembourg, but was little

SIR WILLIAM HOWE.

calculated to break the back of a rebellion. In a series of impressive moves, he compelled Washington to quit New York and its environs and later outmanoeuvred the Continental army below Philadelphia, occupying the American capital in September 1777.

Howe was undoubtedly a capable tactician, but he failed to build on his victories. Time and again the American army slipped from his grasp. His major impediment as a general was that he failed to appreciate the nature of the rebellion. His victories, invariably followed by the occupation of a seaport, seemed impressive, but strategically they did little more than deprive the Americans of vulnerable population centres which they could scarcely utilize anyway. Howe's failure to 'go for the jugular' and destroy Washington's ragamuffin Continentals—the life force of the rebellion—was ultimately to prove decisive.

Anthony Wayne (1745–96), whose division led Sullivan's advance through the town, was an intense, combative brigadier whose remarkable talents had not gone unnoticed. Of Irish Protestant ancestry (his grandfather had led a troop of Williamite horse at the Boyne), he was born on his family's extensive estates in Chester County, Pennsylvania. Like Washington, he spent much of his early life as a surveyor, but in 1767 he settled down to the squire's life on his estate near Waynesborough, Pennsylvania. Before the Revolution he served in the Pennsylvania legislature, but when the war broke out he raised a regiment and marched to join Washington's army at Boston. Subsequently, he served with distinction at Trois Rivières, Brandywine and Germantown.

Wayne's reputation as a fighting general, his impetuosity and personal vanity led to his nickname of 'Mad Anthony'. This epithet, in turn, seems to have clouded his reputation as a thinking officer. To be sure, he was always in the thick of the fighting, but Washington also valued his counsel (as at Monmouth, where he was the only ranking officer to recommend attack), and his presence of mind in executing the attack at Stony Point earned him the acclaim of the army. At Green Spring Farm his quick thinking saved his men from certain destruction in a difficult position.

After the war Wayne dabbled in politics for a short time and then re-entered the army. His last campaign was against the Indian Federation of the Old Northwest, which he defeated at Fallen Timbers in 1794. At his death he was Commander-in-chief of the United States Army.

ANTHONY WAYNE.

THE BATTLE

At dawn the van of Sullivan's wing—Conway's brigade and a handful of light horse under Captain Allen McLane of Delaware—drew close to the British picket at Allen's House in Mount Airy. The sun was glimpsed briefly but then disappeared in a bank of fog and haze which was to complicate the manoeuvres of the American army for the rest of the day. For the present, though, this fog masked the approach of Conway's men, muffling the sounds of the march so much that even the usually alert light infantrymen manning the picket line were not aware that an attack was imminent.

The British were not caught completely off-guard, however. Captain Ewald of the Hessian jaegers had warned Howe of an attack on the right at Luken's Mill, and the Guard Light Infantry had been moved forward to reinforce the post of the 1st Light Infantry at that point. There were also other warnings of an impending attack, but, as Major John André put it, they were 'very little credited'. The capture of some rebel flankers soon lent credence to the notion that a general attack was in the offing, but by then it was too late to do much in the way of preparation.

Just after daybreak the picket guard at Mount Airy was hit by Captain McLane's horsemen. The light infantrymen fired wildly at the ghostlike figures looming out of the fog. None of McLane's partisans was hit, but one of Conway's men had his hand shattered by a musket ball ricocheting off a tree. He was the first casualty of the Battle of Germantown.

McLane's horsemen quickly dispersed the picket and captured two field pieces. Conway's regiments, still in column on the road, hurried their march, but the firing at the picket house had alerted the 2nd Light Infantry at Beggarstown some 200 yards farther down the Germantown Road. A few minutes later Conway's column collided with the light infantry, who were busy forming to receive the attack of what most of their officers believed to be a strong raiding party.

The musketry of the light infantry broke up the head of Conway's column, but that battle-hardened veteran soon had his brigade formed into a line on the right of the road while Sullivan sent the 2nd Maryland Brigade into line on his left. In the meantime, the 40th Regiment of Lieutenant-Colonel Thomas Musgrave had advanced from its camp nearer Germantown and taken position on the left of the light infantry.

The action now became general, and Sullivan, anxious for his flanks, reinforced Conway's brigade with his own division and detailed 'Mad Anthony' Wayne's division off to the left of the road. The sight of the light infantry incensed Wayne's Pennsylvanians (who had been their victims in a devastating night attack at Paoli, just before the taking of Philadelphia). Crying 'Have at the bloodhounds' and 'Revenge Wayne's affair', they attacked with the bayonet. According to Wayne his men 'took Ample Vengeance for that Nights Work. Our Officers Exerted themselves to save many of the poor wretches who were Crying for Mercy—but to little purpose; the Rage and Fury of the Soldiers were not to be Restrained for some time—at least not until great numbers of the Enemy fell by our Bayonets.'

The weight and vigour of Sullivan's attack began to drive the British through Beggarstown and into the precincts of Germantown. Here and there groups ran, but others resisted stubbornly, making a stand at every ditch, wall and fence in the backlots and byways of the town. Nonetheless, the British line was losing its cohesiveness. Captain Frederick von Munchausen, Howe's adjutant-general, rode toward the firing and was astonished to see 'what I had never seen before, the English rapidly flying'. An officer of the 52nd Regiment's light infantry company recalled that his battalion 'was so reduced by killed and wounded that the bugle was sounded to retreat; indeed, had we not retreated at the time we did we should all have been taken and killed, as two columns of the enemy had nearly got round our flank. But this was the first time we had ever retreated from the Americans, and it was with great difficulty we could get the men to obey our orders.'

By this time many of the fields of stubble and buckwheat in the backlots had caught fire, and the dense smoke of these fires combined with the smoke of the musketry and the fog to produce an incredible darkness in which whole units lost their way. Conway's brigade drifted off to the right into the morass and broken ground near Paper Mill Run, while Sullivan's division stumbled forward along the route of the Germantown Road. Wayne's division continued to drive the British to its front 'with the utmost precipitation' and soon outstripped its supports to the right.

In the meantime Lieutenant-Colonel Musgrave had thrown six companies of the hard-pressed 40th Regiment into the formidable stone house of Attorney-General Benjamin Chew which stood about 100 yards back from the Main Street and to the left of the American centre. These men had a brief respite as the battle swept by them, and, in the confusion, they were missed.

Musgrave used his time well and soon had converted the Chew House into a veritable fortress. He exhorted his men to 'sell themselves as dear as possible to the enemy'. Within moments the little garrison was firing on the reserve of the American army as it advanced up the Main Street toward Sullivan's position.

This sudden fire from Chew House caused a great deal more confusion than it should have. For, instead of filing off to the right and left of the house and leaving a small force to watch the men barricaded inside, the reserve division halted and called for artillery. It was at this point that the American commanders began to lose control over the course of the battle. Several things happened almost simultaneously which ultimately destroyed the impetus of the attack.

Firstly, Howe had come up to the ground below Chew House to investigate the continual rattle of musketry. Still under the impression that his advance corps was dealing with a scouting party, he 'got into a passion' when he came upon the broken remnants of the 1st Light Infantry. Spurring his horse toward the men, he chided them in a firm,

fatherly voice (Howe fancied himself to be the 'father' of British light infantry):'For shame, Light Infantry, I never saw you retreat before. Form! Form! It is only a scouting party.' At that moment, however, the Americans manhandled three cannon out of the haze and fired a salvo of grapeshot into the General's party. Howe and his staff prudently retired, but very soon Sullivan had more than the advance corps and a few scattered reinforcements to deal with, for Howe quickly put four brigades in motion toward the fight on the Main Street.

Secondly, just as the British advanced to the counter-attack, Sullivan's men began to tire and run out of ammunition. During the previous hour's advance Sullivan's division had been a virtual walking battery—devastating the enemy with repeated volleys which literally shook the ground. Washington, who accompanied Sullivan's advance for a space, had, in fact, cautioned him to conserve ammunition; now Sullivan's men faced a crisis with barely the means to defend themselves.

Still, there were reassuring developments. A link with Greene's wing had been established, although not, it appears, at the designated place. Part of Stephen's division—probably elements of Woodford's brigade—had deviated from Greene's line of march along Limekiln Road and wandered toward the sound of battle along minor tracks. These men eventually spotted elements of Wayne's division below Chew House, and, unbeknown to the Pennsylvanians, began to follow their advance.

THE ASSAULT ON CHEW HOUSE; FROM A PAINTING BY HOWARD PYLE.

Then, too, the roar of musketry a few miles off to the left signalled the beginning of Greene's attack on the British posts above Luken's Mill. Even though Greene was three-quarters of an hour late— his march had been by a circuitous route, four miles longer than anticipated, and his guide had lost the way—the sound of his fire brought encouragement to the battle-weary men of the centre.

In the meantime, at Chew House, American artillery under General Henry Knox had begun battering the solid grey stone walls with solid shot. At first, the balls had little effect, since the guns had been laid at an oblique angle to the walls of the house, and the shot glanced off—many being deflected into the ranks of Ogden's New York militia regiment which was drawn up nearby. Then Timothy Pickering of Washington's staff rode up to the guns and corrected their position so that they could fire directly at the shuttered windows and door on the ground floor. One of the defenders of the house related what happened next:

'With the first shot they burst open both the hall-doors, and wounded some men with the pieces of stone that flew from the wall. Capt. Hains, a brave intelligent officer, who commanded on the ground floor, reported to Col. Musgrave what had happened, and that he had thrown chairs, tables, and

little impediments he could before the door, and that he would endeavor to keep the enemy out as long as he had a single man left: he was very soon put to the test, for the rebels directed their cannon (sometimes loaded with round, sometimes with grape shot) entirely against the upper stories, and sent some of the most daring fellows from the best troops they had, to force their way into the house....'

At Billmeyer's House, one hundred yards north of Chew's, Washington, Knox and some other officers held a hurried conference. A French engineer, on the basis of his experience in Italy, suggested that Chew House be bypassed, but Knox, the Chief of Artillery, recalled an obscure maxim of war and argued that 'It would be unmilitary to leave a castle in our rear'. Further, Knox stated, the tiny garrison should be summoned to surrender. Pickering argued against Knox, but the porcine artillerist's opinion carried more weight with Washington, and a volunteer was sought to carry the summons to Chew's. A few minutes later Lieutenant William Smith, Washington's deputy adjutant-general, approached the house under a white flag. A volley rang out and Smith fell, mortally wounded, a few yards from the doorway. Clearly, Musgrave's men had no intention of surrendering their 'castle'.

After this incident, the first of several assaults on the house by 'Scotch Willie' Maxwell's brigade took place. For about half an hour Maxwell's men and the artillery alternated in assailing the place. Some of the Americans succeeded in getting into the house by the shambles near the doorway, only to be bayonetted by defenders operating from behind piles of furniture inside. In a short time the lawn was littered with the bodies of more than fifty men. Other parties approached the house using the kitchen outhouse and board fences as cover. A few actually got to the house and attempted to fire it, but they were shot down by men posted in the cellar.

Maxwell's attacks and Knox's bombardment had been spectacular failures. Musgrave's men stood firm within the battered walls of Chew House. There was nothing to do now but pass them by.

The Chew House episode might have been insignificant in itself, but its effect on the troops of Wayne and Sullivan—now hundreds of yards beyond the house and approaching the main

British line in the Market Square area—cost the Americans the battle.

In their advance toward the British camp, the divisions of Wayne and Sullivan had drifted apart and lost contact. Wayne's advance had been quicker—Sullivan's division faced stiffer opposition and was impeded by fences and walls which had to be torn down to allow the men to pass—and both divisions were skirting the town to avoid British units which had shut themselves up in the more substantial dwellings. Nash's brigade of the reserve was dealing with these pockets of resistance but had fallen behind. Thus, a gap of several hundred yards had developed between the two divisions driving hard toward the Market Square. Neither Sullivan nor Wayne, of course, knew anything of the problems developing at Chew House.

For Wayne's troops the opening shots of Knox's bombardment of Chew House had ominous implications. Sullivan's fire had slackened and all but ceased. There were few British to their front on Luken's Mill Road, but parties of Grey's 3rd Brigade had begun to pressure their right near the Main Street. Then the rumblings from Chew House became more pronounced, followed shortly by one crashing volley from the same direction (Sullivan's last, as it turned out). Wayne's division slowed, then halted and faced about. Rumours began to circulate. Sullivan must have been flanked; he was in trouble back there; perhaps the enemy had gained the rear of the American attack. Reluctantly, Wayne ordered his division to return by the route they had come. Suddenly, ahead, barely visible in the blinding smoke and haze, a long, well-ordered line of troops appeared. Shots rang out, then volleys. The line melted away, broken up by Wayne's fire. Then a horrible discovery was made. Those troops were Americans too! Wayne's men had exchanged fire with Adam Stephen's division, which had been trailing their advance for the last half-hour. Now Wayne's men were in worse danger. A terrible cross-fire was being loosed upon them from the Main Street to their left, from behind them and even from the fields in which Stephen's division had stood just moments before. They too began to lose order and run.

It now appears that the British counter-attack from Schoolhouse Lane had penetrated the gap between Sullivan and Wayne. Nash's brigade, near the Mennonite Meeting House, was closer to Sullivan than to Wayne. Nash and Sullivan had been hit first (by Agnew's 4th Brigade), loosed one volley and retreated. Agnew's men continued forward without their brigadier, who had been mortally wounded near the Meeting House, but the 17th and 44th Foot of Grey's brigade had marched unopposed into the void between Sullivan and Wayne. Shortly after Wayne's troops had fired on Stephen's men, Grey's British unit began to fire on Wayne from the fields east of the town. Wayne's division, thoroughly confused and perplexed by the sudden turnabout in its fortunes, trailed back in the direction of Chew House.

Mercifully, the British did not press their advantage. They too were impeded by the rough terrain and stopped constantly to reorder their lines. Patriot-soldier Tom Paine, serving with Sullivan, described the sullen, grudging retreat of the Americans: 'The enemy kept a civil distance behind, sending every now and then a shot after us and receiving the same from us'.

In the meantime, off to the east, the Battle of Germantown entered its last phase. Greene's column, having brushed aside the 1st Light Infantry and the Guard Light Infantry in the woods above Luken's Mill, swept past the 4th Foot near the Mill. Muhlenberg's brigade, led by the 9th Virginia, overran a 'little flush redoubt' near the Mill and, in fighting described by Colonel Charles Stewart as 'cursed hot Work', took three guns defended by the 5th and 38th Foot. Then, with McDougall's brigade on his left and Scott's on his right, Muhlenberg swept down toward the Market Square.

Again it was a case of too little too late. The British line recovered smartly and responded to this new blow with firmness and remarkable precision. The 27th Foot drove north from the area below Luken's Mill and checked. McDougall. Other regiments, led by Major-General Grey, broke away from the pursuit of Sullivan and Wayne and stopped Scott's brigade. Now only Muhlenberg's Virginians were left, and General Grant was leading reinforcements forward against them.

Perhaps unaware that his supports were gone and that a ring of steel was closing about his men, Parson Muhlenberg continued to drive his brigade forward. His troops had by now slashed deep into the British centre, taking 110 prisoners as they traversed the length of the camps along the Mill Road. This was the deepest American penetration of the day, and it might have been fatal had it coincided with Wayne's thrust of the previous hour.

But Muhlenberg's men were done in. They had been marching and fighting for 14 hours, and now even Muhlenberg found himself dozing off in the saddle despite the heat of the action.

At that point British resistance noticeably stiffened. The troops of Agnew, Grey, Stirn and Grant and reinforcements from Philadelphia under Lord Cornwallis concentrated on Muhlenberg's command. The dazed Americans stopped, reformed and then attempted to fight their way back. At Luken's Mill the British had reoccupied the redoubt taken by the Virginians earlier in the morning. Some of Muhlenberg's men, seeing this way barred, took to the fields and by circumventing the force at the Mill made good their retreat; but the 6th and 9th Virginia, having led the advance, were the rearguard in the withdrawal. Too closely pressed to break away to the north, they were forced to ground arms. The British took 400 prisoners, including the entire 9th Virginia Regiment.

Away to the north-east, the pursuit of Greene's battered column continued in earnest, until finally the 3rd Virginia of Woodford's brigade faced about and, by taking a firm stand, ended it.

For the troops of Washington's army there had never been, and probably never again would be, an experience like Germantown. Lieutenant James McMichael of Wayne's command later described an incredible 24-hour period in which he had marched 45 miles, fought for four hours, including a 'furious advance' through smouldering buckwheat fields, and concluded that he 'had previously undergone many fatigues, but never any that so much overdone me as this'. Captain Anderson, of the famous Delaware Regiment, gave a similar account,

69

LIST OF UNITS PRESENT

AMERICANS
General George Washington

RIGHT WING MILITIA CONTINGENT
(Brigadier-General John Armstrong)
Irvine's Brigade
Potter's Brigade
First City Troop (detachment)

RIGHT WING CONTINENTALS
(Major-General John Sullivan)
Conway's Brigade
   (Brigadier-General Thomas Conway)
Sullivan's Division:
   1st Maryland Brigade (Stone)
   2nd Maryland Brigade
Wayne's Division
   (Brigadier-General Anthony Wayne):
   Wayne's Brigade
   2nd Pennsylvania Brigade (Hampton)
Captain Allen McLane's Delaware Horse
Moylan's Light Dragoons (detachment)
Bland's Light Dragoons (detachment)

LEFT WING CONTINENTALS
(Major-General Nathaniel Greene)
McDougall's Brigade
   (Brigadier-General Alexander McDougall)
Greene's Division:
   Muhlenberg's Brigade
   Weedon's Brigade
Stephen's Division
   (Major-General Adam Stephen):
   1st Virginia Brigade (Woodford)
   Scott's Brigade
Cavalry (Count Casimir Pulaski):
   Sheldon's Light Dragoons (detachment)

LEFT WING MILITIA CONTINGENT
(Brigadier-General William Smallwood)
Smallwood's Brigade
Forman's Brigade

RESERVE (Major-General Lord Stirling)
Stirling's Division:
   Nash's Brigade
   Maxwell's Brigade

ARTILLERY (Brigadier-General Henry Knox)
ESTIMATED TOTALS

Continentals	8,000
Militia	3,000
Cavalry	200

ESTIMATED GRAND TOTAL 11,200

Losses: 152 killed, 521 wounded, 400 missing
and captured.

BRITISH
General Sir William Howe

PICKET
40th Regt (Musgrave)
1st Light Infantry
2nd Light Infantry

LEFT WING
   (Lieutenant-General Baron von Knyphausen)
Hessian Jaegers (von Wurmb)
4th Brigade (Major-General James Agnew):
   33rd, 37th, 46th, 64th Regiments
3rd Brigade (Major-General Charles Grey):
   15th, 17th, 44th Regiments
Hessian Brigade (Major-General Stirn):
   Regiment Erbprinz
   Regiment von Donop
Reinforcements (from Philadelphia)
   Grenadier Battalion von Minnigerode
   Grenadier Battalion von Linsing

RIGHT WING
   (General Sir William Howe)
2nd Brigade (Major-General Grant):
   5th, 27th, 55th Regiments
1st Brigade:
   4th, 28th, 49th Regiments
Brigade of Guards
   (Brigadier-General Edward Matthew)
Queen's Rangers (Wemyss)
Reinforcements (from Philadelphia):
   1st, 2nd Grenadiers

CAVALRY
2 squadrons Light Dragoons
ESTIMATED TOTAL 9,000

Losses: 70 killed, 450 wounded, 14 missing
and captured

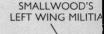

SMALLWOOD'S
LEFT WING MILITIA

STIF

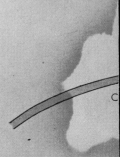

C

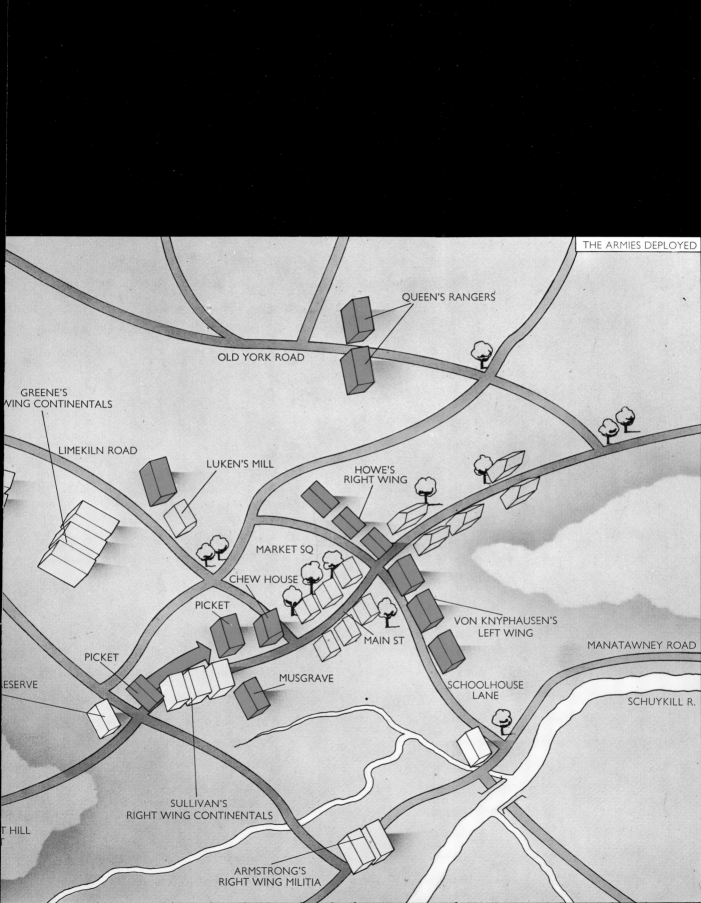

QUEEN'S RANGERS

OLD YORK ROAD

GREENE'S
WING CONTINENTALS

LIMEKILN ROAD

LUKEN'S MILL

HOWE'S
RIGHT WING

MARKET SQ

CHEW HOUSE

PICKET

PICKET

MAIN ST

VON KNYPHAUSEN'S
LEFT WING

MANATAWNEY ROAD

SCHOOLHOUSE
LANE

SCHUYKILL R.

ESERVE

MUSGRAVE

SULLIVAN'S
RIGHT WING CONTINENTALS

T HILL

ARMSTRONG'S
RIGHT WING MILITIA

adding that he and his men had 'eat nothing and drank nothing but water on the tour'. Viewed from any angle, Germantown had been an ordeal for the Americans, another entry in an inventory of hardship which extended back to the painful retreat across the Jerseys of the previous autumn and the miserable winter spent in the hutments of their temporary garrison in Morristown.

Clearly, Germantown had been an American defeat, yet it was not regarded as such by the army. In his report to Congress, Washington stated that the troops had unaccountably 'retreated at an instant when Victory was declaring herself in our favor'. Lieutenant McMichael echoed Washington's sentiments when he declared, 'It was disagreeable to have to leave the field, when we had almost made a conquest. . . .' The men were aware that they had suffered a setback but sensed that rather more had been gained than lost. As General George Weedon put it, 'Though the event miscarried, it was worth the undertaking'.

For the British, Germantown was simply another victory, and 'Major' Washington, to use André's terminology, had been sent scuttling back to his camps on the Perkiomen. But the American ranker gained something invaluable at Germantown. He had seen the enemy's best troops put to flight in a fair contest. He sensed that he was achieving parity with the British regular. In the words of Colonel William Heth, 'Though we gave away a complete victory, we have learned this valuable truth: to beat them by vigorous exertion, and that we are far superior in respect to swiftness. We are in high spirits. Every action of our troops reflects fresh vigor and a greater opinion of their own strength.'

'In war,' Napoleon Bonaparte wrote, 'moral factors account for three-quarters of the whole; relative material strength accounts for only one quarter.' The American soldier had never lacked courage, enthusiasm and the will to endure hardship. Germantown taught him confidence. But the lesson had been dearly bought. American casualties were 152 killed, 521 wounded and 400 missing or prisoners. The British, too, had suffered. Howe officially reported 70 killed, 450 wounded and 14 missing, but unofficial estimates of British casualties ran as high as 800.

Germantown had international significance, too. Vergennes, the French Foreign Minister, and many other influential Europeans were favourably impressed by reports of the battle. John Adams, one of the American diplomats in France, alluded to this fact in a letter to a member of Congress when he wrote:

'General Gates was the ablest negotiator you had in Europe; and next to him, General Washington's attack on the enemy at Germantown. I do not know, indeed, whether this last affair had not more influence upon the European mind than that of Saratoga. Although the attempt was unsuccessful, the military gentlemen in Europe considered it as the most decisive proof that America would finally succeed.'

In retrospect, it is clear that, although surprise was to have been a key element in the American attack, complete surprise was out of the question. The roads leading to the main British camp near the Market Square were adequately posted in every possible direction of approach. Von Wurmb's jaegers

covered the Manatawney Road from their post at Van Deering's Mill behind the Wissahickon, and light infantrymen manned pickets three miles north of the camp along the Skippack Road at Mount Airy. Other pickets watched the Limekiln Road near Luken's Mill, while the Queen's Rangers anchored the right along the York Road. The probability of surprising these men—all excellent light troops—was slight. Moreover, the British light infantry were especially vigilant, remembering their own role in the Paoli Massacre and well aware that the Americans were burning for revenge. Nonetheless, partial surprise was achieved, and was made more effective by the fog and the discipline of the American approach march.

Given the improbability of achieving complete surprise, the rationale behind the American attack becomes suspect. Certainly, the moment the pickets were driven in or resisted, an alarm would be dispatched to the main camp and the soldiers there placed under arms, ready to resist any attack. The quickest infantry could not have deployed and advanced the three miles from Mount Airy to the Market Square in less than three-quarters of an hour under optimum conditions.

The delay occasioned by the resistance of the 2nd Light Infantry and Musgrave's 40th Regiment along the Main Street was compounded by fog and smoke. Sullivan's division, moreover, was further delayed by the built-up nature of the area, and, in their pursuit of the light infantry, the men were 'compelled to remove every fence'. Thus the British, despite Howe's inexplicable underestimate of the seriousness of the attack, had ample time to form and react. The later arrival of Minnigerode's brigade on the left and three battalions under Lord Cornwallis behind the right-centre meant that the British were the stronger party at the crisis of the battle. The British and Hessian troops were fresh, too, since the battle had proceeded toward them, while Washington's men were tired and becoming confused.

Another factor causing the American plan to go awry was the miscalculation of the distances involved. Washington estimated the distance to Germantown from this camp on the Skippack Road at 'about 12 Miles', whereas in fact the distance was 16 miles. Greene's column had to travel even farther, but this does not seem to have been taken into consideration. From the beginning, then, the timing of the attack was wrong, based as it was on false assumptions. Furthermore, the planned co-ordination between Sullivan's and Greene's columns existed only on paper. This elementary oversight might be excused had the Americans been operating in an unfamiliar area, but the Continental army had camped in Germantown both before and after the Battle of Brandywine (1–8 August and 12–14 September 1777), and there were many officers familiar with the district.

Thus the plan of attack, aside from its complexity and ambitious objectives, might have succeeded only if surprise could have been achieved and co-ordination preserved among widely separated columns. That Washington and his officers believed such a plan would succeed, and, indeed, believed that in the event they came within an ace of success, is indicative of the amateurism still pervading the American high command at that period.

THE AMERICANS SURROUND COLONEL MUSGRAVE'S REDCOATS, BARRICADED INSIDE CHEW HOUSE
AN OFFICER IS SEEN SETTING FIRE TO THE MAIN DOOR.

VON RIEDESEL'S HESSIAN COLUMN ADVANCES TO THE AID OF THE BRITISH FORCE IN THE CLEARING AT FREEMAN'S FARM; INDIAN SCOUTS ARE SHOWN IN THE FOREGROUND.

19 September – 7 October 1777
Near Saratoga, in steadily worsening conditions,
Burgoyne twice ventures his army in battle, but heavy
losses compel him eventually to surrender. In
Europe, Britain's enemies celebrate the
rebel triumph and the French sign their deadly
alliance with the Americans.

SARATOGA

THE
BACKGROUND TO
THE BATTLES

The 1776 campaign closed with British armies in full retreat on two fronts. The first setback occurred in October when Sir Guy Carleton, the Governor of Canada, attempted to invade New York State by way of Lake Champlain. Carleton's drive was blunted before it reached Fort Ticonderoga, its first objective, when the British gunboat fleet battled with an improvised American flotilla commanded by General Benedict Arnold. In the first fleet action of the war, fought off Valcour Island on 11 October, Arnold's gunboats were roughly handled and forced to flee southward, but the British fleet was so severely damaged that it put about and sailed back to Canada. At this point, Carleton had second thoughts about proceeding with the invasion and withdrew from the New York frontier. Less than two months later Sir William Howe's New Jersey campaign ended in a shambles, with Washington winning the twin victories of Trenton and Princeton, and the British quitting New Jersey and withdrawing to their base of operations in New York City.

One soldier who shared in the disappointments of the 1776 campaign was General John Burgoyne, Carleton's second-in-command. When the Northern Army returned from its abortive invasion of New York, Burgoyne took leave from his Canadian post and journeyed to England to argue for a scheme of invasion which, he maintained, would end the rebellion within a year by isolating New England, the hotbed of revolutionary sentiment, from the other colonies. Burgoyne's plan was embodied in a document entitled *Thoughts for Conducting the War from the Side of Canada*. This paper, which was submitted on 28 February 1777, suggested a massive, three-pronged invasion of New York State by British armies operating along the major waterhighways—the Lake Champlain-Hudson River Valley and the Mohawk Valley. The town of Albany, which was located at a point where the lines of advance converged, was to be the objective of all three armies.

Two armies would move from the British base at Montreal in Canada. The major strike force, commanded by Burgoyne himself, would descend on Albany by way of Lake Champlain and the Upper Hudson, following the centuries-old invasion route through the Adirondack wilderness. A second, smaller force, commanded by Lieutenant-Colonel Barry St Leger, would go by boat to Oswego on Lake Ontario and then follow the Iroquois Trail inland to the objective. The third pincer, to be detailed from Howe's main army, would operate northward from New York City along the Hudson. Once the three armies had joined forces in Albany Burgoyne, presumably, was to hold the Champlain-Hudson line with a string of outposts and invade New England, while Sir William Howe acted against Washington with the main army.

Burgoyne's project was by no means novel. Similar schemes had been proposed before, but none

had been championed by a soldier of his charm, wit and brilliance. Then, too, Carleton, who might normally have commanded the operation, had been discredited, and both the King and Lord Germain, the Secretary of State for America, were looking for a more enterprising commander. Burgoyne, though he denied the charge, undoubtedly used his political influence to further undermine Carleton and secure an independent command for himself. Almost from the moment of his arrival in England he was closeted with either Germain or the King, lobbying fiercely for the adoption of his grand strategy. In due course, the plan was approved.

There remained, it seemed, only the question of what Carleton's place in the scheme would be. Germain wanted him removed from the Canadian command, and Burgoyne no doubt would have preferred to operate unfettered, but the King balked at the idea. In the end, Sir Guy was retained, but Burgoyne's instructions indicated precisely that his role would be limited strictly to providing logistical support for the expedition.

Politics aside, Burgoyne's plan was deceptively simple: it paraded an impressive, fatally attractive concept. The Ministry's armchair strategists were captivated; even so, they failed to translate their optimism into action, and the strategic planning of the venture was slipshod in the extreme. Howe's cooperation, which was essential to the success of the invasion, was never firmly secured. Sir William was willing to pay lip-service to Burgoyne's project, but he had a plan of his own, intending to make a major effort against Philadelphia, the rebel capital. As a sop to Burgoyne he would, he informed Germain, leave a weak corps under Sir Henry Clinton at New York City to make 'a diversion occasionally upon Hudson's River'. Incredibly, Germain approved this considerable modification to Burgoyne's plan, contenting himself with cautioning Howe that 'whatever he may meditate, it will be executed in time to co-operate with the army ordered to proceed from Canada'.

Howe, of course, was convinced that he would be in a position to return from Pennsylvania and assist Burgoyne's progress. On the other hand Clinton, his deputy, argued strenuously against the move, pointing out, correctly, that 'Philadelphia had better close than open the campaign, as it required an army to defend'. But Clinton's well-reasoned argument went unheeded. Howe persisted in his design, launching his invasion of Pennsylvania in July. The effect of this move was to cripple Burgoyne's offensive before it had fairly commenced.

Burgoyne, meanwhile, concentrated his invasion army at St Johns on the Richelieu River above Lake Champlain. Inevitably, there were delays, and the troops were not ready to sail until 21 June—a month behind the schedule outline in the *Thoughts*. Still, the army was formidable, and Burgoyne confidently expected to be in Albany by the end of summer. He had 9,861 men in a mixed force of

British and German regulars, Canadians, Provincials and Indians. The splendidly equipped siege train, with which he hoped to reduce Fort Ticonderoga, his first objective, consisted of 138 guns and was the largest ever assembled on the North American continent.

Impressive as this martial array was, it was also ill-suited to the demands of warfare in a wilderness. Burgoyne had taken precautions to increase the mobility of his regulars, but the army marched overburdened by all manner of useless paraphernalia. The worst offender was Sir John himself, whose personal baggage filled three wagons. The 400 Indians, led by the Chevalier de St Luc and Charles de Langlade, were scarcely any help. Burgoyne admonished them to fight in a civilized manner, but admitted that they were 'spoiled children' who probably could not be controlled beyond the confines of the camp. Then, too, the small forces of

scouts, but the British commander meant to employ them 'particularly upon detachments for keeping the country in awe and procuring cattle'. 'Their real use,' he noted, 'will be great in the preservation of national troops.'

Sir John, however, did not expect to have to fight his way through the wilderness. He was convinced that Fort Ticonderoga was the only obstacle barring his way to Albany and that once his siege guns had battered the defenders of the old fortress into submission, his army's progress would be transformed into a triumphal march.

Burgoyne's assessment of the strategic situation was not too wide of the mark. Both sides considered Ticonderoga and its satellite forts to be the key to the campaign. The fort stood on a spit of land at a point where Lake Champlain narrowed to the width of a cannon shot and also guarded the portage to Lake George, the most desirable route to the Upper

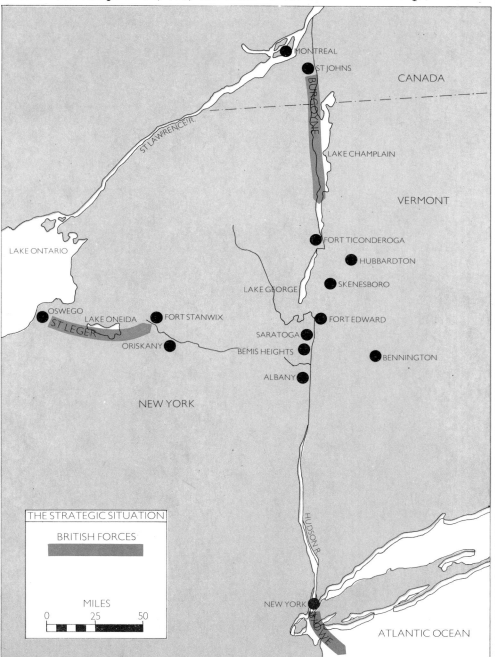

Hudson. Ironically, the Americans had done little to improve the fort, and in 1777 it was little more than a tumbledown pile; this edifice was garrisoned by 2,000 sick and dispirited troops commanded by Major-General Arthur St Clair. It was, however, the only fortified locality between the British and Albany, and Congress regarded its defence as vital.

Beyond Ticonderoga, the Americans could also look to a field force of some 2,000 men. This, the Army of the Northern Department, was camped at Fort Edward about 40 miles south of Ticonderoga. Its commander, Major-General Philip Schuyler, was an aristocratic New Yorker with a reputation as a stern disciplinarian—though in the few months preceding the opening of the campaign he had been unable to mould the New England militia into an effective fighting force. The New Englanders, who constituted the bulk of the troops available for the defence of the region, hated him as a New Yorker and suspected him of Toryism, while Major-General Horatio Gates, his predecessor and chief rival for the command, had intrigued against him in Congress. Thus Schuyler, though able and resourceful, faced the almost impossible task of opposing Burgoyne's invasion with a weak, demoralized and near mutinous army. 'I would not complain,' a junior American officer

Tories and Canadians accompanying the expedition were misused. These men knew the countryside and might have been of assistance as light infantry or

lamented, 'but, in the name of heaven, what can be expected from a naked, undisciplined, badly armed, unaccoutred body of men, when opposed to a vast superiority of British troops?'

Burgoyne lost no time in exploiting his adversary's weakness. Advancing on both shores of Lake Champlain, the British army invested Fort Ticonderoga on 2 July. St Clair realized that he could not hold the fort's outworks against the British host and withdrew his men to the 'Old French Lines' nearer the main fort, where he resolved to make a stand against the inevitable assault. Across the lake at Mount Independence, Ticonderoga's sister fortress, Brigadier-General Roche de Fermoy faced the approach of Burgoyne's left wing under Baron von Riedesel.

Ticonderoga's chances of withstanding a formal assault by the British army were probably quite good. The Marquis de Montcalm, with a veteran army of 4,000 regulars, had defended the same line of breastworks against seven assaults by Abercromby's British troops in 1758. St Clair's force was slightly smaller than Montcalm's (Schuyler had latterly managed to send reinforcements) but, against that, many of the Americans were sick. Nevertheless St Clair hoped at least to buy time for Schuyler and Major-General Benjamin Lincoln to rally the militia to the defence of the Hudson Valley.

Burgoyne, however, did not repeat the blunder of 'Mrs Nanny Cromby'. One of his officers, probably Lieutenant Twiss, the army's chief engineer, discovered that Ticonderoga had a fatal weakness: the Americans had neglected to fortify Mount Defiance, a steep, wooded eminence just south of the fortress. This hill overlooked and commanded the forts on the lake. It had not been fortified because it was generally regarded as inaccessible. However, Major-General William Phillips, the hard-bitten artillerist who was Burgoyne's second-in-command, ended further speculation on that point. When Twiss reported his findings, Phillips is said to have exclaimed: 'Where a goat can go, a man can go, and where a man can go, he can drag a gun.' Working round the clock under Phillips's direction, a fatigue party cut a crude path up the hill, and by the morning of 5 July, the British had emplaced two guns on the boulder-strewn summit.

Phillips's feat placed Ticonderoga and Fort Independence at the mercy of the British gunners, who could lob shells into both forts at their leisure. St Clair had no alternative but to order the evacuation of the position under cover of darkness. That night the American army slipped away toward Vermont, retreating to the eastern shore of the lake over a sturdy pontoon bridge used to maintain communications with Fort Independence. The main army marched for Castleton, Vermont, covered by a strong rear guard of 1,000 men commanded by Colonel Ebenezer Francis. The sick and wounded, together with the army's baggage, fled down the lake in an immense flotilla of boats.

The American retreat did not go unnoticed. Some time before dawn Burgoyne was alerted to the situation; he dispatched Brigadier-General Simon Fraser's advance corps in pursuit of St Clair, supported by von Riedesel's slow-moving Germans. The British commander himself broke through the boom and bridge of boats and led his gunboats in a wild chase after the retreating foe.

Fraser's detachment overtook St Clair's rear guard at Hubbardton, Vermont, on 7 July, and a brisk battle ensued. One American regiment fled almost immediately, but Francis, supported by Colonel Seth Warner's famous Green Mountain Boys, broke up a British assault with accurate volleys of musketry and counter-attacked in turn. For a time, Fraser's men were in danger of being swept away, but von Riedesel saved the day, advancing to the assistance of the British at the head of three battalions of stalwart Brunswickers and driving back the American right wing at the point of the bayonet. Colonel Francis was killed, and his men quit the field, dispersing into the surrounding forest. The Americans lost about 360 men in the engagement, and Fraser reported casualties of 183 killed and wounded. Nevertheless, Fraser's men did not pursue much beyond Hubbardton, and St Clair continued his retreat undisturbed. On 12 July he joined Schuyler at Fort Edward.

Burgoyne, meanwhile, had smashed the American flotilla at Skenesboro, adding another triumph to his auspicious string of victories. Thus, in the space of a few days, the Continental Army had been dealt a staggering blow. Besides the capture of the forts, which in itself was enough to create a panic, the Americans had lost a great quantity of military stores and provisions, 5 galleys, 200 boats, and 130 cannon. Materially, at least, the main American Army was crippled, and King George III, when he heard the news, shouted for joy: 'I have beat them, I have beat all the Americans.'

At this juncture, however, Burgoyne made a mistake in judgment that spelled disaster for his campaign. Instead of retracing his steps to Ticonderoga and resuming his advance southward by way of Lake George and the wagon road to the Hudson, he chose to march directly on Fort Edward through 23 miles of rough, thickly forested terrain. Just why Burgoyne opted for the latter route has never been satisfactorily explained. He believed, correctly, that the Lake George route was the 'most expeditious and commodious' line of advance but stated subsequently that he did not wish to make a retrograde movement, since to do so would give the appearance of a retreat and 'abate the panic of the enemy'. One interesting but far-fetched theory has it that Major Philip Skene, Burgoyne's chief Tory aide, prevailed upon the general to advance directly into the wilderness so that he, Skene, would acquire a good road through his 25,000-acre land grant. Whatever the motive, the result of the decision was to reduce the British advance to a crawl. The army covered the remaining 23 miles in 24 days and had to build 40 bridges, including one causeway two miles in length.

Schuyler, of course, did everything in his power to retard the British advance. His troops felled trees across the forest path and blocked up and diverted the numerous streams and rivulets of the area, turning the countryside into a vast, tangled morass. He also pursued a scorched-earth policy, stripping the farms of forage and burning what could not be carried off.

Burgoyne's advance, if slow, was nevertheless inexorable. The panic over the loss of Ticonderoga had not subsided, and Schuyler was having trouble keeping his army together. Two Massachusetts regiments marched away when their enlistments expired and Schuyler declared that half his troops were 'utterly dispirited and insubordinate'. Despairing, he retreated down the Hudson to the mouth of the Mohawk, there to make one last stand.

Suddenly, however, the strategic situation changed when St Leger's division, which Burgoyne hoped to join in Albany, marched straight into a hornets' nest. Advancing from Oswego by way of Lake Oneida and Wood Creek, the British column arrived at Fort Stanwix, an American post guarding the western entrance to the Mohawk Valley, on 3 August. St Leger expected to have an easy time with Fort Stanwix but, instead, found that the garrison was prepared to resist to the very last.

St Leger's force, which was just 1,642 men strong, was the smallest of the three invading armies; even so, it was fairly formidable. The greater portion of the men (apart from the 200 British regulars) were skilled bush fighters; they included Indians, Tory backwoodsmen, and Hessian jaegers. The fort's defenders, some 750 men under the command of Colonel Peter Gansevoort, might have perished had they attempted to meet the British in the open, but they were secure enough behind the earthen walls of their post because the invaders had no heavy artillery. St Leger summoned the fort to surrender, but received no reply and was forced to interrupt his progress toward Albany to engage in a formal siege.

GENERAL BURGOYNE ADDRESSING THE INDIANS.

In the meantime, General Nicholas Herkimer collected the militia of Tryon County and, together with a handful of friendly Oneida Indians, marched to raise the siege. On 6 August Herkimer's 800-man relief column blundered into a cleverly laid ambush in a swampy ravine near Oriskany, just six miles from the fort. In the engagement that followed— one of the most savage and closely contested battles of the war—St Leger's Tories and Indians were driven off, but Herkimer was mortally wounded and his little army, crippled by 650 casualties, was forced to withdraw.

This raging battle at Oriskany demoralized St Leger's Iroquois, who had lost many of their favourite chiefs. Unused to the routine of a siege, they became surly and unmanageable, and on 22 August, when they learned of the approach of a second relief column, composed of Continentals commanded by Major-General Benedict Arnold, they rioted and decamped. St Leger was forced to raise the siege and retreat to Oswego, thus ending the threat to the Mohawk Valley.

St Leger's defeat cheered the Americans, but they still had to contend with Burgoyne, who seemed determined to continue his advance in the face of stiffening resistance and despite the breakdown of his army's inadequate supply system. The British were forced to wander far from their line of advance in search of forage, and the destruction of one such expedition produced the first American victory of the campaign.

On 11 August Burgoyne ordered Lieutenant-Colonel Frederick Baum and 800 men, mostly Germans and Tories, to march to Bennington, Vermont, and seize the Patriot magazine there, which was rumoured to be weakly guarded. Baron von Riedesel opposed the expedition, which would carry Baum's troops over 30 miles deep into territory Burgoyne himself believed populated by the 'most active and rebellious race of the Continent', but Skene, anxious to recruit his Tory corps to full strength, assured Sir John that 'the friends to the British cause are as five to one, and they want only the appearance of a protecting power to show themselves'.

Baum's detachment never reached Bennington. His march was harassed by American snipers, who fired 'in the usual way from bushes'; to make matters worse, the Indians, mercurial as ever, behaved as if they were at an aboriginal carnival, cutting the throats of beef cattle taken along the way to get at the cowbells, which fascinated them. Finally, on 14 August, Baum encountered the main American force under Colonel John Stark, the stubborn, independent hero of Bunker Hill. The Germans skirmished with Stark's men, driving them back toward Bennington, but Baum called off the pursuit when more and more Americans appeared under arms outside the town. Then, with nightfall approaching, he ordered his men to fortify a hillock and sent to Burgoyne for reinforcements. The next day torrential rain prevented a resumption of the battle and, significantly, delayed the march of Lieutenant-Colonel Heinrich von Breymann's relief column of 550 men.

On the 16th the weather cleared, and Stark, shouting 'We'll beat them today or by night Molly Stark's a widow', attacked. Baum's men were overwhelmed in the first rush, but von Breymann's column was nearby, and the stern German grenadiers maintained the unequal contest until nightfall when they withdrew under pressure from Warner's Green Mountain Boys. The battle—really two separate engagements—was an unmitigated disaster for Burgoyne's army. Stark's losses were slight, just 70 men, but the American commander reported enemy casualties of 207 killed and over 700 captured. Baum's corps was destroyed, and von Breymann's battered column had barely escaped a similar fate.

Bennington pricked the bubble of invincibility that had carried the British army to Fort Edward on the Hudson. For the first time, Burgoyne became despondent, and his troops, according to Sergeant Lamb of the 9th Regiment, lost confidence in themselves. The battle, Lamb said, 'deranged every plan for pursuing the advantages which had been previously obtained'. Still plagued by chronic shortages of forage and military stores, Sir John was forced to halt his advance yet again, while the army revictualled in preparation for its next thrust. Then, on 13 September, the British resumed their march, crossing the Hudson by a pontoon bridge near Saratoga.

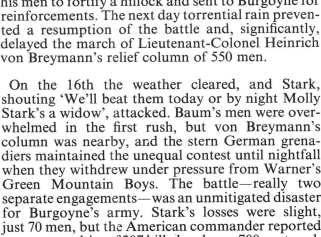

THE COMMANDERS

Major-General Horatio Gates (1727–1806) remains to this day one of the least understood major figures of the Revolutionary Era. Historians have pictured him as a cowardly snob; a man utterly devoid of military talent who managed to gain high command by undermining the reputation of General Schuyler, the aristocratic New Yorker who preceded him as commander of the Northern Department. This estimate of Gates's character is probably much too severe, but like many broad sketches it contains enough of the truth for there to be no mistaking the subject.

Before the Revolution Gates served as a field officer with the British Army in North America and Martinique. His service record was excellent, and he eventually rose to the rank of major in the regular army. But because of his humble birth (his mother was a housekeeper to the Duke of Leeds), his prospects of attaining high rank were negligible. Following the Seven Years' War, he sold his commission and, in 1773, bought a plantation in Virginia.

When war broke out in 1775, Gates became the Continental Army's first adjutant-general. His staff work was thorough, and in due course he was rewarded with a field command. This command, it happened, was that of the Northern Department, nominally the fief of General Philip Schuyler. Schuyler was not prepared to be jobbed out of his position, and for over a year the two men bickered over the command, Gates eventually winning.

At Saratoga, Gates's role was secondary. He wanted to meet Burgoyne's invasion with a passive defence, but Arnold and Morgan took the initiative and, by aggressive action, staggered, and then stopped the British advance. Gates won the victor's laurels, but the credit for the victory belongs to his subordinates.

Lieutenant-General Sir John Burgoyne (1723–92) was one of the more colourful personalities of his time. Handsome, witty, and ambitious, he possessed all the virtues and most of the vices freely displayed by men of his position in 18th-century England.

The son of an army captain, Burgoyne managed to rise above the relative insignificance of his birth by eloping with Lady Charlotte Stanley, the daughter of the Earl of Derby, one of England's most powerful peers. The Stanley connection undoubtedly helped to further his career, since through it he gained access to the court, where he was a favourite of both George II and George III.

He was, nevertheless, a dashing, competent officer, and he eventually achieved fame as a leader of light dragoons in Portugal during the Seven Years' War. On his return from active service he purchased a seat in Parliament, settled in London, and divided his time between Westminster, writing plays, and sitting at gaming tables.

The war in America provided Burgoyne with an opportunity for advancement, and he was among the first to step forward when the King asked for officer-volunteers. As a subordinate at Boston, he witnessed the Battle of Bunker Hill and grudgingly admitted that the Americans fought well; despite this, he professed to regard the rebels as a 'rabble in arms', who could easily be defeated by regular troops. His estimate of the rebels' military capabilities in fact blinded him to the realities of warfare in North America, and so contributed to distortions in the planning of the 1777 campaign.

To his dying day, he never understood the real reason for his defeat at Saratoga. Incredibly, he tried to place the blame on the Hessians, declaring: 'Had all my troops been British . . . I should have made my way through Mr. Gates's army.'

HORATIO GATES.

SIR JOHN BURGOYNE.

THE BATTLES

With St Leger defeated and Howe gone to Philadelphia, Burgoyne was left to shift for himself in the back country of the upper Hudson. His decision to abandon his army's line of supply with Canada and plunge on, alone and unaided, toward Albany was a gamble—the last and fatal blunder, as it turned out, in a chain of errors extending back to the misdirected pursuit following Ticonderoga. Undoubtedly, his immense vanity and ambition affected the decision. He knew the operation was hazardous, 'depending', he admitted, 'on adventure and the fortune that often accompanies it', but he cloaked his ambition by pleading that his instructions left him no choice but to proceed. He complained that his army, reduced by losses and detachments to a strength of just 6,000 men, might be penned up and destroyed by Americans gathering to his front and on his left flank; at the same time, he dismissed earlier defeats as insignificant. Bennington, for example, he described as 'a common accident of war, independent of any general action, unattended by any loss that could affect the main strength of the army, and little more than the miscarriage of a foraying party'.

In truth, Sir John was the victim of his own 'no retreat' philosophy. 'Britons,' he had boasted, 'never retreat.' Now, with his army revictualled and poised to strike the final blow, he could not bring himself to order a withdrawal. The decisive battle of the campaign remained to be fought. To retreat before the rival armies had met and tried issues in a pitched battle would be unthinkable. Burgoyne knew his career was at stake. He did not wish to repeat Carleton's mistake of the previous campaign.

In the American camp, meanwhile, General Schuyler was made the scapegoat for the loss of Ticonderoga, and removed from command. Major-General Horatio Gates, the new commander, arrived in camp on 19 August. When he assumed command, the American army, preserved from destruction by Schuyler's delaying tactics, reinforced, and buoyed by the success at Bennington, was ready to take the offensive.

The reinforcements, which the 'damned Dutchman' had been begging for all summer, were particularly important. Besides the militia, which streamed into camp in increasing numbers now that the harvest had been gathered, there were Arnold's 1,200 Continentals, fresh from the victorious campaign against St Leger, and a detachment of 500 riflemen from Washington's army. These riflemen, whom Washington described as 'chosen men, selected from the Army at large, well acquainted with the use of rifles, and with that mode of fighting which is necessary to make them a good counterpoise to the Indian', were commanded by Colonel Daniel Morgan, a burly Virginian who had been a teamster on Braddock's expedition and who had fought with Arnold at Quebec.

Significantly, both Arnold and Morgan were impetuous, offensive-minded leaders. The headstrong Arnold had a formidable battlefield presence. A private soldier described him as 'A bloody fellow . . . He didn't care for nothing; he'd ride right in. It was "Come on, boys!" 'twasn't "Go, boys!" . . . there wasn't any waste timber in him. He was a stern looking man but kind to his soldiers.' Fortunately for his men, Arnold's daring was tempered by a sound tactical sense: he had an almost uncanny appreciation of the drift of a battle. Morgan, too, was a remarkable figure—a brawling, untutored frontiersman who signalled his riflemen in battle with a turkey call, a kind of whistle used by hunters to attract the game birds. Both friends and enemies regarded him as the finest bush-fighter in the world.

On 12 September the American army occupied Bemis Heights, a low plateau 24 miles north of Albany and athwart the route of Burgoyne's advance. Gates ordered his chief engineer, the Polish adventurer Tadeusz Kosciuszko, to fortify the site. During the next few days fatigue parties directed by Kosciuszko felled trees, cleared land, and constructed an extensive three-sided earthwork.

As the Americans laboured to complete their defensive arrangements on Bemis Heights, Burgoyne's army struggled south along the rude wagon track bordering the west bank of the Hudson. By 18 September the whole force was at the Sword House, just five miles north of Gates's lines. There Sir John divided the army into three columns in order to approach the American position on a broad front and sweep the woods of rebel skirmishers who were denying his foraging parties access to the interior.

The next day, at 10 am, Sir John's men marched out, advancing blindly into the primeval wilderness in quest of their elusive, unseen enemy. The indefatigable Simon Fraser led the right flank column, which was composed of 2,000 men, including the army's élite British grenadiers and light infantry. Burgoyne himself accompanied the centre column of 1,100 men, while Baron von Riedesel commanded the 1,100 men of the left flank column, which advanced along the river road.

If Burgoyne had a plan, it has eluded historians. The suggestion that he meant to seize an unfortified hill flanking Gates's lines is speculative. Most of his Tory and Indian scouts had deserted after Bennington and since then his army had groped forward cautiously; like the mythical Argus, it was 'all eyes and no sight'. The woods fringing the river road were the province of Morgan's riflemen, and except in large parties, the British dared not venture too far into them. Thus deprived of certain knowledge of his enemy's strength and dispositions, Burgoyne sought to 'feel' for the American position by means of a reconnaissance in force. The battle that followed was unplanned and unexpected.

The British advance continued without incident until about 1 pm, when the reinforced picket of the centre column ran foul of Morgan's corps in a wooded ravine, situated just south of an abandoned fifteen-acre farm clearing known as Freeman's Farm. Within moments of the first sharp, echoing blasts of rifle fire, the few dozen dazed survivors of the picket stumbled from the woods and ran pell-mell for the safety of friendly infantry on the far side of the farmhouse and barns. Morgan's men followed the retreating Redcoats as far as the timber farmhouse where they, in turn, were dispersed by repeated volleys from Burgoyne's main force, which was deploying in the scrubby field beyond. As the Yankee sharpshooters recoiled in confusion from this shock, 81

AMERICANS
Major-General Horatio Gates

RIGHT WING
(Major-General Horatio Gates,
subsequently Major-General Benjamin Lincoln)
Paterson's Continental Brigade (Brigadier-
General John Paterson)
Nixon's Continental Brigade (Colonel John
Nixon)
Glover's Continental Brigade (Brigadier-
General John Glover)

CENTRE
(Brigadier-General Ebenezer Learned)
Learned's Continental Brigade
4th New York Regiment (Colonel James
Livingstone)

LEFT WING
(Major-General Benedict Arnold)
Poor's Continental Brigade (Brigadier-General
Enoch Poor)
Connecticut Militia
Morgan's Continental Rifle Corps
(Colonel Daniel Morgan)
Dearborn's Light Infantry Battalion (Major
Henry Dearborn)

ESTIMATED TOTAL
The strength of Gates's army fluctuated as
militia units came and went. On 19 September,
the day of the first battle, the army had an
estimated strength of 7–10,000 men.

Losses: Approx. 300 killed and wounded at
Freeman's Farm, 200 in the second battle.

BRITISH
Lieutenant-General Sir John Burgoyne

ADVANCE CORPS
(Brigadier-General Simon Fraser)
British grenadier and light infantry companies
24th Regiment
Fraser's Rangers
2 companies of Canadians

RIGHT (BRITISH) WING
(Major-General William Phillips)
1st Brigade (Brigadier-General Henry Powell):
9th, 47th, 53rd Regiments
2nd Brigade (Brigadier-General James Hamilton):
20th, 21st, 62nd Regiments

LEFT (GERMAN) WING
(Major-General Baron Friedrich von Riedesel)
1st Brigade (Brigadier-General Johann von
Specht): Regiments von Riedesel, Specht, Rhetz
2nd Brigade (Brigadier-General Wilhelm von
Gall): Regiments Prinz Friedrich, Erbprinz

RESERVE
(Lieutenant-Colonel Heinrich von Breymann)
Light Infantry Battalion von Barner
Jaeger Company Schottelius
Grenadier Battalion von Breymann
Dragoon Regiment Prinz Ludwig

ARTILLERY
4 companies Royal Artillery
1 company Hesse-Hanau artillery

AUXILIARIES
Companies of Loyalists and Indians

TOTALS (based on the return for 1 July 1777)

British	3,724
Germans	3,016
Artillery	473
Canadians/Tories	250
Indians	400

GRAND TOTAL 7,863
with 30 cannon, 6 howitzers and mortars

Losses: Approx. 600 killed and wounded at
Freeman's Farm, a similar number in the second
battle. Many deserted between the two battles.
On 17 October Burgoyne surrendered 5,791
officers and men and 35 guns.

CONFRONTATION AT FREEMAN'S FARM,
19 SEPTEMBER 1777

THE ARMIES DEPLOYED

THE SECOND BATTLE, 7 OCTOBER

MORGAN,
LATER REINFORCED
BY POOR

FREEMAN'S
FARMHOUSE

BURGOYNE

VON RIEDESEL'S
RELIEF COLUMN

FRASER

MIDDLE
RAVINE

GATES'S CAMP
ON BEMIS HEIGHTS

HUDSON R.

RIVER ROAD

BREYMANN'S
REDOUBT

BALCARRES'S
REDOUBT

GREAT
REDOUBT

ACLAND
VON RIEDESEL
FRASER
MORGAN

POOR

ARNOLD

GATES

MIDDLE
RAVINE

HUDSON R.

RIVER ROAD

82

more and more British troops came up until, shortly, the entire 300-yard expanse of the clearing was filled with red-coated infantry deployed shoulder-to-shoulder in a tight semi-circular formation. On the far right and somewhat to the rear were the men of the 9th Regiment, who protected the link with Fraser's corps, which occupied high ground about half a mile west of the farm. In the clearing itself, from right to left, Burgoyne formed the 21st, 62nd, and 20th regiments—about 900 men in all. These troops were supported by the column's artillery contingent of four 6-pounders.

The American riflemen had been dispersed, 'scattered God knows where', in Colonel Morgan's words, by their brief, impetuous charge into the clearing and unexpected brush with Burgoyne's force; but Morgan soon rallied them with his turkey call, and when the British resumed their advance, they were quickly brought to a halt by accurate long-range rifle fire from the woods. 'Men, particularly officers, dropped every moment on each side,' recalled Sergeant Roger Lamb of the 9th Regiment. 'Several of the Americans placed themselves in high trees, and as often as they could distinguish a British officer's uniform, took him off by deliberately aiming at his person.' Staggered by this galling fire, the British infantry fell back. Burgoyne, who bravely exposed himself all day, ordered his gunners to rake the woods with case shot and then set off to rally the infantry for another advance.

Morgan, meanwhile, directed some of his men to infiltrate Burgoyne's right flank, but this attack was smashed by Fraser's light infantry and grenadiers, and most of the Americans broke contact and moved back to the fight at the

AN AMERICAN MARKSMAN, CONCEALED IN A TREE, PICKS OFF AN ADVANCING REDCOAT.

clearing. Fraser lost a great opportunity by not counter-attacking immediately. Morgan's corps—500 men in all—might then have been driven off in disorder; but, as one British officer explained, 'it was deemed unadvisable to evacuate the heights where they [the Advance Corps] were advantageously posted'. As it was, Fraser's strong élite force remained mostly inactive in a defensive posture for the greater part of the day.

At about 2 pm, Morgan was reinforced by Poor's New Hampshire Continentals, sent to the scene of the action by Arnold. (Whether Arnold himself took the field that day is debatable, but he did play an important role in wringing reinforcements for Morgan's embattled men from a reluctant, almost timid Gates.) The arrival of Poor's men changed the character of the action. The British regiments in the clearing were lashed by a tremendous, sustained fire of musketry as the Americans took the offensive. Poor and Morgan launched six major attacks and

several times drove the British beyond the farmhouse and into the woods fringing the clearing to the north, but each time Burgoyne's three regiments counter-attacked vigorously and pushed the Americans back into the pine wood south of the farm. For three hours the fight swayed to and fro across the clearing.

As the afternoon wore on, Burgoyne's men were steadily destroyed. The Americans, too, suffered losses, but they were continually reinforced by fresh drafts of militia from the camp and were better able to sustain the action. In time it became a very real possibility that the British centre would collapse. In the American camp, Arnold sensed that the decisive moment had arrived. Declaring, 'I will soon put an end to it', he led Ebenezer Learned's Continental brigade up to the fight at the farm. He had not gone very far, however, when one of Gates' aides rode up and recalled him. Without Arnold's direction Learned's men marched too far west and missed the fight at Freeman's Farm entirely. Instead, they rambled toward Fraser's position where they became involved in an inconclusive skirmish with the British advanced corps.

Even without Learned's assistance, however, Morgan and Poor were steadily and inexorably destroying the British centre. By 5 pm, according to Baron von Riedesel, 'The three brave English regiments . . . formed a small band surrounded by heaps of dead and wounded'. One regiment alone, the 62nd, lost 212 men in the battle—over two-thirds of its strength. At this juncture, help arrived from an unexpected quarter. Von Riedesel, who on his own initiative had marched from the river road toward the sound of gunfire, led two regiments of Brunswickers in a wild bayonet charge against the exposed right flank of Poor's brigade. Caught unawares, the Americans pulled back into the woods and abandoned the fight against Burgoyne.

Von Riedesel's attack virtually ended the Battle of Freeman's Farm. The Americans lingered in the woods for a while but retired to the Bemis Heights position at nightfall. Burgoyne's men bivouacked on the field of battle, where they spent a tense, sleepless night under arms. The battle had cost the British army about 600 men—roughly double the number of casualties sustained by the Americans. In Burgoyne's view, nonetheless, British arms had triumphed. His men had driven the Americans from the field after a fierce contest; he therefore decided to renew the assault on the 20th.

Few men were as adept at self-deception as 'Gentleman Johnny'. Lieutenant Thomas Anburey, a grenadier officer, took a more objective view: he observed that the Americans had fought with 'courage and obstinacy' and he feared that the 'real advantages' of the day rested with Gates's men. The British army, he noted, was 'so much weakened by this engagement as not to be of sufficient strength to venture forth and improve the victory, which may, in the end, put a stop to our intended expedition; the only apparent benefit gained is that we keep possession of the ground where the engagement began'.

Anburey's analysis was correct. Burgoyne's plans were dashed when Fraser informed him that the troops were too fatigued to continue. A short while later he learned that General Sir Henry Clinton was preparing to attack the American forts on the lower Hudson at Peekskill and might soon be in a position to assist the Northern Army's advance on Albany. With roughly a month of provisions left, Burgoyne decided to postpone his contemplated advance until he should receive news of Clinton's progress in the Highlands. In the meantime, he ordered his troops to fortify their position against the possibility of a surprise attack by the Americans.

Three crude but formidable earth and log redoubts were constructed to protect the approaches to the camp. The two most important works were at the western end of the line, near the site of the battle of the 19th. One, manned by Lord Balcarres's British light infantry, was just south of Freeman's Farm and anchored Burgoyne's right flank. The other, garrisoned by Colonel Breymann's German Reserve Corps (the survivors of Bennington), stood on a knoll about half a mile north-west and to the rear of the Balcarres Redoubt. This fortification was meant to prevent the Americans from working their way through the woods into the army's rear area. Fraser's and Breymann's troops held the ground in the vicinity of the two flanking redoubts, while the rest of the army was strung out in two miles of fortified camp extending to the Hudson. Thus situated, Burgoyne's troops idled for the better part of three weeks.

During this period the condition of the British army deteriorated considerably. Rations were short, forage scarce, and disease prevalent; American snipers and their Stockbridge Indian allies picked off the unwary and every day gathered in dozens of deserters in the woods. By early October the army's situation had become critical, and Burgoyne knew that he could no longer afford to wait for Clinton. Against the advice of his most senior officers, he ordered a new advance against the Americans, to be put in motion on 7 October.

Burgoyne at first proposed to commit the better part of his 6,000 men in a final effort to defeat Gates's 11,000, but Fraser and von Riedesel objected, pointing out the hazards of such a plan, really an all-or-nothing gamble. Finally, Burgoyne caved in and agreed not to hazard another major battle until the American position had been thoroughly reconnoitred. So, instead of 4,000 men, just 1,500 were allocated to the advance; this made it no more than a grand scouting party, as the probing force of 19 September had been.

At 11 am on the 7th Burgoyne led his men forward to the decisive fight of the Saratoga campaign. By noon he had advanced to a wheatfield just half a mile south-west of the Balcarres Redoubt, where he had halted and ordered his columns to deploy. Fraser's corps, including Balcarres's light infantry, the Canadians and Tories, and two guns, filed off to the right; von Riedesel, with a force of Germans, the British 24th Regiment, and four guns, took position in the centre; and Phillips, with Major Acland's grenadiers and four guns, was placed on the left. Satisfied with his dispositions, Burgoyne climbed to the roof of a log cabin and attempted to gain a view of the American lines.

The British approach had been detected by American pickets, and Gates's adjutant-general, Lieutenant-Colonel James Wilkinson, had galloped forward to investigate. Wilkinson returned with a complete report of the British deployment and urged Gates to launch an attack against Burgoyne's vulnerable right flank, which rested on a wood and was commanded by a 'lofty height'. For once, Gates acted with resolution and determination. Hastily, he sketched a plan. Morgan, with the rifles and light infantry and two brigades of militia, was to march to the wooded hill on the British right and attack Burgoyne's flank and rear. Simultaneously, Poor's Continentals were to engage Acland's grenadiers on the British left. When Burgoyne's men turned to meet these attacks, Learned's brigade would be launched against their centre. After he had described his plan, Gates turned to Wilkinson and commanded: 'Well, then, order on Morgan to begin the game'.

The one element missing from Gates's plan was Benedict Arnold. The fiery divisional commander had quarrelled with Gates following Freeman's Farm, and Gates had relieved him of his command. However, as soon as the sound of gunfire began to echo through the woods, Arnold, hatless and 'in a state of furious distraction', rode from the camp to direct the attack. Again, Gates tried to recall him, fearing that his rashness might lead to some calamity, but this time Arnold was not to be restrained.

Meanwhile, Morgan and Poor launched their attacks. Poor's men struck first, surging up the gentle slope of the wheatfield toward Acland's stolid grenadiers, arrayed with their supporting artillery at the crest. The ensuing battle followed the bitter pattern of Freeman's Farm. The Americans came on furiously, threatening to overwhelm the British by their frenzied attack. But the grenadiers resisted firmly, meeting each charge with searing volleys and levelled bayonets. After an hour of savage fighting, though, the British, battered by repeated volleys and sadly reduced in numbers, were forced to fight back-to-back in tiny rally squares while the American tide boiled around them. Finally, Major Acland fell, both legs shattered by a musket ball; his demise signalled the general capitulation of Burgoyne's left.

On the British right, Morgan's men, driving Captain Alexander Fraser's auxiliaries ahead of them, rushed 'like a torrent' into Balcarres's light infantry. Attacked from three sides at once, the British line crumpled and bent—but did not break. Almost incredibly, General Fraser succeeded in rallying his shaken men and, succoured by the 24th Regiment, formed a new line farther back.

A few minutes later Learned's brigade, led by Arnold and supported by Colonel Ten Broeck's 3,000 Albany County militia, swarmed over von Riedesel's Germans. Attacked by five or six times their number, the British and their German allies were swamped. The entire line buckled and then collapsed, the survivors retreating 'in the greatest

possible disorder' for the camp. Fraser, whom Arnold described as being 'of himself a host', attempted to salvage the situation, but Morgan directed Tim Murphy, a legendary Indian fighter, to pick him off. Murphy's third shot brought Fraser from his saddle, mortally wounded.

As the wreckage of Burgoyne's force poured back to its fortified camp, Arnold, behaving 'more like a madman than a cool and discreet officer', sought to capitalize on the afternoon's success by leading new attacks against Balcarres's and Breymann's Redoubts. Sweeping forward, the Americans struck first at Balcarres's Redoubt. Rebuffed there, Arnold turned and directed his troops northward against Breymann's. There the Germans gave the Americans one volley and then mutinied, abandoning their works to the wild torrent of frontiersmen led by Morgan and Arnold. Breymann himself was shot down and killed, possibly by one of his own men,

their lines on the night of 8–9 October, but their march was hampered by torrential rains, and it took two days to cover the eight miles to Saratoga, where the bridge of boats provided an escape route to Canada. The Americans, advancing up both sides of the river, easily outdistanced Burgoyne's men and prevented a breakout by emplacing guns on the bluffs above the bridge of boats. By the 14th, Burgoyne's tiny force was surrounded by 20,000 Americans, and Sir John, recognizing the hopelessness of his situation, proposed a capitulation. On 17 October, he surrendered his command of 5,791 officers and men and 35 cannon.

This event, Major Dearborn recorded in his diary, was 'the greatest Conquest Ever known'. Dearborn may be forgiven this characteristic piece of excess, for on this occasion he was not hopelessly far from the mark; the outcome at Saratoga was to have repercussions greatly beyond the fact that it was the

THE BURIAL OF BRIGADIER-GENERAL SIMON FRASER, MORTALLY WOUNDED IN THE SECOND BATTLE BY ONE OF MORGAN'S RIFLEMEN; THE PAINTING IS BY J. GRAHAM.

and Arnold was dangerously wounded. Still in a frenzy, he refused to leave the field. When a surgeon begged him to retire and have his wound treated, he replied that he would hear 'no such damned nonsense' and that he would 'see the action through'.

Finally, dusk brought an end to the battle. Burgoyne, staggered by the loss of 600 men (the Americans lost just 200), including many of his best young officers, and the key Breymann Redoubt, withdrew his troops across the Great Ravine and prepared to retreat. The British stole away from

first substantial American victory of the war. Across the Atlantic, at the Court of Versailles, the French King Louis XVI, who up till then had condoned only clandestine aid to the colonists, threw off the cloak of neutrality and approved a formal treaty of alliance with the American nation. Soon the greater part of Europe, including Spain, Holland and Prussia, followed the French example and declared war on the American side. Russia, Denmark and Sweden, too, emerged as openly hostile to Great Britain.

28 June 1778
Washington, intercepting Clinton during
the latter's withdrawal overland from Philadelphia
to New York, plans a devastating blow against the
British. However, the American advance guard is
badly directed by General Lee and Washington is
forced to intervene. In temperatures of more than 100°F,
the two main armies then fight a draining but
inconclusive four-hour battle.

MONMOUTH

THE
BACKGROUND TO
THE BATTLES

The news of Sir William Howe's marginal victory at Germantown, following as it did in the wake of reports of Burgoyne's disaster at Saratoga, did little to mollify the anger of the British public at the mismanagement of the 1777 campaign. There were many in London, especially among Loyalist supporters, who loudly blamed Howe for the loss of the Northern Army, and demands mounted to have him removed as commander-in-chief. Another argument raised against him was that after Germantown he had, for the third time in as many major encounters, allowed Washington's battered army to slip away unmolested.

In fairness to Howe, it should be noted that his main concern in the six weeks or so following Germantown had been to open a supply route to Philadelphia along the Delaware River. When his army had entered Philadelphia after the Battle of Brandywine, it had bypassed the strong forts blocking the river below the American capital. So long as the Americans held these forts, however, all the British army's supplies had to be brought overland along an exposed route from Chester. If this route were cut, as it might be by a detachment from Washington's army or by American forces operating from Delaware, the British might find themselves besieged in Philadelphia.

Consequently, the Howe brothers (Sir William and Admiral Lord Howe) spent much of late October and November fighting to clear the river below Philadelphia. Washington might have intervened to prevent the reduction of the river forts, but his army was too weak to take the offensive. On 20 November the Americans evacuated Fort Mercer on the Jersey shore, and the riverine supply route that Howe had so keenly desired was finally open. Nevertheless, the heroic resistance of the river forts had been of great value to Washington in distracting Howe's efforts for the better part of two months.

Finally, on 4 December, the British sallied forth from Philadelphia to do battle with Washington's force, which was entrenched near Whitemarsh above the city. Howe apparently intended to draw Washington into a set-piece battle in the open, but the American commander refused to be budged from his position, and on 8 December the Redcoats returned to their camps in Philadelphia. This abortive campaign ended military operations for 1777. The British wintered in Philadelphia, and Washington's army retired to winter quarters on the bleak, windswept plateau of Valley Forge on the Schuylkill River.

The situation of the rival armies during the winter of 1777–78 presents a study in contrasts. The British were quartered comfortably in Philadelphia, where General Howe and his mistress, Betsey Loring, presided over a lively social season. Dashing young officers like Ban Tarleton and Captain John André enjoyed the time of their lives squiring beautiful Tory maidens to an endless round of galas, fêtes, balls, and other *divertissements*. Howe's indolence and the debauched life of the garrison angered the upright Quakers of the city and dismayed the large Loyalist element, but the British commander was an unabashed libertine and notoriously averse to winter campaigning. He was, also, weary of the war. As early as the preceding October he had asked Lord George Germain, Secretary of State for the Colonies, to relieve him of the command—an office which he described as 'this very painful service'.

At Valley Forge, in the meantime, Washington's army was undergoing an ordeal that threatened its very existence. Food was scarce in the camp, and several times the army seemed to be on the brink of starvation. This situation was all the more remarkable because farm produce and beef on the hoof were plentiful in the countryside and, indeed, everywhere in the colonies; but farmers would not sell to army contractors who could pay them only in depreciated Continental currency (a contemporary saying was 'Not worth a Continental!'), and Washington was too scrupulous to allow his forage parties to plunder. Clothing, too, was a problem; because of shortages men suffered from exposure or actually froze to death in what was, comparatively, a mild winter. One despairing soldier, driven almost to distraction by the vicissitudes of life in the camp, wrote: 'Poor food—hard lodging—Cold Weather—fatigue—Nasty Cloaths —nasty Cookery—Vomit half my time—smoak'd out of my senses—the Devil's in it—I can't endure it—Why are we sent here to starve and freeze . . . ?'

Somehow, the army survived. The quartermaster and commissary departments were reformed and made more efficient. The food situation improved, clothing was procured, and in due course, when Congress offered a bounty, enlistment figures began to increase. The most remarkable change, however, was the introduction of a workable, uniform drill by the army's new Inspector-General, Baron Friedrich von Steuben.

Von Steuben was a Prussian veteran who, though he styled himself a lieutenant-general in the King of Prussia's service, had never risen above the rank of captain. Nor was he, in fact, a nobleman. Nevertheless, he was a brilliant organizer. He came to Valley Forge in February 1778 as a volunteer, but so impressed Washington that he was placed in charge of a temporary department of inspections. The Baron's most immediate concerns during the weeks that followed were to reform the army's drill and organization and to eliminate the scandalous waste that had compromised its effectiveness.

The von Steuben drill was a simplified and streamlined version of the British *Manual Exercise* of 1768 —then the most prevalent of the variety of drills employed by the Continental Army. The Baron took 120 picked men from the various corps of the army and each day drilled them himself 'like children

87

learning their alphabet'. When these men had mastered the drill they returned to their own units and passed on what they had learned. Thus, under von Steuben's tutelage, the entire army became expert in the new drill. The results were astounding. In the space of little more than a month the hardened veterans of the Continental Line acquired the ability to manoeuvre smoothly and quickly in any battlefield formation. The army became a deadly machine, equal to or better than any corps of European regulars.

In late March, with the army in the midst of its preparations for the next campaign, came news of the signing of the long-awaited treaty of alliance with Bourbon France. The French had been secretly aiding the Americans almost from the beginning of the war, but the treaty transformed the conflict from a local quarrel to a world war and meant that Britain could no longer concentrate her efforts against America alone.

The effects of the French alliance were felt almost at once. Great Britain was thrown on the defensive and forced to reconsider her war strategy. The Royal Navy, Britain's first bastion of defence, had been in decline for a decade and was unprepared for the responsibilities of global war. French naval power now forced the British to divert their energies from the subjugation of America to the defence of the empire, the nation's trade, and, indeed, even the British Isles themselves. In the reassessment of priorities that followed, the prosecution of the American war was relaxed.

At this juncture the British government decided to abandon Philadelphia to the rebels and concentrate the main army at New York, a post less susceptible to French naval intervention or American attack. At the same time the army was directed to suspend offensive operations pending the outcome of negotiations between Congress and the Carlisle Commission, a peace mission empowered to grant all the principal demands of the Americans except independence.

General Howe's resignation was finally accepted in February, but Sir Henry Clinton, his replacement, did not assume command until 24 May. During the interim period the British army continued its season of idleness in the rebel capital. Washington, however, had received reports of the impending evacuation: American patrols were stepped up, and the armies became engaged in a bitter war of detachments. The American army's aggressive posture denied the British access to the countryside beyond Philadelphia and its much-needed forage and provisions. Reduced to a state

of near-siege, the British struck back vigorously, employing light troops and partisan corps like Major John Graves Simcoe's Queen's Rangers.

On 18 May, Washington escalated this 'small war' by detaching Lafayette and a corps of 2,100 men from the main army with orders to take up a position at Barren Hill near Philadelphia and prevent British foraging parties from molesting the countryside. Because of the nature of his mission Lafayette's position was much exposed to British attack—a fact that did not escape the notice of Howe, who perceived a chance to trap and destroy a third of Washington's army.

The British commander lost no time in reacting. Early on the morning of 19 May, he dispatched 7,000 troops in three columns toward Barren Hill. The British intended to converge on Lafayette's camp and snare the young Frenchman's corps between their bayonets, to the front, and the

THE STRATEGIC SITUATION

AMERICAN FORCES

BRITISH FORCES

MILES
0   10   20

MORRISTOWN
NEW YORK
LONG ISLAND
BASKINGRIDGE
STATEN ISLAND
DELAWARE R.
RARITAN R.
SOUTH AMBOY
SANDY HOOK
PENNSYLVANIA
PRINCETON
ENGLISHTOWN
SCHUYLKILL R.
FREEHOLD
TRENTON
MONMOUTH COURT HOUSE
WASHINGTON
WHITEMARSH
VALLEY FORGE
ALLENTOWN
ATLANTIC OCEAN
GERMANTOWN
CLINTON
PHILADELPHIA
NEW JERSEY
HOWE
WILMINGTON

Schuylkill River to the rear. The plan was well conceived and tolerably well executed, but Lafayette's scouts detected the presence of the enemy at the last moment, and the Marquis, after bluffing an attack, successfully withdrew across the river by a ford.

The affair at Barren Hill was the first test of the 'new' American army. Lafayette's skilful retreat from certain disaster was a tribute to von Steuben's tuition, since the Marquis's complex manoeuvring in the face of the enemy would have been impossible without confident, well-drilled and disciplined troops.

Howe left Philadelphia by ship for England on 25 May. Clinton, who had assumed command the day before, faced a difficult task. The Ministry, as usual, had managed to create a confusing situation by insisting on its plan of abandoning the field while the Carlisle Commission negotiated with Congress.

Incredibly, Clinton was expected to evacuate the main army by sea to New York and, at the same time, detach 8,000 men for expeditions against French and Spanish possessions in the West Indies and the Floridas. In fact, there were not enough transports on hand to convoy even half the troops in the garrison, let alone the army's baggage and the thousands of Loyalists demanding safe passage out of Philadelphia.

Clinton was left with no alternative but to disobey the Ministry's orders. He formulated a plan of his own—a daring one, but possibly the best under the circumstances. The impractical expeditions were postponed. The fleet, still commanded by Admiral Lord Howe, was instead entrusted with the task of ferrying the army's accumulated baggage, some demoralized German regiments, and Philadelphia's Tory population to New York. Clinton and the main army were to slip across the Delaware into New Jersey and withdraw overland.

Clinton's plan for the retreat across the Jerseys depended for its ultimate success on the ability of the army to out-march Washington's troops, who were certain to follow and attempt to disrupt progress. On 5 June, the British destroyed their fortifications and all the excess baggage that they could not send by sea or easily move overland— and thereby announcing the imminence of their departure to Washington. Then, on 18 June, Admiral 'Black Dick' Howe's fleet lumbered down the river, and Clinton led the army into New Jersey.

The Americans were slow in responding to the British march from Philadelphia, and Washington's army did not itself cross the Delaware until the 21st. Nevertheless, the American commander had taken precautions against a surprise march. Earlier in the month, he had dispatched 'Scotch Willie' Maxwell's brigade across the river to link with General Philemon Dickinson's militia contingent. The combined force, which totalled 1,800 men, was instructed to harass and obstruct Clinton's march.

Almost from the beginning, the British withdrawal was dogged by misfortune. The weather was unbearably hot and humid, and Maxwell's men did everything in their power to add to the discomfort of the Redcoats. Trees were felled across the road, bridges broken down, wells stopped up, and shots fired from ambush. Soon, discipline broke down, and the soldiers began to loot and pillage indiscriminately—even breaking into the homes of known Tories. The troops became so rapacious that Lieutenant-Colonel Clark of the Royal Fusiliers commented in morning orders for the regiment for 21 June that he was 'mortif'd at observing the great Irregularity and excesses that have been committed within these few day . . . '. Soon after, on the 23rd, Clinton was forced to order the 'immediate execution' of any man caught looting.

Clinton had bigger worries than his troops' indiscipline, however. The march column, burdened by a 12-mile-long baggage train, was progressing at an intolerably slow pace, while Washington's fast-moving Continentals, marching on a parallel route to the west, would soon be in a position to block its progress toward South Amboy, where transports waited to ferry the men to New York. Then, too, there were unverified reports that Gates, the American commander in the New York Highlands, was moving south in the direction of the Raritan, where he could take up a position to prevent the British army from reaching the Hudson. Clinton was not opposed to fighting, but he did not relish the idea of having to attack the American army on ground of its own choosing in the hilly Princeton area. So, on 25 June, he altered his line of march and swung his men northeast onto the sandy track that led to Freehold.

Sir Henry's new objective was Sandy Hook Bay, a harbour at the southern entrance to Lower New York Bay. The new route took the British army away from Washington's line of march but slowed the column considerably, the entire army being now forced to march along one narrow country lane. Washington, if he moved quickly, could still attack the British rear; with this in mind, Clinton changed the order of march. Von Knyphausen's division, followed by the baggage train, was placed at the head of the column, and Lord Cornwallis's division, the army's élite corps, became the rear guard.

The American command, meanwhile, was finding it difficult to decide what, if anything, it proposed to do about Clinton's withdrawal. At a council of war held on 24 June, Major-General Charles Lee spoke eloquently and forcefully of the dangers of attacking the British army. However, Washington, Lafayette and Wayne disagreed, arguing instead for an attack on the British rear guard at the first favourable opportunity. But Lee, who was supported by a majority of the generals, held fast to his opinion, and the council adjourned after agreeing to do nothing more than detach a force of 1,500 men 'to act as occasion may serve, on the enemy's left flank and rear'.

During the next few days, however, Washington detached more and more men away from the main army to join the advance corps. Soon this agglomeration of units grew so large that it constituted nearly half the troops in the American army, and Washington decided that it needed a commander of its own to co-ordinate its movements. Lee was offered the command, but he declined, stating that he thought it 'a more proper business of a young volunteering general [meaning Lafayette], than that of the second in command of the army'. At this, Washington placed Lafayette in command of the advance corps with orders to 'take the first fair opportunity to attack the rear of the enemy'.

The Marquis joined his new command on the 26th. The advance corps was now very close to the British column, which had been observed moving slowly in the direction of Freehold, and Lafayette was eager to attack. Even so, neither Washington nor Lafayette wanted to bring on a general engagement while the advance corps was somewhat isolated from the main army; Lafayette was therefore ordered to march toward Englishtown and delay his offensive until the main army drew within supporting distance. Lafayette arrived in Englishtown on the 27th and promptly established contact with Washington's force, which lay at Cranberry, just three miles away. At this juncture, Lee rode into the Marquis's camp and announced that he was assuming command. He had, apparently, changed his mind about commanding the advance corps when he saw that it had grown to a strength of some 5,000 men.

89

THE COMMANDERS

Charles Lee (1731–82), the commander of the American advance corps at Monmouth, may well have been the most bizarre character of the Revolutionary era. Tall, thin and physically ugly, his grotesque appearance was matched only by his outlandish personality. A contemporary described him as 'careless in his manners, even to a degree of rudeness . . . His voice was rough, his garb ordinary, his deportment morose. He was ambitious of fame, without the dignity to support it. In private life he sank into the vulgarity of the clown.' In fact, Lee's temperament was so erratic that it seems to have disquieted most of those with whom he came into contact—even the Indians, who nicknamed him 'Boiling Water'.

Lee had few admirers and no friends, but his military knowledge and experience overawed his fellow officers, who were inclined to treat him with a degree of respect and deference which genuinely endangered Washington's hold on the army on more than one occasion.

Despite his brilliance, Lee was a troublemaker. As the second-ranking general in the Continental service, his philosophical disagreement with Washington over the conduct of the war during 1776 might have proved disastrous but for the fact that he was captured at Baskingridge, New Jersey, on 12 December. Exchanged in April 1778, in time for the Monmouth campaign, his presence with the army proved to be something of an embarrassment for Washington. Lee's controversial mishandling of the advance corps at Monmouth led to his court-martial and suspension from command. Not content with this verdict, he subsequently wrote an abusive letter to Congress which led to his dismissal from the service. He died in 1782, as much a victim of what he himself described as the 'distemper of my mind' as any physical ailment.

Lieutenant-General Sir Henry Clinton (1730–95) was no stranger to America. His father, an admiral in the Royal Navy, was governor of New York for a decade, and young Henry began his military career as a lieutenant in a company of provincial militia. After service at the Siege of Louisbourg, he made his way to London, where he benefited from the family connection with the Dukes of Newcastle by securing a commission in the Coldstream Guards. During the Seven Years' War he served on the staff of the Duke of Brunswick, one of Europe's finest soldiers, and distinguished himself in several engagements.

Clinton emerged from the war as one of Britain's bright young soldiers. Like Howe, Burgoyne and Cornwallis, he seemed destined for greatness. At the outbreak of the Revolution he volunteered to serve in America even though he disagreed with the Government's American policy.

Sir Henry's service in the American War was strangely uneven. He performed brilliantly as a subordinate to Howe, but as Commander-in-chief, from 1778, he was inconsistent. When he was present at the scene of operations, as at Monmouth or Charleston, he acted decisively, but when he attempted to direct operations from a distance, as in the Yorktown campaign, he was erratic and indecisive. His biographer, William B. Willcox, has attributed his changeable fortunes to a neurotic quirk in his character.

RIGHT:
SIR HENRY CLINTON.

ABOVE:
GENERAL CHARLES LEE IS SURPRISED AND CAPTURED BY BRITISH CAVALRY IN DECEMBER 1776 AT BASKINGRIDGE, NEW JERSEY. HE WAS EXCHANGED IN APRIL 1778.

AMERICAN ARTILLERY ON COMB'S HILL PREPARES TO FIRE ON THE OUTFLANKED BRITISH LINE.

WASHINGTON RELIEVES LEE OF THE AMERICAN COMMAND.

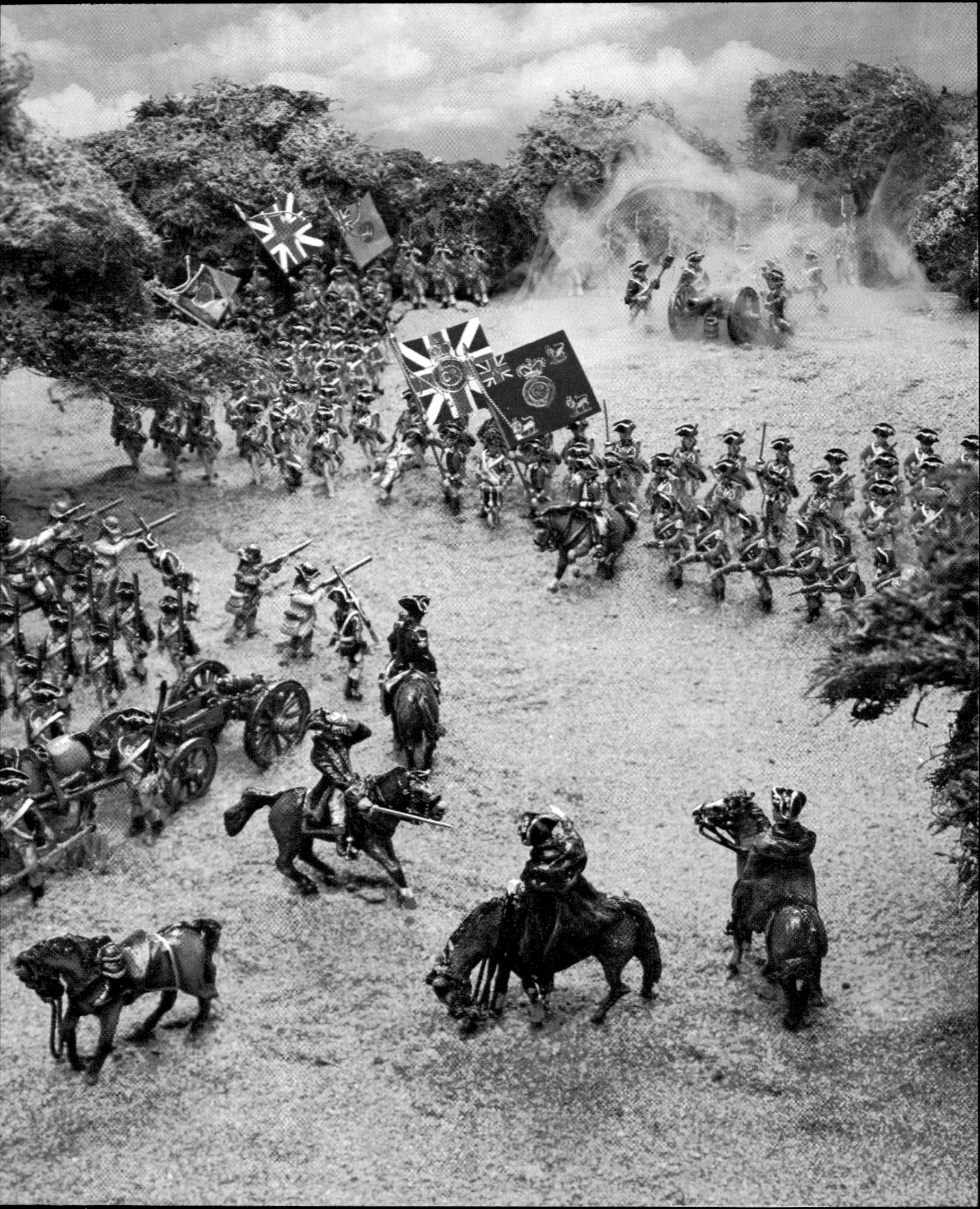

THE BATTLE

If Lee's behaviour in first rejecting and then demanding the command of the advance corps was odd, then his actions following his assumption of the command were even odder. Washington conferred with him in Englishtown at about noon on the 27th and ordered him to attack Clinton's column the next day 'when the front was in motion, or marched off'. But, when Lee held his council of war during the evening of the 27th, he gave no orders for an attack. Instead, he cautioned his subordinates 'to keep in readiness to march at a moment's warning in case the enemy should march off'. Still later in the evening Lafayette visited Lee at his headquarters and inquired about the general's plans for the morning attack. Lee, however, had little to tell the Marquis. He had no plan but 'thought it would be better to act according to circumstances...'.

Washington's overall plan was masterful; if it succeeded, the British army would be crippled. The Americans were risking very little, because Lee's attack was to be launched against the rear of the British column—roughly 6,000 men under Clinton and Cornwallis. General von Knyphausen's division of 5,000 men, which formed the advance guard, would have long since marched away from the field of battle toward Sandy Hook. These men, separated from the rear guard by the baggage train, would be in no position to double-back and assist their comrades. Lee's advance, if successful, would pin Clinton down and force him to fight steadily increasing numbers of Continentals. The British could not stage a fighting withdrawal, because their wagons would block the only retreat route from the field—the narrow, sandy pass at Middletown. If Clinton chose to attack, the main army could march to Lee's assistance and overwhelm the British in a counter-attack.

The wild card in the whole scheme was, of course, the unpredictable Charles Lee. Ever since his exchange in the spring (see 'The Commanders') he had counselled against fighting the British in a set-piece battle. He was convinced that the Continentals, even with von Steuben's training, would be 'defeated in every Recontre which depends on manoeuvres'. Nevertheless, on the present occasion he would be expected to manoeuvre sharply and cleverly when the advance corps came to grips with the enemy.

The British broke camp early on the morning of the 28th. Von Knyphausen's division marched before dawn, at 4 am, and the baggage train followed within the hour. Cornwallis's division fell in on the Sandy Hook Road at 5 am. As Cornwallis's men marched away from the encampment, a strong body of American militia filed from the woods near the Cranberry Road, north-west of Freehold, and formed as if to attack the British column. These men were engaged by Simcoe's Queen's Rangers, who charged and drove them away after a brief mêlée in which Simcoe was wounded. Then more Americans appeared. A troop of light dragoons was spotted near Freehold, and some infantry debouched from the woods to the north of the town. The British unlimbered some 3-pounder battalion guns and opened fire on the infantry, which fell back. The dragoons, however, continued to press forward, skirting some woods and drawing dangerously close to Cornwallis's line of march. Two or three troops of the 16th Light Dragoons (Burgoyne's old regiment) wheeled from the column and trotted toward the impetuous American horsemen. For a few minutes it looked as if the two bodies of horse would collide in an old-fashioned stirrup-to-stirrup cavalry duel—a rarity in the Revolutionary War. But, as the British closed on the Americans, their ranks were swept by an unexpected volley from American infantry lying in ambush nearby, and the red-coated dragoons were forced to retreat toward the main column.

The repulse of the 16th Light Dragoons convinced Clinton that the Americans were beyond Freehold in force. The other rebels that had shown themselves were acting boldly, too, pushing forward in formation and challenging the British covering parties. This was a departure from their tactics of the previous week, when they had done little more than engage in desultory skirmishes with the British rear guard.

Even as Clinton pondered the possibilities, still more Americans advanced from the pine woods east of the Cranberry Road and south of McGellaird's Brook (the East Ravine). One column, according to Captain André, was 'marching very rapidly and in good order'. These men, acting in concert with the troops near Freehold, seemed determined to envelop the British column as it snaked away in the direction of Middletown.

Clinton's anxiety increased. While a major clash seemed unavoidable, the light troops covering the column's withdrawal were plainly too few in number to cope with the Americans. Immediately, he sent orders to Cornwallis's division to face about, form and advance to the support of the screening troops. Cornwallis obeyed this command promptly, swinging the bulk of his force into a line of battle on Briar Hill, a low eminence about $1\frac{1}{4}$ miles east of Freehold. The rest of the division formed south of the hill and closer to the town. Cornwallis's manoeuvre was completed just in time, for the nearest American troops were only a quarter of a mile from the hill when the Redcoats seized it. A delay of just 15 minutes might in fact have been enough to seal the fate of Clinton's army.

The troops crowding in upon the British column were, of course, the men of General Lee's advance corps. The 'flying army', as General Wayne termed this force, had spent the night under arms a few miles from the British camp; scattered detachments were even closer, hanging on the fringes of Clinton's position and watching for the first signs of enemy movement. By 5 am both Washington and Lee had been informed of von Knyphausen's departure, whereupon Washington had requested Lee to 'move forward and attack the enemy, unless very powerful reasons prevented'. The main army, Washington added, 'had thrown aside their packs and was advancing to his support'.

Lee moved his men toward Freehold shortly after he received Washington's order, but the brigades

93

AMERICANS
General George Washington
ADVANCE CORPS (Major-General
Charles Lee; second in command,
Marquis de Lafayette)
Brigades and detachments of: .

Brigadier-General Scott (detachment)	1,440
Brigadier-General Wayne (detachment)	1,000
Brigadier-General Maxwell (brigade)	900-1,000
Brigadier-General Varnum (brigade)	300-600
Brigadier-General Scott (brigade)	300-600
Colonel Jackson (detachment)	200

Detachment of Light Horse
14 field guns

MAIN ARMY
Brigades of:

Woodford	385
North Carolina	369
Poor	639
Huntington	509
1st Maryland	657
2nd Maryland	529
Muhlenberg	575
Weedon	449
1st Pennsylvania	352
2nd Pennsylvania	401
3rd Pennsylvania	343
Glover	512
Learned	294
Patterson	357
ESTIMATED TOTAL	11,000

NOTE. Morgan's detachment (500) and Dickinson's New Jersey militia (800) are not included here, since those corps did not take part in the main battle.
Losses: 69 killed (including 37 from fatigue and sunstroke), 161 wounded, 132 missing (most of whom subsequently rejoined the army).

THE BATTLE OF MONMOUTH

① Lee's advance corps half-heartedly engages the British, then Lee for no clear reason orders a general retreat.

CLINTON

MONMOUTH COURT HOUSE

LEE

MIDDLETOWN

EAST RAVINE

SOUTH AMBOY

LIST OF UNITS PRESENT

BRITISH
Lieutenant-General Sir Henry Clinton
FIRST DIVISION
(Lieutenant-General Earl Cornwallis)
Brigades and detachments of:
    16th Light Dragoons (detachment)
    1st Light Infantry (detachment)
    Brigade of Guards
    Queen's Rangers (detachment)
    1st and 2nd Grenadiers (detachment)
    Hessian Grenadiers (detachment)
    3rd, 4th and 5th British brigades
SECOND DIVISION
(Lieutenant-General Baron von Knyphausen)
17th Light Dragoons
2nd Light Infantry
Hessian jaegers
1st and 2nd British brigades
Stirn's and von Loo's Hessian brigades
Pennsylvania Loyalists

West Jersey Volunteers
Maryland Loyalists
REARGUARD
Detachments of:
    16th Light Dragoons
    Queen's Rangers
    1st Light Infantry
    British Grenadiers
    Hessian Grenadiers
2 3-pounder guns
ARTILLERY
12 6-pounders
2 12-pounders
2 howitzers

ESTIMATED TOTAL: 12-13,000 ALL RANKS
Losses: 294 killed and wounded (including 59
dead of fatigue and sunstroke) 64 missing., Over
600 deserted on the march to Sandy Hook.

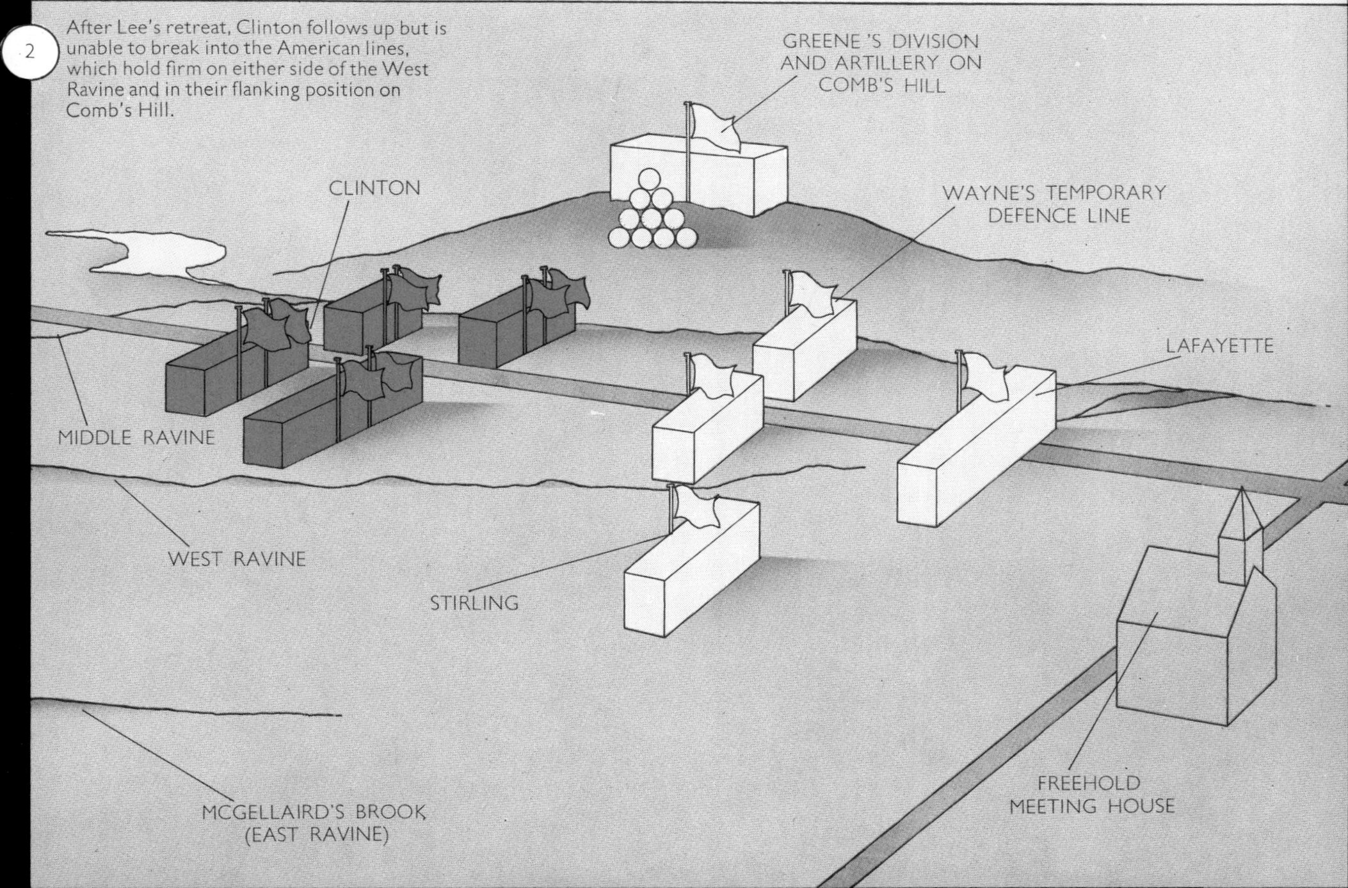

(2) After Lee's retreat, Clinton follows up but is
unable to break into the American lines,
which hold firm on either side of the West
Ravine and in their flanking position on
Comb's Hill.

GREENE'S DIVISION
AND ARTILLERY ON
COMB'S HILL

CLINTON

WAYNE'S TEMPORARY
DEFENCE LINE

LAFAYETTE

MIDDLE RAVINE

WEST RAVINE

STIRLING

FREEHOLD
MEETING HOUSE

MCGELLAIRD'S BROOK
(EAST RAVINE)

and detachments of the corps marched in random order without any overall direction. This slipshod march was the first tell-tale sign that Lee was discharging his command in a careless manner. Further confusion ensued when the column of march stacked up before a bridge to the west of the town.

By 10 am Lee had ranged his 5,000-man detachment in line of battle beyond Freehold. Some of the American units were briskly engaged, but others stood in immobile lines while the British recovered from the surprise of the attack and formed to advance on them.

The battle had hardly begun when Lee lost control of his corps. He failed to take advantage of his position close to the British flank and rear, and although he confided to an aide at one point that he 'would have them all prisoners', he lost the initiative to Clinton when Cornwallis's division swept forward from Briar Hill. His preconceived idea of acting 'according to circumstances', was now creating havoc all along the line. He had no plan of co-ordinated action, and in the absence of orders, individual units were left to shift for themselves. Finally, with a wave of his hand, he ordered a retreat.

This order caused consternation in the ranks. Few of the units of the advance corps had even been engaged, and none had been ordered to attack the enemy. Even the British were surprised by General Lee's withdrawal. Captain André recalled: 'The Rebel Corps as soon retreated, nor was a shot fired until we had recrossed the Cranberry Road'.

MONMOUTH COURT HOUSE, FROM A PAINTING BY MRS CARRIE SWIFT, OF FREEHOLD, NEW JERSEY.

The American retreat began almost absent-mindedly. Some units never received an order to fall back but withdrew when they discovered the British lapping around a flank or marching in their rear. General Wayne's Pennsylvanians, for example, retired in a compact mass, 'being often hard pushed, and frequently surrounded'.

Significantly, though, Lee's withdrawal did not develop into a rout. The men marched away from the British advance (in some cases seemingly in the midst of it), recrossed the East Morass and retired to a new position behind a ravine formed by Wemrock Brook (the Middle Ravine) two miles west of Freehold.

Clinton did everything in his power to drive the Americans before his advance like a herd of cattle, but the Continentals simply refused to be hurried. Their retrograde manoeuvre was performed skilfully, and several units fought delaying actions while the bulk of the command moved to the rear along the Englishtown Road. Nonetheless, the first stage of Sir Henry's hastily conceived plan of battle had succeeded admirably. By striking at Lee's centre, he had caused the American com-

mander to recall his flanking detachments. Now, as his red-coated infantry struggled forward in the wake of Lee's retreat, he saw an opportunity to destroy the entire advance corps and, perhaps, the main army under Washington as well.

Clinton noted that Lee's corps would, inevitably, have to make a stand. The withdrawal, which up till then had been conducted on a broad front, was entering difficult terrain. The plain to the west of Freehold was intersected by two ravines, and Lee's retreat was slowed when the men crowded toward the narrow causeway crossing the first defile. The British commander knew that Washington was in the vicinity and he knew also that Washington had to support Lee's corps or watch it perish while attempting to negotiate the second defile—the West Ravine. If the main American army crossed this obstacle to sustain Lee or cover his withdrawal, it, too, might be destroyed by a vigorous attack. All that remained to be done, or so it seemed, was to continue the advance,

But just at this point the British offensive began to peter out. The day was hot, unbearably so. The temperature had risen to over 100°F, and there was no wind to relieve the discomfort of the men, who fought burdened by heavy packs and clothed in tight-fitting woollen coats. Not surprisingly, the heat began to take its toll. All over the sun-baked plain men stumbled from the ranks and died of heat prostration or exhaustion. The most significant casualty of the heat, however, was Clinton's entire advance, which literally wilted away under the stifling noonday sun and slowed to a crawl. Lee's men, who were lightly equipped, now outpaced their pursuers.

Washington, who was riding ahead of the main army on its advance from the vicinity of the Tennent Meeting House, had no idea of the disaster that had overtaken his advance corps until he rode into the midst of Lee's retreating men near the causeway over the West Ravine. When questioned, none of the men could explain why they were retreating, except to say that General Lee had ordered it. Washington was already in a fury when Lee himself rode up trailed by a column of exhausted, disorganized men, and Washington demanded an explanation. Tench Tilghman, one of Washington's aides, described the agitated conversation of the two generals at Lee's court-martial:

'General Lee answered . . . "Sir, Sir?" I took it that General Lee did not hear the question distinctly.

'Upon General Washington's repeating the question, General Lee answered, that from a variety of contradictory intelligence, and that from his orders not being obeyed, matters were thrown into confusion, and that he did not chuse to beard the British army with troops in such a situation.

He said that besides, the thing was against his own opinion.

'General Washington answered, whatever his opinion might have been, he expected his orders would have been obeyed, and then rode on toward the rear of the retreating troops.'

Tilghman's account of this incident, though otherwise accurate, omits to mention that Washington dismissed Lee with an uncharacteristic verbal blast.

Washington quickly regained his composure, however, and with the assistance of his staff and General Wayne, he set about organizing a temporary line of defence along the crest of a hill just east of the West Ravine. At the same time, orders were dispatched to the units of the main army to deploy along the ridge west of the defile. The temporary defence line, which was commanded by Wayne, was meant to hold just long enough to allow the rest of the troops to deploy.

During the next four hours or so the two armies wrestled to a standstill in a confusing sequence of actions fought under the broiling sun on the dusty, relatively open plain between the Middle and West Ravines. The British flung themselves repeatedly at Washington's strong position behind the West Ravine, and the Americans sought to counter-attack when the Redcoats seemed to be tiring.

Clinton's first attack during the afternoon phase of the battle was launched against Wayne's line, which was posted in an exposed position on a wooded hill behind Wemrock Brook. Both Washington and Clinton appreciated the tactical value of this hill, which commanded the ground where the British would have to form for their attack on the American main line of resistance. It is probable that Sir Henry led the attack personally; one observer described him as 'galloping like a Newmarket jockey at the head of a wing of grenadiers'. Wayne's men fought hard to maintain their position, but the British turned their flanks and forced them to quit the hill.

Wayne's men drifted back to a new position behind a hedgerow and orchard about 1,000 yards east of the West Ravine. Here they were joined by other troops and more guns sent forward by General Henry Knox, the chief of artillery. Clinton's troops did not, or could not, pursue the American withdrawal. The assault had been costly, though according to André more men had died from 'heat and fatigue . . . than from the Enemy's shot'. Still, Clinton persisted, and he ordered his artillery forward while his men regrouped and prepared for the next assault.

A few minutes later the British struck Washington's left, his most vulnerable flank. The attackers were the men of the 3rd brigade, the 1st Light Infantry, and the Queen's Rangers. But the defenders were equal to the task. Lieutenant-Colonel Edward Carrington's artillery battalion concentrated its fire on the leading regiments as they struggled to extricate themselves from a morass and disrupted their advance. Then General Enoch Poor's crack Continental brigade poured volley after volley into the British column and forced it back across the ravine.

The American artillery played a similar, though more decisive, role on the right, where Clinton attempted to storm a position held by Nathanael Greene's veteran division. Here Knox's guns occupied a secure position on Comb's Hill, which flanked and overlooked the British staging area. Sir Henry's grenadiers never really had a chance of succeeding. From the moment their line surged forward it was savaged by an enfilading fire which scythed men down in bunches.

Having failed on both flanks, Clinton next drove his men straight at Wayne's position in the centre. Two attacks failed, broken up by deadly volleys from behind a hedgerow, but Lieutenant-Colonel Henry Monckton, the commander of the 2nd Grenadiers, urged his men to make one last attempt, and for the third time the British line advanced up the slope toward the ominously silent hedgerow that marked the American line. As the British pressed forward Wayne cautioned his men to hold their fire. 'Steady, steady!' he shouted. 'Wait for the word, then pick out the kingbirds [officers].' Finally, when the British line had drawn to within a few yards of the hedge, he barked the command to fire, and the grenadiers were raked by a withering blast of flame and smoke. This blast killed Monckton outright and shattered his command, which was sent reeling down the slope. Just moments later, however, the grenadiers were back, enraged by the loss of their leader and the battalion's colours. Wayne's men counter-attacked with the bayonet, and a wild, almost grotesque mêlée ensued over Monckton's corpse. Finally, the Americans withdrew across the bridge over the West Ravine (carting Monckton's body with them), and the British rested on their arms at the body-strewn hedgerow position.

By this time the British army had pretty much fought itself out, and Clinton was forced to admit that there was no hope of seriously threatening Washington's main line. 'It was not for me to give him the advantage . . . by attacking him so posted', he wrote later. 'Nor indeed could I have done it, as the troops were fairly spent.' There was, however, a considerable danger that the Americans would counter-attack, since a good proportion of Washington's army had not been engaged. Wisely, Clinton withdrew his men to a new position behind the Middle Ravine. There the British formed a line which Sir Henry thought he 'might have held against the world'.

At this juncture Washington attempted an attack. Two brigades, Poor's and Woodford's, advanced from opposite ends of the American line, but before they had gone too far these men, like Clinton's grenadiers, collapsed in exhaustion, and the attack was never made.

This abortive advance ended the Battle of Monmouth, the war's longest and most gruelling combat experience. Both armies suffered equally—each losing about 350 men. Strangely, the heat claimed more lives than musketry or roundshot.

Monmouth was a drawn battle. Clinton quit the field at midnight and rejoined von Knyphausen's division the next day, By 1 June, the entire army had gained Sandy Hook, where, secure behind the sandhills of Navesink, they awaited evacuation to New York by Admiral Howe's fleet. When Washington withdrew from the field, he marched his army northward to White Plains above New York City, where the men remained until they departed for the Yorktown campaign in 1781.

17 January 1781
Daniel Morgan's Americans reverse the tide
of defeat with a stunning victory over 'Barbarous
Ban' Tarleton; their success reanimates the
Patriot cause in the South.

COWPENS

QUEBEC

MONTREAL

BOSTON

NEW YORK

PHILADELPHIA

COWPENS ★

CHARLESTON

SAVANNAH

ATLANTIC OCEAN

THE
BACKGROUND TO
THE BATTLES

Until 1778 the South had been a secondary theatre of operations. But, following Monmouth, the war in the North had virtually ended, and British planners in Whitehall, sensing a deadlock against Washington in New Jersey, were understandably drawn toward this untrammelled and inviting territory where Loyalist sentiment was reputedly strong.

From the American point of view, the South posed special strategic problems. The weight of the Patriot effort had always to be opposed to the serious British threat in the New York–New Jersey area, and few regulars could be spared to protect the South in the event of the British using their superior naval mobility— their 'canvas wings', to quote Washington — to strike swiftly and gain a foothold on the Southern Coast. Except for Virginia and Maryland, which contributed greatly to the American cause in both the North and the South, the underpopulated Southern States seemed incapable even of defending themselves, and, until 1778, the cause of Congress prevailed in the South by only the most tenuous of margins.

The Tories, very strong in the South, had risen prematurely in 1776 and had been soundly beaten at Moore's Creek Bridge near Wilmington, North Carolina, on 27 February. This action delivered North Carolina to Congress. In June, Admiral Sir Peter Parker's British fleet, transporting an invasion army under Sir Henry Clinton, attacked Fort Moultrie, a palmetto-log improvisation defending the harbour of Charleston, South Carolina. In the gun duel that followed, HM frigate *Actaeon* was set afire, Parker's flagship was riddled (and the Admiral's breeches were blown off), while Clinton's army looked on impotently from nearby Long Island, prevented from crossing and joining the assault by deep water and shoals. Three weeks later Clinton's army ended its miserable vigil on Long Island. Racked by malaria, dysentery and typhus, gored and hulled by the guns of the palmetto fort, the British expedition had had enough of South Carolina. Parker and Clinton slipped away, and the South gained two years of peace as the fighting shifted northward.

But this brief respite perhaps aided the British,

since it encouraged disaffection and apathy among the Americans. The next British descent on the South occurred in late December 1778, when a force commanded by Lieutenant-Colonel Archibald Campbell took Savannah, Georgia, from a minuscule American army commanded by General Robert Howe. Then, in January 1779, Brigadier-General Augustine Prevost, the British commander in Florida, marched north on the Old Post Road to Savannah with reinforcements for Campbell, who subsequently took Augusta (29 January 1779), a strategically important inland town situated on the Savannah River.

As the mild Southern winter set in, General Benjamin Lincoln's Charleston-based army of Continentals and militia attempted to retake Georgia, but the British were too strong. Still later in 1779 Lincoln tried to retake Savannah with the assistance of Admiral Count d'Estaing's French fleet. Although the Allied army outnumbered Prevost's defenders and might have taken the town outright, a great deal of time was wasted in formal siegecraft, and Prevost managed to strengthen his works against the inevitable assault. On 9 October, four weeks into the siege, an attack was launched. Although executed with great bravery, it was met by a galling fire and an equally spirited defence. After an hour of determined fighting, the broken remnants of the Allied army trailed back to their own trenches, leaving over 400 of their number within or near the British works. Count Casimir Pulaski, the Polish cavalier serving with the Allies, was mortally wounded in the assault. By the end of the month the French fleet had departed, and Lincoln, bereft of heavy artillery (the fleet's guns had been utilized as a siege train), lifted the siege and withdrew to Charleston. Georgia was to remain under British occupation until 1782.

The repercussions of this failed siege of Savannah were profound. With d'Estaing's troublesome fleet gone from the Southern Coast, Lord George Germain's plan for a full-scale invasion of the South could proceed. Moreover, the defeat had upset the equilibrium that the belligerents had managed to establish during the preceding year. General Moultrie stated that the repulse 'depressed

SERGEANT JASPER'S HEROIC ACTION DURING THE DEFENCE OF FORT MOULTRIE, JUNE 1776; UNDER FIRE FROM THE BRITISH FLEET, HE REPLACED A FLAG ON THE BASTION.

our spirits, we began to be apprehensive for the safety of these two Southern States; it also depreciated our money so low that it was scarcely worth anything'.

In New York Sir Henry Clinton began preparations for a second try at taking Charleston. About 8,500 men of his New York garrison (then nearly 29,000 effectives) were detached for the expedition, which was to be convoyed by Rear-Admiral Marriot Arbuthnot's fleet. Clinton embarked on 26 December 1779, leaving the New York post to the care of the capable Hessian General von Knyphausen and taking with him, as his second-in-command, Lord Cornwallis. After a nightmare voyage that lasted over a month, during which the ships were scattered by storms, the bulk of the invasion fleet (minus a portion of the ordnance, some of the artillery horses and all of the cavalry mounts, which were lost to the storms) reassembled off Tybee Island near Savannah. In February 1780, a landing was made at John's Island, near Charleston, and the Redcoats began to work their way toward the city just 30 miles distant but separated from them by an impeding maze of rivulets, malarial swamps and salt marshes.

At this point General Lincoln might well have abandoned Charleston as untenable, but political considerations forced him to stay and defend the city against the imminent British siege. By 12 March Clinton's army had crossed the Stono and Ashley Rivers and had taken a position on Charleston Neck blocking the landward approaches to the city. On 9 April Admiral Arbuthnot's fleet ran past the guns of Fort Moultrie and took position in the harbour, facing the city. The investment was completed when the American post at Monk's Corner, Charleston's last link with the outside world, was surprised and taken by a detachment under the command of Lieutenant-Colonel Webster. After receiving reinforcements from Savannah, the methodical Clinton began formal siege operations on 1 April, and the city fell on 12 May.

On 29 May 1780, just 17 days after the surrender of Charleston, Lieutenant-Colonel Tarleton, an enterprising young officer of Clinton's command, surprised and slaughtered a force of Virginia regulars at the Waxhaws near the North Carolina line. This regiment, Abraham Buford's 11th Virginia, was the last Continental unit in South Carolina. By June the British had established complete control in the State, and General Clinton, who departed for New York that month, could boast, 'There are few men in South Carolina who are not either our prisoners, or in arms with us'.

Lord Cornwallis, Clinton's successor in South Carolina, was more adventurous and less systematic than his superior. He disdained Clinton's plan for a plodding, methodical advance northward along the coast and, instead, pushed deep into the Piedmont Plateau with advance elements covering his left flank in the 'up-country' mountain region. Cornwallis's principal effort was directed toward the subjugation of North Carolina, but he was distracted by numerous irregular bands led by such notable partisans as Francis 'Swamp Fox' Marion and Thomas 'Gamecock' Sumter, which preyed on his extensive lines of communication and supply, waylaid his detachments and terrorized Loyalists. Then, if Marion, Sumter, et al were not enough trouble, an American army materialized in North Carolina, led by Horatio Gates, the victor of Saratoga. It consisted of a corps of 1,400 Continentals under Baron De Kalb and about 2,000 militia. Gates, who seems to have taken leave of his senses for the space of the subsequent campaign, took this 'Grand Army', as he called it, southward. After a march in which the men were forced to endure terrible hardships and privation because of Gates's ignorance of the countryside, the 'Grand Army'—tired, hungry and ravaged by dysentery—met the British near Camden, South Carolina, on 16 August 1780. The Battle of Camden was sheer disaster—in fact, the worst battlefield disaster suffered by any American army in the war. Gates's militia, facing British regulars, bolted. Many of the men escaped through the surrounding swamps. Gates, who fled the field with the militia, rode all the way to Hillsborough, North Carolina (200 miles from Camden) in three days. The remnants of his army reassembled there over the next month.

Cornwallis advanced to Charlotte, North Carolina, on 26 September and began active preparations for the conquest of the State. His plans were dashed when, on 8 October, one of his detachments operating in the 'up-country', Major Patrick Ferguson's Tory corps, was completely destroyed by rifle-armed frontiersmen at King's Mountain. After King's Mountain, Cornwallis fell back to Winnsboro, South Carolina, postponed the invasion of North Carolina and went into winter quarters. Gates's army entered Charlotte after the British withdrawal, built a miserable camp in which it was hoped the men could survive the winter and awaited the arrival of a new commander—Gates having been recalled to answer charges concerning his mismanagement of the Camden campaign.

ALLIED COMMANDERS AT THE ABORTIVE SIEGE OF SAVANNAH (SEPTEMBER — OCTOBER 1779): GENERAL BENJAMIN LINCOLN AND (INSET) ADMIRAL COUNT D'ESTAING.

THE COMMANDERS

Brigadier-General Daniel Morgan (1736–1802) was born in Hunterdon County, New Jersey. A runaway at the age of seventeen, Morgan became a child of the frontier, growing to maturity in the rough-and-tumble environment of the Virginia Piedmont region. In 1755 he was a wagoner on Braddock's ill-fated expedition to Fort Duquesne. Violent, illiterate, and, no doubt, insubordinate, Morgan soon ran foul of army justice and was court-martialled for striking an officer. He was sentenced to receive 499 lashes and proudly bore the scars of this punishment all his life. Later he survived being shot through the jaw in an Indian ambush.

Following the French and Indian War (1754–63),

DANIEL MORGAN.   BANASTRE TARLETON.

deserved promotion. Denied this by Congress's inane promotion policy and plagued by poor health, he took a leave of absence.

A year later, following Gates's defeat at Camden, Washington cast about for men who could salvage the deteriorating situation in the South. The leadership of the Southern Army had to be vested in the best officers available. Nathanael Greene of Rhode Island was sent, and Daniel Morgan was made his second-in-command.

Lieutenant-Colonel Banastre Tarleton (1754–1833) was the son of a merchant and one-time mayor of Liverpool. He was educated at University College, Oxford, but then, like many another young rakehell, spent the months preceding the outbreak of the war gambling away his father's fortune.

The troubles in America rescued this youthful *roué* from the life he had been pursuing in the gambling dens and coffee-houses of London. Rather down in his fortunes, Tarleton welcomed the opportunity to withdraw gracefully from the dissolute circle in which he moved; moreover, the war represented a fresh outlet for his boundless energy. In the spring of 1775 Tarleton purchased a cornet's commission in the 1st Dragoon Guards, and later he volunteered to go to America with Lord Cornwallis.

Some measure of Tarleton's brash temperament may be gathered from an account of his last appearance at the Cocoa Tree, his favourite West End haunt. There he brandished a sabre and declared: 'With this sword I'll cut off General [Charles] Lee's head!'

Once in America, Tarleton assumed command of a unit of Tory dragoons, and these later supplied the nucleus of his famous British Legion, a mixed force of foot and dragoons formed on 1 August 1778. In December 1779, the Legion embarked from New York for Charleston, South Carolina, with Sir Henry Clinton's expeditionary corps.

In the South, Tarleton added to his already considerable reputation as a commander of light troops. His forays into the hinterland were planned and executed with dazzling rapidity and brilliance. But his volatile disposition permitted excesses and gratuitous violence, most notably in the massacre of Virginia militia at the Waxhaws on 29 May 1780. After this incident Tarleton was known throughout America as 'Bloody Ban' or 'Barbarous Ban', and, though feared, was marked for the noose if captured.

Morgan settled into a calmer, more domesticated existence in Winchester, Virginia, where he learned to read and write and became a respected leader in the local community. By 1771 he held the rank of captain in the Frederick County militia, and at the outbreak of the Revolutionary War he was appointed captain of one of the original ten rifle companies raised for Continental service.

Morgan and his riflemen participated in the gruelling Quebec campaign, and the 'Old Wagoner', as he was by then known, was captured in the assault on the Lower Town in December 1775. Exchanged, he rejoined Washington's army, was commissioned colonel of a rifle corps, and was sent north with his men to reinforce Gates's army at Saratoga. There, as we have seen, Morgan and his corps were the very heart of the American effort at Freeman's Farm, the 'shirt men' contributing mightily to the defeat of Burgoyne's army.

Morgan returned from Saratoga expecting a well-

MORGAN'S CAMPAIGN WEST OF THE CATAWBA

General Nathanael Greene, the new commander of the Southern Army, arrived in Charlotte on 2 December 1780. Greene was a Quaker—the son of a Rhode Island iron founder. He had begun the war as a private in the Kent County Guards (a Rhode Island militia unit) but had risen rapidly to a position of prominence in the Northern Army. Greene was a proud man who possessed few Quaker virtues. He was nonetheless self-assured and confident—qualities which would sustain him in the coming months, for when he assumed command of the Southern Army he faced a task that might have driven a lesser man to despair.

The force at Charlotte, Greene found, was 'but the shadow of an army in the midst of distress'. It had 'only an imaginary existence'. Camden had wrecked this army, especially the pitiably small corps of regulars (Congress could spare no more). Of the 2,000 men in camp only 600 were regulars; the rest were militiamen. All were hungry, ill-clothed and unpaid. The army had no baggage, no artillery, no stores and no money.

Greene at once set about creating a new fighting force more like the partisan corps of Sumter and Marion than the classic regular army reinforced by militia that Gates had taken to Camden. He wanted, he said, a 'flying army'—an entire army equipped and utilized like the advance guard and light troops of regular armies. The new force was not to be frittered away in pitched battles with British regulars but was, rather, to be used for harassment, attacks on posts and detachments, and for raids deep into enemy territory. It was to live off the land, foraging over the countryside and keeping constantly on the move to avoid enemy traps. Although these aims may seem limited, there was, given the material he had to work with, little else the new commander could do.

Greene had scarcely been with the army two weeks when he drafted orders to Brigadier-General Daniel Morgan, his second-in-command, instructing him to march to the south-west with a small detachment of the main army and join with some militia operating in the hills on the west bank of the Catawba River. Morgan's mission, consistent with Greene's idea of a 'flying army', was to 'give protection to that part of the country and spirit up the people, to annoy the enemy in that quarter . . . collect the provisions and forage out of the way of the enemy . . .'

The employment of this force outside of foraging and 'showing the flag' west of the Catawba was left entirely to Morgan's discretion. But, since Greene planned to take his portion of the army away from Charlotte in the opposite direction, Morgan had to take care to maintain his lines of communication with the dangerously distant troops of the main army. A glance at the strategic map will show in an instant just how injudicious and unorthodox—or brilliant—Greene's new disposition of the army was. Cornwallis, at

Winnsboro, would occupy a central position midway between the separate elements of the American army. If he were quick enough, he might destroy either; and any such defeat would effectively doom the American cause in the South.

Morgan's tiny force left the Charlotte camp immediately on receiving Greene's order (16 December). If Cornwallis had intelligence of Morgan's movements, he was slow to react. Greene remained at Charlotte until 20 December, when he began his march to Cheraw on the Pee Dee River; thus at first Morgan's march might have resembled a harmless foraging expedition. But then, on 30 December, a mounted detachment of Morgan's corps surprised and slaughtered 250 Georgia Loyalists at Hammond's Store. This encounter roused Cornwallis to action. The British commander sensed that Ninety Six, the western anchor of his broad disposition, was the object of Morgan's sortie. But, if Morgan were moving on Ninety Six, he was doing so in a broad arc. Cornwallis, by moving his men up the Catawba, could block Morgan's retreat in the upper reaches. A force of light troops under Lieutenant-Colonel Tarleton was detached from the main British army and sent sweeping to the north-west to block Morgan's advance.

Morgan did not know he was being chased until 12 January, when Major Joseph McJunkin of Washington's dragoons rode into his camp with a message from Colonel Andrew Pickens, the commander of the State militia, that Tarleton was drawing close. Pickens, who was known to the Indians as 'Skyagunsta' (Border Wizard Owl), had been operating with Morgan since the affair at Hammond's Store. The news of Tarleton's approach disturbed Morgan. His men were dispersed, most of them gathering forage. Pickens was at Fairforest, near Hammond's Store, and Washington and the mounted troops were refitting at Wofford's Iron Works (now Glendale). Messengers were dispatched at once to these troops with orders to join Morgan and the main body at Hannah's Cowpens, a local landmark on the Old Cherokee Trail. On the 15th, in the midst of these hurried preparations, Morgan found time to scribble a letter to Greene.

'Upon a full and mature deliberation', he wrote, 'I am confirmed in the opinion that nothing can be effected by my detachment in this country, which will balance the risks I will be subjected to by remaining here. The enemy's great superiority in numbers, and our distance from the main army, will enable Lord Cornwallis to detach so superior a force against me, as to render it essential to our safety to avoid coming to action.'

There was, however, one hope. This difficult country was laced by streams, creeks and rivers. One of these watercourses, the Broad River, curved across Morgan's rear about five miles from the Cowpens rendezvous. The Broad, as its name

implies, was wide enough to prevent an army fording it without difficulty. If Morgan could concentrate his scattered units in time and slip across the Broad, a small rearguard might force Tarleton to detour; this could be enough to save the Patriot army.

On the night of 15–16 January Morgan was at Gentleman Thompson's (now Thicketty Station). On the morning of the 16th some of Pickens's men brought word that Tarleton was closer than Morgan had expected. In fact, Tarleton's advance elements were but five miles away. So, before dawn, the Americans were rousted from their breakfast fires, formed, and marched toward the Broad River.

Ban Tarleton was at his best in the chase. As in the march to the Waxhaws, he drove his men to the limits of their endurance. He was now so close that Morgan knew he could not get his army over

was that it was free of the dense, impenetrable undergrowth of the surrounding district; indeed, it was very much like a park. Morgan's men made their camp in a swale between the two hills and waited for Pickens's militia to arrive.

After surveying the Cowpens, Morgan decided to fight a unique defensive battle there. Much, of course, depended upon Pickens and the militia. If they would fight, the Patriot army might have a chance of winning the day.

All that evening Pickens's men drifted into camp. They were lean, vigorous men, veterans of dozens of scrapes with Tory militia, many of them 'over-mountain' men who had fought at King's Mountain. Morgan did not have great confidence in their ability to stand firm in a set-piece battle, but they did increase his force to over 900.

Colonel Andrew Pickens joined Morgan in a council of war that evening. If Morgan had had doubts about the militia, their grizzled commander, a descendant of Huguenot refugees, soon disabused him. 'I will fight with my command alone,' he said, 'if for nothing else, to show the people that we do not give up the State!' Further retreat, Pickens argued, was out of the question—it would only discourage his militia. He ended by saying, 'My men have come to fight!'

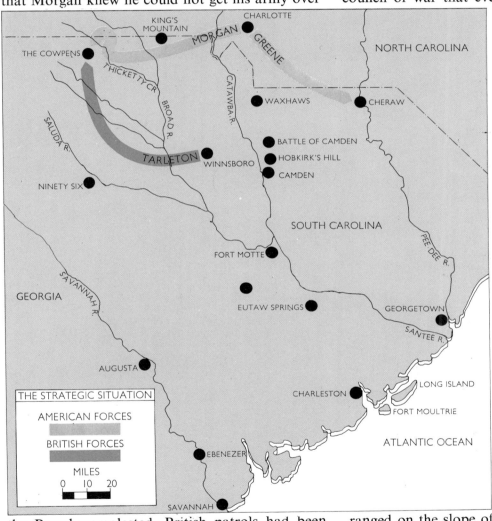

THE STRATEGIC SITUATION

AMERICAN FORCES

BRITISH FORCES

MILES
0   10   20

Pickens's bellicosity cheered Morgan. Over-burdened as he was by the cares and tribulations of the past few days, he nonetheless began an animated description of how he proposed to fight the coming battle.

Morgan's plan was simple. He knew that Tarleton's attacks (for the latter always took the initiative) invariably consisted of straightforward, impetuous rushes right at his quarry. With this in mind, Morgan planned to break the impetus of the attack with musketry from successive lines of infantry

the Broad unmolested. British patrols had been active and stragglers had been taken. To try and evade the British in the thickets, hills and ragged forests of the area was, Morgan saw, out of the question.

Some time in the mid-afternoon the head of Morgan's column emerged from the tangled underbrush of Thicketty Creek and debouched onto a wooded meadow which sloped gently up toward two round hills. This was Hannah's Cowpens—a fairly extensive undulating grassland used by local cattlemen to graze the herds of cattle which roamed the area freely throughout the year. One significant aspect of the Cowpens

ranged on the slope of the first hill. Washington's dragoons and McCall's mounted infantry were to be held in reserve behind the second hill—a trump card to deal with Tarleton's dragoons or strike the British infantry at an opportune moment.

Later in the evening Morgan, Pickens and some of the other officers moved among the campfires. 'Stand fire as long as you can,' Pickens cautioned the militia. 'When you can't stand any more, don't run. Quietly retreat, then form again. Mark the epauletted men [the officers] and shoot at them.'

Five miles to the south, Tarleton's men rested. Their commander was confident that Morgan, his back to a river, was inextricably trapped.

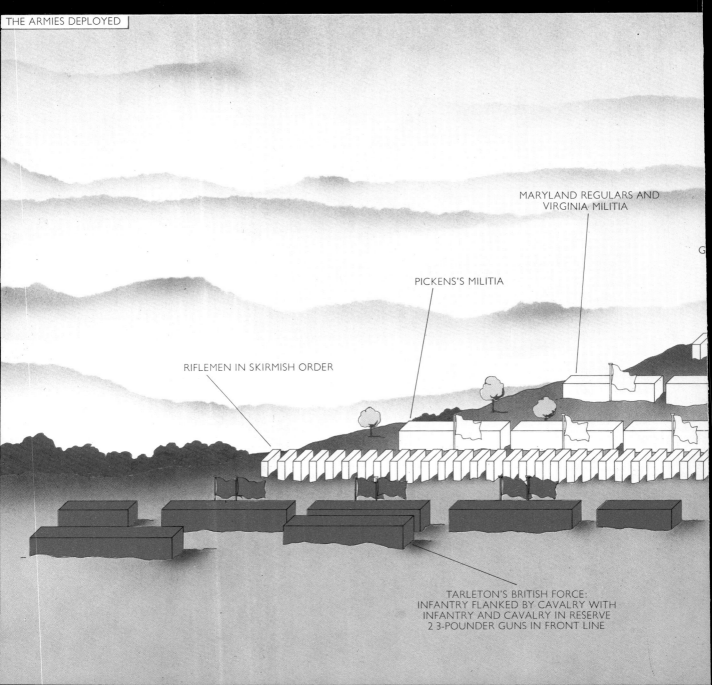

MARYLAND REGULARS AND
VIRGINIA MILITIA

PICKENS'S MILITIA

RIFLEMEN IN SKIRMISH ORDER

TARLETON'S BRITISH FORCE:
INFANTRY FLANKED BY CAVALRY WITH
INFANTRY AND CAVALRY IN RESERVE
2 3-POUNDER GUNS IN FRONT LINE

LIST OF UNITS PRESENT

AMERICANS		BRITISH/TORY	
Brigadier-General Daniel Morgan		Lieutenant-Colonel Banastre Tarleton	
MILITIA CONTINGENT		7th Foot (Royal Fusiliers)	200
(Colonel Andrew Pickens)		71st Foot—Frasier's Highlanders	200
South Carolina Volunteers	270	(Major McArthur)	
(Pickens, with Brannon, Thomas,		3 companies of light infantry	—
Hays, Hammond)		Tarleton's British Legion	550
North Carolina Volunteers	—	(infantry and dragoons)	
(Major James McDowell)		17th Light Dragoons	50
Georgia Volunteers	60	Royal Artillery section (two 3-pounder	
(Major Cunningham)		'galloper' guns)	
REGULARS (Lt.-Col John E. Howard)		ESTIMATED TOTAL 1,100	
1st Maryland of the Continental Line	290	Losses: 110 killed, 702 wounded and captured.	
Virginia Militia (Beatie, Triplett)	100		
Augusta (Va.) Riflemen	100		
(Tate, Buchanan)			
CAVALRY (Lt.-Col William Washington)			
Washington's Light Dragoons	80		
McCalls' Mounted Militia	45		
ESTIMATED TOTAL 1,000			
Losses: 12 killed, 60 wounded.			

MORGAN AND STAFF

WASHINGTON'S CAVALRY

THE BATTLE

Tarleton's men were up at 3 am and moving within the hour. The bulk of the British army was made up of Tarleton's own British Legion, a veteran Tory unit which, like its commander, was used to winning. There were two battalions of British regulars, the 71st Foot (Frasier's Highlanders), commanded by Major McArthur, and the 7th Royal Fusiliers, an ancient regiment with a proud record. These line battalions were complemented by three companies of light infantry, a troop of the 17th Light Dragoons and a Royal Artillery section of two light 3-pounder 'galloper' guns. Altogether Tarleton had with him some 1,100 men, including the best light troops in Cornwallis's army.

Not long after Tarleton had begun to move, his advance was detected by Pickens's tireless scouts. When word of the advance was relayed to Morgan an hour before dawn, the 'Old Wagoner' once again moved among his men, this time bellowing, 'Boys, get up! Banny is coming!'

By dawn the Patriot army was drawn up in battle order. A short while later, at 6.30, the British army could be seen filing into its line of battle just 300 yards from the skirmishers of Morgan's first line. Pickens, in the meantime, moved among the riflemen of the first line attending to last-minute details. 'If the cavalry advances,' he cautioned, 'every third man must fire, while the other two hold their loaded rifles in reserve. Take careful aim and fire low.'

At 6.45 the British line began to advance. True to form, Tarleton rushed his men forward before they had time to order their line of battle. As the somewhat ragged line advanced, the men gave a cheer. Not to be outdone, Morgan's men answered with Indian whoops.

Almost immediately the riflemen in Pickens's skirmish line opened fire. A half-dozen of Tarleton's green-jacketed Legion cavalrymen toppled from their saddles at the first volley, and as the riflemen reloaded, the dragoons turned and rode back toward the British infantry. McDowell's riflemen continued to fire, and officers and men in the ranks of the British infantry began to fall. The 7th Royal Fusiliers were still beyond effective musket range, but their ranks were filled with inexperienced recruits who began to fire back at the Patriot riflemen. The hollow, ineffectual pop-pop of the 7th's musketry was soon stopped by the officers, but the bark of the American rifles continued. Several British officers now lay dead in the tall grass, but the Redcoats had begun to close on the rifles. Suddenly, the riflemen broke away and ran back towards Pickens's main body of militia, drawn up 200 yards behind them.

Tarleton's men now crowded toward Pickens's line, and the Legion dragoons returned to the fray. Coolly, Pickens's men held their fire until the British had approached to within 50 yards of their line. Then the militia line spat fire from end to end. More officers and sergeants fell among the British. At 40 yards, the British halted and fired a volley. Pickens's men returned this fire and began to file off to their left. The British maintained their formation and attempted to follow the Americans, who by now were sprinting away over the shoulder of the hill. Every so often a militiaman would turn and fire, but Pickens's line was gone, replaced by a disorganized mass running helter-skelter away from the heat of battle.

As Pickens's command bolted, Tarleton's dragoons cantered forward after them. For a moment the dragoons experienced every cavalryman's dream—chasing broken infantry with the sabre. One of the militiamen, James Collins, seeing the horsemen bearing down on his unit, thought to himself, 'My hide is in the loft'. Just then the British cavalry was hit by a compact mass of white-coated dragoons under Colonel William Washington. According to Collins:

'Colonel Washington's cavalry was among them like a whirlwind, and the poor fellows began to reel from their horses without being able to remount. The shock was so sudden and so violent that they could not stand it and immediately betook themselves to flight. There was no time to rally, and they appeared to be as hard to stop as a drove of wild Choctaw steers going to a Pennsylvania market. In a few moments the clashing of swords was out of hearing and quickly out of sight.'

Washington's sudden charge from his hidden position behind the second hill was reminiscent of Seydlitz's famous charge at Rossbach (1757). Moreover, it hit with the same savage and decisive force. For most of Tarleton's dragoons, the battle ended with this sharp encounter.

The British attack on Pickens and Washington's counter-charge had consumed less than five minutes. Tarleton's infantry watched Pickens's men disperse, sorted themselves out, and began to advance on Morgan's third line 200 yards farther up the hill. The advance was still enthusiastic, still spirited, but now, as Morgan had foreseen, it had become undisciplined. Most of the officers and sergeants were down, victims of McDowell's rifles and Pickens's musketry. The men of the understrength light infantry battalion on the right had been swept away by Washington's charge, and many of the men were sabred on the return of the Patriot dragoons. The Legion infantry and the men of the 7th Regiment had become intermingled but still pressed forward toward the Continentals on Morgan's left. Looking on from the bottom of the hill, Tarleton believed the day won. He waved the 71st Highlanders forward in support of the infantry.

Based on appearances alone, Tarleton's optimistic estimate of the situation was correct. He was enough of a realist to know that the Legion infantry and the 7th would be roughly handled by the Marylanders, but they would nonetheless occupy the attention of the Continentals while the 71st turned the American right, which was held by the small detachment of Virginia militia. Moreover, he still had on hand 200 fresh—if unenthusiastic—dragoons to complete the destruction of Morgan's army.

But, as Tarleton's men streamed forward toward that last resolute line of blue and homespun brown that barred the way to victory, there were significant developments taking place in the swale

behind the hill. Washington had returned to reform his troopers, and Pickens was likewise engaged in rallying his men. If these soldiers could be persuaded to return to the battle, Morgan would have 300 relatively fresh men to throw in at the decisive moment.

The last act of Cowpens began at about 7.25 am. The Legion infantry and the Royal Fusiliers had by now struggled to within 40 yards of the Marylanders. Here they met with one searing volley after another. Men fell in heaps, but still the British maintained their line and returned the fire. At this point John Eager Howard, commanding the American line in Morgan's absence (he was helping to rally Pickens's men), began to grow apprehensive. The cause of his concern was not the battle to the front of his Maryland regiment, but the advance of the British 71st. As Howard perceived, the steady drive of the High-

instructions to reload as they withdrew.

Morgan returned at this time, and he was undeniably disturbed by what he saw. But Howard soon calmed his fears 'by pointing to the line and observing that men were not beaten who retreated in that order'. Morgan then ordered Howard to prepare his men to face about and fire a volley from a position near the crest, and the 'Old Wagoner' rode toward the crest to mark the position. Some time during these confused moments a messenger from Washington rode up to Morgan with a brief but important message: 'They are coming like a mob—face about and give them a fire and I will charge them!' Morgan nodded his assent and the messenger rode back to the dragoons.

The Patriot line continued its retreat to the position marked by Morgan. The British were but 30 paces behind. Suddenly, the hoarse bellows of American officers shouting orders rent the air, the

ALTHOUGH THEIR IMPACT ON THE WAR AS A WHOLE WAS SLIGHT, CAVALRY PLAYED A DECISIVE ROLE AT COWPENS. THIS PAINTING IS BY S. KEMMELMEYER.

landers would take them beyond the right flank of the Virginia militia, from which point they could wheel and rush the American line, rolling it up from one end to the other. Already the 71st was inclining toward the right flank of the Virginians.

Howard reacted quickly to this new crisis. Riding to the Virginians, he ordered them to refuse their right flank company, i.e. turn about and move to a position where they could face the Highlanders as they closed. Other officers in the American line observed this movement and, incredibly, ordered their men to face about and retreat to a new position near the crest of the hill. Soon, the entire American line was retreating, though the men maintained good order and obeyed

line abruptly faced about and delivered a sudden volley into the very faces of the British soldiers following it. This fire was too much for the brave men of Tarleton's command. They gave way in confusion. Howard then ordered the Continentals to finish the British with the bayonet—an order which, he observed, 'was obeyed with great alacrity'.

On the American right Pickens's men burst from the swale and barrelled into the flank of the Highlanders, completing the destruction of that unit. Simultaneously, Washington's troopers drove into the British line from the left, passing the Marylanders, sabring and slashing away at the last knots of resistance. Everywhere now the British infantry began to ground their arms—further

107

resistance was futile. As the British were herded into manageable groups many of the militia began to shout, 'Tarleton's Quarter!' 'No quarter!' But Pickens and other officers prevented an ugly scene by yelling, 'Give them quarter!'

The battle was practically over. Tarleton watched in disbelief as his infantry surrendered and the brave artillerymen manning the 'gallopers' were cut down by Washington's horsemen. Casting about for a means to retrieve some honour from this desperate situation, he ordered his dragoons to charge. But the men baulked. In Tarleton's words, 'All attempts to restore order, recollection, or courage, proved fruitless. Above two hundred dragoons forsook their leader, and left the field of battle.' But a handful of courageous dragoons did advance, colliding with Washington's horsemen near the guns and driving them back for a distance until the Continentals again pressed forward and finally dispersed them.

A TRIUMPH OF SABRE OVER BAYONET.

As Tarleton and a small band of survivors rode from this last mêlée a troop of American horse led by Washington rode among them. Never one to resist a duel, Tarleton turned and fired his pistol at Washington, wounding him in the knee. A second later Washington caught Tarleton's hand with his sabre, and the British commander turned and fled. Many months later Tarleton recounted the action for Mrs. J. B. Ashe of Halifax, North Carolina, stating that he would like to meet Colonel Washington, whom he had heard was squat and ugly. Mrs Ashe, who was familiar with the Patriot version of the story, reprimanded him, saying bluntly, 'If you had looked behind you, Colonel Tarleton, at the Battle of Cowpens, you would have enjoyed that pleasure.'

The battle ended at about 8.00 am, just over an hour after it had begun. The long slope of the hill up which the British had toiled was littered with the dead and wounded of Tarleton's command; many of the bodies lay in windrows where successive volleys had scythed them down. Near the crest Howard sat on his charger holding seven swords surrendered by British officers. The destruction of Tarleton's force was complete. Of the 1,100 men he had led onto the field at dawn, less than 300 escaped to the main army. The British casualties attested to the sharpness of the action and the valour of the advance: 110 were killed, over 200 wounded and 500 made prisoner. Among the booty taken by the Patriots were the two 3-pounder field guns, 800 muskets, 100 horses, much of Tarleton's baggage, including a travelling forge, and 'all the enemy's music'. Morgan's losses totalled just 12 killed and 60 wounded.

If nothing else, the Cowpens was decisive in the sense that it was not an American defeat. Had Morgan's detachment been destroyed at the Cowpens, Greene's army, which was scarcely larger, must have inevitably abandoned the Carolinas for good or faced certain ruin at the hands of Cornwallis. As it was, Cornwallis, roused to a fury by Tarleton's report of the disaster, chased Morgan and Greene to the Virginia line (1–14 February 1781). In this 'Race to the Dan (River)', Greene stayed always one day's march ahead of Cornwallis's larger army. Greene's corps of light troops under Colonel Otho H. Williams skilfully covered the retreat, contesting each ford on the numerous rivers and streams of the Carolina Piedmont region. Cornwallis destroyed most of his baggage to speed his march but failed ultimately because, as Tarleton put it, 'the unfortunate affair at the Cowpens deprived him of almost the whole of his light troops'. Without light troops a properly organized and conducted pursuit was impossible.

Despairing of effecting anything against the wily Greene, Cornwallis returned to Hillsborough, North Carolina, to recruit Loyalists, rest his army and prepare for the spring campaign. But the Battle of Cowpens turned out to be just the beginning of a long train of British disasters in 1781. On 22 February Greene slipped into North Carolina again. His army had grown to a strength of 4,400 men, although only 1,600 were regulars. Greene now sought battle, and on 15 March, at Guilford Court House, Cornwallis obliged him. At Guilford, Greene disposed his men in three lines as Morgan had done at Cowpens—militia in the first two lines and regulars in the third. Cornwallis, with 2,000 men, attacked each line in succession. The battle lasted two hours, and Cornwallis lost a third of his army. 'The enemy gained his cause,' wrote Greene, 'but is ruined by the success of it.'

Following his Pyrrhic performance at Guilford, Cornwallis withdrew his army (now barely 1,500 strong) to Wilmington on the coast. Thereupon Greene marched his army into South Carolina to reconquer the Palmetto State. The campaign which followed was a masterly illustration of how to win by losing. The American commander lost both pitched battles of the campaign, but with the help of Marion, Sumter and 'Light Horse Harry' Lee, he had, by mid-September, forced the British to withdraw completely from their posts and garrisons in South Carolina and Georgia, except for those at Charleston and Savannah.

The Cowpens-Guilford Court House and South Carolina campaigns of 1781 restored the South to the United States and ended forever British plans to gain eventual victory by detaching that territory and using it as a secure base from which to carry the war to the Middle Atlantic States. Ultimately, victory was gained through a remarkable combination of patient effort and stubborn courage—qualities that Greene might have had in mind when, after his defeat at Hobkirk's Hill (25 April 1781), he wrote, 'We fight, get beat, rise, fight again'.

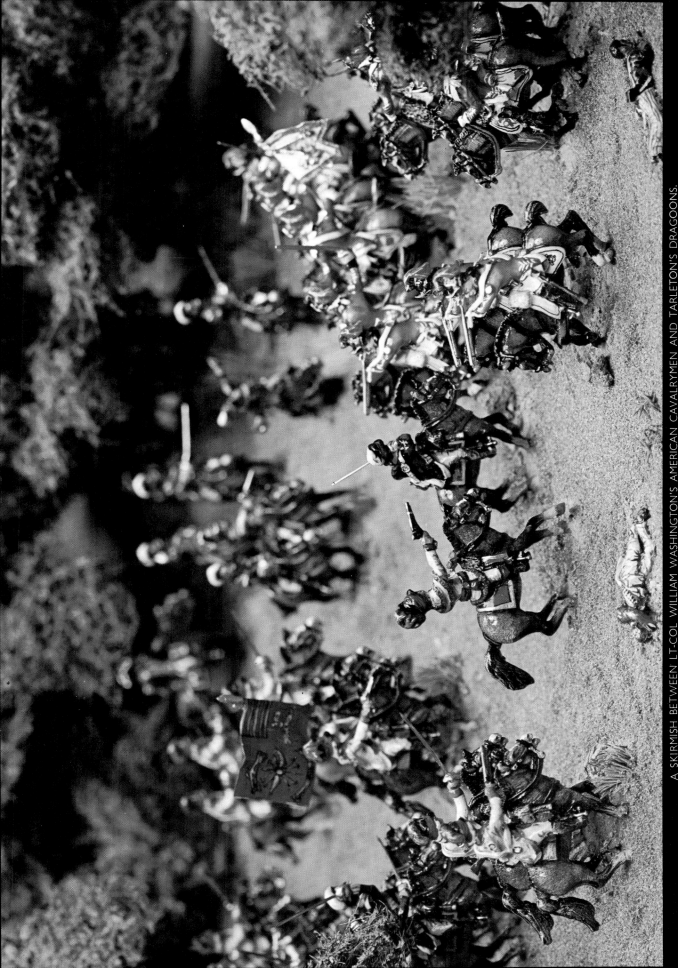

A SKIRMISH BETWEEN LT-COL WILLIAM WASHINGTON'S AMERICAN CAVALRYMEN AND TARLETON'S DRAGOONS.

THE ALLIES MAKE THEIR ASSAULT
ON THE BRITISH REDOUBTS NOS. 9 AND 10.

28 September–19 October 1781
A crushing victory at last for the Allies.
The combined weight of de Grasse's fleet, and the
armies of Washington, Rochambeau and
Lafayette, breaks the back of the British
war effort and effectively guarantees
victory for the American cause.

YORKTOWN

THE
BACKGROUND TO
THE SIEGE

Following his costly victory at Guilford Court House (15 March 1781), Lord Cornwallis withdrew his battered army to Wilmington, North Carolina, on the Cape Fear River. General Nathanael Greene, commanding the main American army in the South, followed Cornwallis as far as Ramsey's Mill and then, sensing that the British army was incapable of taking the field, turned away to campaign against Lord Rawdon in South Carolina.

In the meantime, at Wilmington, Cornwallis surveyed the wreckage of his command. Not five months before he had bragged that 'for the numbers there never was so fine an Army'. But Cowpens, the Race to the Dan and Guilford Court House had bled the army white. During the period 15 January–1 April 1781 Cornwallis had lost 1,501 men. Less than 1,500 survivors followed him into Wilmington. He was too weak to risk another confrontation with Greene, who stood between his force and that of Lord Rawdon; but to stay at Wilmington would, he thought, invite destruction should Greene return there. So, consumed by fears for the safety of his little army and thoroughly disgusted with the course the war had taken in the Carolinas, Cornwallis proposed to march his force to Virginia and join the substantial army already there under the command of General Phillips.

Cornwallis's plan had a great deal of merit. There was no doubt that the Carolinas, if they were isolated, could not long resist British power. But, for the plan to work, Rawdon would have to cope with Greene, the cleverest and most resourceful American commander, and the British would have to maintain naval supremacy over the French in the Chesapeake, so that Cornwallis's army would not be cut off from its source of supply.

Cornwallis outlined his plans to General Clinton, the British Commander-in-chief in New York, and Lord George Germain, the Secretary of State for the Colonies, and, without waiting for a reply, set his army in motion for Virginia. Germain approved the plan, but Clinton was apprehensive for the safety of Cornwallis's army and kept up a continual barrage of letters warning Cornwallis that in carrying operations into Virginia he was courting disaster. But Clinton never firmly and explicitly ordered Cornwallis away from Virginia; in fact, as time passed, his orders helped to persuade Cornwallis to remain there—even as the Allied trap closed around his force.

Cornwallis's troops entered Petersburg, Virginia, Phillips's headquarters, on 20 May. There Cornwallis learned that Phillips, a close friend, had died of malarial fever just three days before. The British army in Virginia, including subsequent reinforcements sent to Cornwallis, numbered 7,500 men—the largest British force in America excepting Clinton's main army in New York.

Opposed to Cornwallis in Virginia was an American army of about 3,000 men under the Marquis de Lafayette and Baron von Steuben, the Prussian drillmaster. Lafayette's army was too weak to do more than annoy Cornwallis, but he did this skilfully in the weeks following the latter's arrival in Virginia.

Once in Petersburg, Cornwallis, with his customary vigour, prepared his army for an offensive against Lafayette's force, which was encamped near Richmond. Benedict Arnold, the turncoat brigadier who had taken command of the Petersburg force after Phillips's death, was sent to New York. His continued presence with the army was an embarrassment Cornwallis could do without. By 24 May the British army was on the march toward the James River, which was crossed at Westover, below Richmond. Instead of fighting, Lafayette deftly side-stepped a general engagement and retreated north toward Racoon Ford on the Rappahannock River. Early in June Cornwallis realized that Lafayette—'the boy', as he contemptuously referred to him—was pursuing an oriental strategy not unlike that which Greene had employed in the Race to the Dan. If he continued to pursue the young Marquis, his army would be worn down by forced marches and lured farther from its supply bases on the coast; in time Lafayette would be reinforced, and militia would gather on the flanks of the British line of march. Then, deep in the interior of Virginia, cut off from reinforcements and resupply, the British army would be cut to pieces by superior American forces. Saratoga, King's Mountain and Cowpens provided vivid examples of this favourite American strategy.

This time, however, Cornwallis resolved not to be an actor in the scenario. His fears were confirmed when he learned that on 10 June Lafayette had been reinforced by 1,000 Pennsylvania Continentals under Anthony Wayne. Two days later 600 'Over Mountain' men under Colonel William Campbell entered Lafayette's camp. To the amazement of the Americans, Cornwallis called off the pursuit, launched a few punitive raids and then retreated toward Williamsburg on the peninsula between the York and James Rivers.

When Cornwallis retired eastward, Lafayette followed. The young Frenchman, enjoying his first independent command, could hardly believe his good fortune. Writing to Washington on 28 June he said:

'The enemy has been so kind as to retire before us. Twice I gave them a chance of fighting (taking care not to engage them farther than I pleased) but they continued their retrograde motions. Our numbers are, I think, exaggerated to them, and our seeming boldness confirms the opinion. I thought at first, Lord Cornwallis wanted to get me as low down as possible, and use his cavalry to advantage . . . General Greene only demanded of me, to hold my ground in Virginia. I don't know but what we shall, in our turn, become the pursuing enemy.'

Cornwallis, in the meantime, had established his army at the old colonial capital of Williamsburg.

The Virginia campaign, as far as he was concerned, was over. He now sought to remove himself and his army from the province. Any future operations in Virginia could, he thought, best be conducted by amphibious expeditions launched from New York. Had Clinton consented to the evacuation of Cornwallis's army at that point, the tragedy of Yorktown might have been averted. Instead the British Commander-in-chief directed Cornwallis to establish a post on the peninsula and embark part of his army to reinforce the New York garrison.

Clinton, in fact, was in one of his periodic panics. His intelligence service had intercepted some letters which showed that Washington and Rochambeau were planning a descent on New York. Although his army outnumbered any combination the Allies might bring against him, Clinton felt that his position would be immeasurably improved by the addition of 3,000 of Cornwallis's men.

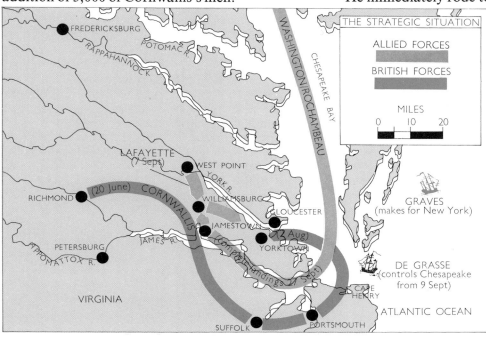

On 6 July Wayne's Continentals, the vanguard of Lafayette's army, attacked Cornwallis's screening troops at Green Spring. Wayne had only 800 men and three light cannon, but he thought his force was more than adequate to deal with the small British detachment that his scouts had reported seeing. A fierce skirmish developed as the Americans pushed forward into the morass in front of the woods where most of Cornwallis's men were hiding. The British waited until Wayne's men were fully committed before launching their counter-attack. Columns of red-coated infantry began to snake around Wayne's flanks while other regiments crowded into the firing-line facing the American attack, and opened a blistering fire on the Pennsylvanians.

Lafayette, who had taken position on a hill where he could see the troops concentrated in the British rear, realized at once that Wayne's men were trapped. He immediately rode to Wayne's position to help in extricating the beleaguered Continentals, but his efforts might have gone for naught had not Wayne himself decided boldly to order a charge. The British were closing rapidly when Wayne's men reformed and then, unexpectedly, advanced furiously with bayonets levelled. 'Mad Anthony's' audacious move caught them off balance. The nearest Red-coats stopped and wavered. In the confusion that followed, most of the Americans managed to escape. Lafayette then retreated six miles and prepared for the worst; but Cornwallis did not follow up. Instead, he pulled his army across the James and continued his march to Portsmouth.

Lafayette lost 200 men at Green Spring Farm; and he very nearly lost his army. The British lost about half as many men; even so, Lafayette contrived to claim a victory, in his letters speaking only of the British retreat. Greene, however, discerned the truth of the matter and observed wryly that the 'victory' would 'look well in a gazette'.

When Cornwallis arrived at Portsmouth, he found that Clinton had changed his mind about the reinforcements and, instead, wanted him to remain in Virginia with all his troops and fortify 'a station in Chesapeake for ships of the line, as well as frigates'. After a survey Cornwallis settled on the small village of Yorktown on the York River. Yorktown had an excellent harbour and was not as exposed to a sudden descent by a French fleet as a post on Hampton Roads might be; nevertheless, the new position did have its faults. The major problem, Cornwallis saw, was that neither Yorktown, nor its sister port of Gloucester across the river, was particularly well situated to resist a siege. However, by 2 August, Cornwallis's men were once more on the peninsula of Virginia, busily fortifying their new post. Lafayette, in turn, moved to West Point, about a day's march away, and awaited developments.

In order to comply with Clinton's order, Cornwallis would be obliged to move his army across the James River to the deep-water base at Portsmouth, where the embarkation could be carried out without fear of harassment by Lafayette's army. On 4 July the British army quit Williamsburg and marched to Jamestown, where the troops were to be ferried across the James River for the march to Portsmouth. Lafayette followed the British line of march and walked right into a trap Cornwallis had set for him at Green Spring Farm near Jamestown.

The young Frenchman, increasingly frustrated by the 'kind of runaway war' he had been forced to fight, had seen an opportunity to attack Cornwallis's army as it was engaged in the crossing of the James. If the British rearguard were attacked vigorously, Cornwallis would be at a disadvantage and his army might be crippled. Under ordinary circumstances Lafayette's judgment would have been correct and his prospects of success excellent; but Cornwallis was not an ordinary general. He had anticipated Lafayette's move. Only a small portion of the British army crossed the James. The rest took up a defensive position behind swamps and high ground near the river, with the bulk of the troops screened from the eyes of Lafayette's force by a wood.

113

THE COMMANDERS

Jean-Baptiste-Donatien de Vimeur, Count de Rochambeau (1725–1807), the commander of the French army at Yorktown, had been plucked from a well-deserved retirement to lead the French expeditionary corps to America. A thorough professional with nearly forty years of service behind him, Rochambeau was brave, competent and tactful, qualities which recommended him for this sensitive command over better connected court favourites.

Rochambeau's career was not typical of those who attained high command under the French monarchy. He did not lack means and his family background was impeccable, but he had won promotion more on the basis of merit and ability than through purchase or favour. He was not a court soldier; indeed, he seems to have been quite remote from Versailles and its entanglements. He did not seek the American command and must have been thoroughly surprised by the news of his appointment, as he had no friends in the King's apartments and his scruples prevented him from seeking preferment through politics and ritualistic scheming.

In selecting Rochambeau for the American command, the King and his ministers were, for once, advancing a capable professional. The incompetence of Count d'Estaing, the commander of the first French expeditionary force sent to America, embarrassed the monarchy and caused no small amount of bitterness and resentment in America. A second error of judgment might have sabotaged the war effort. Certainly, Rochambeau's service record indicated that he was the best choice for such an awkward assignment.

Once in America, Rochambeau co-operated fully with Washington, who acted as Commander-in-chief of the Allied army. There was no bickering, no jealousy and none of the petty intrigue which, historically, had emasculated alliance armies. Washington soon came to regard Rochambeau and the elegant officers of his staff as brothers. This spirit of co-operation produced the victory at Yorktown. Much of the credit for the success of the operation must go to the able but self-effacing French commander, whom Washington complimented indirectly when he wrote, 'It may, I believe, with much truth be said that a greater harmony between two armies never subsisted'.

Charles, Earl Cornwallis (1738–1805) was undoubtedly the most competent British general officer holding an army command during the Revolutionary War. Bold, able and courageous, he fought most of his battles in the straight-ahead fashion favoured by those generals whose military experience had been gained in the 'bayonet school' of European warfare. This reckless tactic won the day at Camden, when half the American army ran away at the first shots, but backfired at Guilford Court House as successive lines of infantry savaged the Earl's advancing regiments. Guilford wrecked Cornwallis's army and led ultimately to the Earl's abandonment of the Carolina campaign for Virginia and Yorktown.

Once in Virginia, Cornwallis found only frustration, as Lafayette imitated Greene's Fabian strategy and wore the British army down with marches and

countermarches. As the Allied forces closed about his beleaguered army, he and Sir Henry Clinton, the Commander-in-chief, continued their unfortunate quarrel—a dispute which had been simmering since the Carolina campaign. Cornwallis lost the initiative in Virginia, and hazy, often contradictory orders

ALLIED COMMANDERS AT THE SIEGE OF YORKTOWN: ON THE LEFT OF THE MAIN GROUP, POINTING, IS ROCHAMBEAU; ON HIS LEFT ARE WASHINGTON AND THE YOUTHFUL LAFAYETTE. INSET IS LORD CORNWALLIS.

from Clinton kept him there as the trap closed. But even in defeat he was formidable. Baron von Closen, an aide to Rochambeau, visited him after the surrender and remarked that 'His appearance gave the impression of nobility of soul, magnanimity and strength of character; his manner seemed to say, "I have done nothing with which to reproach myself, I have done my duty, and I held out as long as possible".'

Yorktown was Cornwallis's only defeat. Following the Revolution, he campaigned successfully in India, where he won many battles.

THE SIEGE OF YORKTOWN

While Lafayette and Cornwallis sparred in Virginia, Washington and Rochambeau, the French commander, planned the strategy that would ultimately lead to Cornwallis's capitulation at Yorktown. Washington's army was on the Hudson, engaged in a 'war of observation' against Clinton's powerful force at New York City. Rochambeau's crack army of 5,000 French regulars was at Newport, Rhode Island, where it had landed on 11 July 1780. Although the Allied commanders had agreed to work together, with Clinton's army as the possible object of their joint endeavour, Rochambeau was reluctant to stir far from the security of his base at Newport so long as the British maintained naval supremacy along the east coast. De Barras's French fleet at Newport was too weak to do much against Admiral Graves's British fleet, which was stationed at New York. Then, on 13 June 1781, Washington learned from Rochambeau that a French fleet under de Grasse, with 26 ships of the line, would appear along the coast in July.

The news was electrifying. Finally, after months of waiting, the Allies would have their longed-for naval supremacy. But de Grasse's stay on the coast would be brief. He had orders to be in the Caribbean by October. The Allied armies would have to move swiftly to exploit the temporary advantage that the presence of de Grasse's fleet would give them. Filled with excitement, Washington wrote to Rochambeau: 'Your excellency will be pleased to recollect that New York was looked upon by us as the only practicable object under present circumstances; but . . . we may perhaps find others more practicable and equally advisable'.

Rochambeau's army joined Washington's in Connecticut on 8 July. The remainder of the month was spent in harassing Clinton's outposts and demonstrating against New York. As we have seen, the vigorous activity of the Allied army during this period caused Clinton to request reinforcements from Cornwallis—an order he subsequently rescinded when he received a reinforcement of 2,000 Hessians from Europe.

Then, on 14 August, Washington learned that de Grasse's objective was Virginia. Immediately, plans were laid for a move against Cornwallis. Lafayette was instructed to keep the British penned at Yorktown, while the main army moved southward. Elaborate measures were taken to deceive Clinton, and the Allied army began its march toward Virginia on 19 August.

De Grasse made the Virginia Capes on 30 August. His voyage from Brest by way of the West Indies had been unremarkable. Admiral Graves, who had been forewarned of de Grasse's approach, had not patrolled south of the Virginia Capes and so did not intercept the French fleet. Sir George Rodney, whose British fleet ruled the waves in the Caribbean, had unaccountably allowed de Grasse to slip by him. Subsequently, de Grasse enjoyed a few days of undisturbed tranquillity in the Chesapeake during which he landed more than 3,000 troops from his fleet and refitted.

De Grasse's approach had not gone undetected.

Graves, reinforced by Sir Samuel Hood's squadron from Rodney's fleet (Hood had sailed right past the French fleet on his voyage northward), arrived off the Capes on 5 September. The British admiral had no idea what he might encounter in the Chesapeake. Undoubtedly, as his ships bore down upon the mouth of the bay, Graves mulled over the possibilities. The scouting frigates gambolled far ahead of the van. What would they report? The French might not be anywhere in sight. Then again, de Grasse's fleet might be in the bay. Suppose de Barras, with his fleet of eight 'liners', had managed to join de Grasse? By mid-morning the first reports of the French presence in Hampton Roads were signalled to Graves. The French were in the Chesapeake, anchored 'promiscuously' in three straggling lines. Graves decided to engage.

De Grasse was in an embarrassing situation. While Graves's ships were driving straight for the French anchorage near the mouth of the bay, the French fleet itself was in disarray. Many of the ships had put men ashore to forage and were short-handed. Somehow, though, de Grasse managed to organize his fleet, and a line of battle was improvised. Shortly after noon the van of the French fleet cleared Cape Henry for the open sea beyond.

The French were eager to engage, but de Grasse had nothing resembling a proper line of battle. The enthusiasm of his captains, who wasted a good deal of time jockeying for position closest to the enemy, made matters worse. Graves, had he been of a mind to exploit the disorder in the French line, might have destroyed the divisions of de Grasse's fleet piecemeal. Instead, he ordered his line to wear toward the French and then slowed—while the French formed their line. An hour and a half later, at 4.15 pm, when de Grasse was fully prepared, the British fleet closed for action.

Graves's vanguard, led by the *Shrewsbury*, with 74 guns, approached the French line at an oblique angle, so that the French were able to rake each British ship in succession. Moreover, Graves, in the *London*, a 90-gunner, made the signal to 'engage close' at a most inopportune moment and then raced out of line toward the enemy. The sudden movement of the flagship threw the ships of the van into disorder and prevented some of them from firing on the French for fear of hitting the *London*. A confusing battle followed. Many ships in both fleets were not significantly involved, but those that were engaged fought fiercely at close-quarters for over two hours. Then, at sunset, the battle ended. Neither fleet had lost heavily, but many of Graves's ships were badly damaged.

The two fleets remained in contact over the next few days. De Grasse was in good spirits and anxious to resume the action, but Graves worried constantly over his 'mutilated' fleet, which he thought incapable of sustaining another action. On 9 September the two fleets drifted apart: Graves made for New York, while de Grasse put about and sailed for the Chesapeake. Graves's retreat sealed the fate of Cornwallis's army, since de Grasse's fleet blocked the last possible escape route from the Yorktown peninsula.

On 10 September, de Grasse re-entered Hampton Roads, where another fleet was spotted at anchor. The French approached cautiously, fully aware that Graves's copper-bottomed vessels might have gained the Chesapeake ahead of their own ponderous battleships. The French recognition signal was hoisted and answered. The ships in the bay—eight warships and ten transports—belonged to de Barras, who had come from Newport with the army's provisions and siege train. De Barras had been something of a wild card in the whole operation. No one really knew whether he would come south (as he had promised to do) or cruise the waters off Newfoundland in search of prize money (as he had authority to do). His presence in the bay not only added strength to de Grasse's fleet, the transports he had brought with him could be put to immediate use to ferry the main Allied army from ports along the Chesapeake to the peninsula.

The remainder of the month, until 27 September, was spent in assembling the Allied army at Williamsburg, where Lafayette established his headquarters on 7 September. Lafayette had moved to the old colonial capital, which was about twelve miles from Yorktown, to prevent Cornwallis escaping into North Carolina. Cornwallis, indeed, might have slipped across the James River and marched into the Carolinas in early September; but he, like everyone else concerned, awaited word of the outcome of the naval action. When he finally received news of Graves's defeat, escape was out of the question. By late September neither Cornwallis nor Clinton nor Graves was in a position to do anything which might affect the outcome of the operations in Virginia.

On 28 September the Allied army marched on Yorktown in two columns. The last few days of the month were spent in investing (surrounding) the British position and in driving back minor British outposts.

The town of York (as it was called) stood on bluffs above the south bank of the York River. The ground surrounding the town was sandy and marshy but was generally level. The only high ground in the neighbourhood of the town was the plain known as the Pigeon Quarter which was slightly elevated over the rest of the terrain. From the Pigeon Quarter the ground sloped gently down to the town and the bluffs at the river bank.

Cornwallis's position was circumscribed by creeks which cut deep ravines through the loamy

ADMIRAL DE GRASSE

ground. Ordinarily, these ravines might have added great strength to the British position, since they formed a natural moat, but Cornwallis did not have enough men to hold an extended line, so this natural feature could not be fully exploited. The weakness of the garrison, which numbered just 7,500 men, had forced Cornwallis to resort to a system of detached redoubts for his outer line of defence. This outer line was vital to the garrison. So long as it held, the Allies could not open saps (zig-zag approach trenches) against the main line of defence ringing the town. Also, the Allies' big guns could not concentrate their fire against the garrison in the town until the ground covered by the detached forts was taken and converted into suitable positions for batteries.

The major detached positions in the British defensive network were:

1. The Fusiliers' Redoubt (so called because it was garrisoned by the 23rd Royal Welsh Fusiliers), which anchored the British right near the river.

2. Four small, incomplete forts, which covered the Hampton Road and the high ground of the Pigeon Quarter.

3. Redoubts No. 9 and No. 10 on the British left, which covered the approach to the village from the south-east.

Inexplicably, Cornwallis chose to weaken his position by abandoning the Hampton Road forts on the morning of 1 October. The French promptly occupied these works and converted them to their own use.

Tarleton's Legion and Simcoe's Queen's Rangers garrisoned Gloucester Point on the northern bank of the York River about one mile distant from Yorktown. This weak post, which completed Cornwallis's defensive arrangements, was watched by French marines, the Duc de Lauzun's Legion and Weedon's Virginia militia. The whole Allied force in this sector was commanded by the Marquis de Choisy.

The Allied army facing Yorktown was divided into two wings. The French wing, on the left, was commanded by Rochambeau. It consisted of 7,500 men, including St Simon's West Indian detachment of three regiments (Touraine, Gatinais, and Agenais), which de Grasse had brought from the Caribbean, and Rochambeau's own expeditionary corps of four regiments (Saintonge, Soissonnais, Royal Deux-Ponts, and Bourbonnais), which had marched from Newport. The American wing held the right of the Allied line. It was commanded by General Benjamin Lincoln and consisted of 5,500 Continentals in three

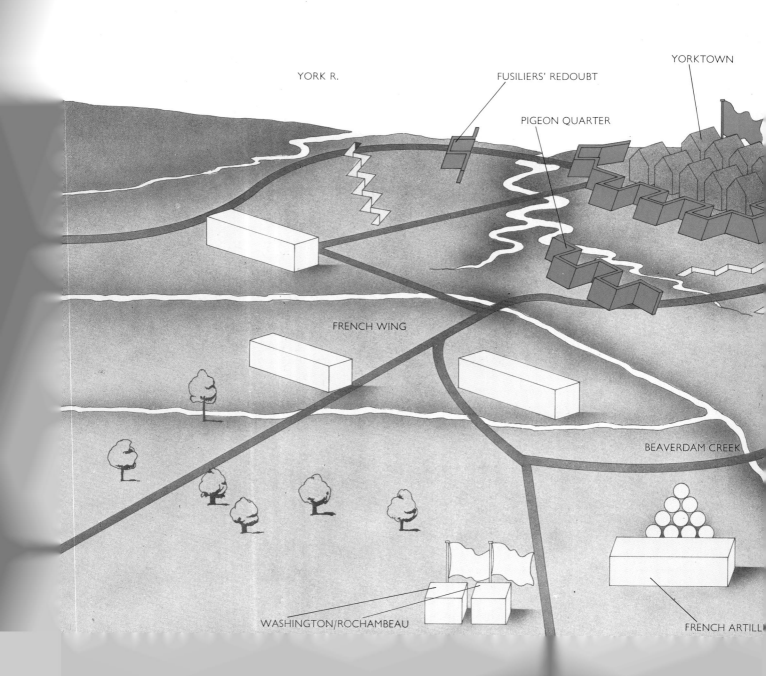

YORK R.

FUSILIERS' REDOUBT

YORKTOWN

PIGEON QUARTER

FRENCH WING

BEAVERDAM CREEK

WASHINGTON/ROCHAMBEAU

FRENCH ARTILLE

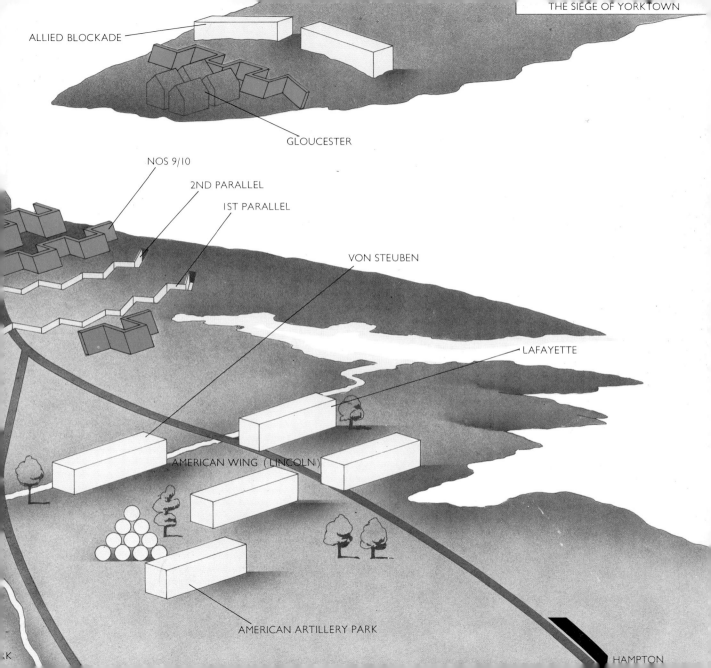

ALLIED BLOCKADE

GLOUCESTER

NOS 9/10

2ND PARALLEL

1ST PARALLEL

VON STEUBEN

LAFAYETTE

AMERICAN WING (LINCOLN)

AMERICAN ARTILLERY PARK

.K

HAMPTON

divisions and 2,000 Virginia militia under Governor Thomas Nelson, Jr.

Because of the nature of the ground, the Allies did not construct a continuous siege line. Instead, they opened their first parallel (a siege line extending parallel to the enemy's works) about 1,200 yards from Redoubts No. 9 and No. 10, and erected batteries opposite the Fusiliers' Redoubt. Otherwise, Cornwallis was blockaded by his own abandoned outworks and the extensive ravine nearly surrounding his inner line.

Eighteenth-century sieges were stylized, formal affairs, conducted according to a centuries-old ritual in which each step, from investment to surrender, was spelled out for the generals in universally accepted rules. The rules were so precise that they even prescribed who got what when the town was taken and given over to pillage. The artillery, for example, always got the church bells, which, of course, could be recast as cannon.

According to the rules, a besieged garrison was obliged to hold its lines until the enemy's artillery had opened a breach in the walls of the town. At that point, the garrison commander was supposed to surrender 'at discretion', and his men would be accorded the honours of war, that is, they would be permitted to march from the town 'with matches lit' (an old phrase referring to the matchlock musket), drums beating, and colours flying. It was considered bad form for the garrison commander to hold out longer once a breach had been made, because the besieging army might then have to resort to an assault on the works. This, of course, meant that the besiegers would lose a lot of men in taking the town. If the town were taken by storm, then it was given over to the soldiers for a time and subjected to an orgy of looting and uncontrolled rapine. Thus, even though Cornwallis's position was hopeless, he was obliged by the rules of the game to hold his lines until the Allies had brought up their artillery and by bombardment rendered his works untenable.

By 9 October, the entrenching parties of the Allied army had finished the laborious task of digging emplacements for the heavy guns and mortars of the siege train, and the bombardment of the British works was begun. According to legend Washington fired the first shot of the bombardment at dusk on the 9th, but French batteries near the Fusiliers' Redoubt were probably in action during the afternoon.

The Allied bombardment continued incessantly over the next several days and nights. The French gunners, who were masters of the artillerist's art, impressed their American colleagues by their skilful use of ricochet fire. By 'skipping' round shot over the British works they often made one ball do the work of several. Within the British lines the bombardment created scenes of indescribable devastation. Johann Doehla, a Hessian soldier, noted that: 'One could . . . not avoid the horribly many cannon balls either inside the city . . . many were badly wounded by the fragments of bombs [mortar shells] which exploded partly in the air and partly on the ground. . . .' Lieutenant Bartholomew James of the Royal Navy was particularly impressed by the intensity of the bombardment. On 11 October he wrote:

'I now want words to express the dreadful situation of the garrison. . . Upwards of a thousand shells were thrown into the works this night, and every spot became alike dangerous. The noise and thundering of the cannon, the distressing cries of the wounded, and the lamentable sufferings of the inhabitants, whose dwellings were chiefly in flames, added to the restless fatigues of the duty, must inevitably fill every mind with pity and compassion who are possessed of any feelings for their fellow creatures.'

Nothing within the British lines was safe from the bombardment. Cornwallis was forced out of his headquarters at the Nelson house, which, by the end of the siege, was levelled. On the night of 10 October the spectacle of the bombardment was further enlivened when St Simon's gunners turned some of their pieces nearest the river on the little squadron of transports and frigates which had conveyed Cornwallis's army from Portsmouth. In rapid succession the 44-gun frigate *Charon* and two transports were fired by hot-shot from the French battery. The frigate *Guadeloupe* and another transport managed to escape to the Gloucester side, where they sheltered under a bluff.

Cornwallis's situation had by now become desperate. The Allied artillery had easily established its superiority—both in number of guns and weight of metal. Ammunition in the British batteries was short, and many of the cannon had been dismounted or battered beyond repair. To add to the troubles of the British garrison, on the night of 11–12 October the Allies began work on a second parallel, just three hundred yards from Redoubts No. 9 and No. 10.

The Allied artillery fire at this stage was so effective that the British could do little to impede the progress of the working parties constructing a siege line under their very noses. By 14 October much of the work on this second parallel had been completed; but before the line could be made secure and extended to the river, the two British advanced redoubts would have to be taken by storm.

The task of assaulting these works was entrusted to picked men from the best units in each army. Redoubt No. 10, nearest the river, was the object of the American contingent, which consisted of 400 men from Lafayette's Light Infantry Division. This detachment was commanded by Colonel Alexander Hamilton. The French force, commanded by Colonel Guillaume des Deux-Ponts, was to assault Redoubt No. 9. It also numbered 400 men and was made up of the grenadiers and chasseurs of the Gatinais and Royal Deux-Ponts regiments. The assault was set for 8 pm on the evening of 14 October.

That night, at 8 o'clock exactly, six cannon were fired in rapid succession—the signal for the attack—and both assault columns moved briskly toward the British works. On the right the American light infantry advanced swiftly with bayonets levelled and unloaded muskets. Night attacks with the bayonet had been a speciality of the Continental light infantry ever since 'Mad Anthony' Wayne had led these same men in a daring assault on the British fort at Stony Point on 15–16 July 1779. As for the unloaded muskets, these derived from the bitter lesson administered by the infantry of the British General 'No Flint' Grey to Wayne's own Pennsylvanians at Paoli, in the bloody prelude to Germantown.

120

The French, on the left, went forward with equal gallantry. For the men of the Gatinais, there was a great deal at stake. The Gatinais Regiment had been formed from the old Auvergne Regiment, which had disappeared in an army re-organization. The men had never liked the change in regimental names. Rochambeau, who had commanded the Auvergne during the Seven Years' War, had promised the troops of the Gatinais that he would petition the king to restore the name Auvergne to the regiment if the men took the British redoubt. Then, as the men scrambled 'over the top', Rochambeau cheered them on with cries of 'Auvergne sans tache [Auvergne, without blemish]!'

Both assaults went in without a hitch. The Americans secured their objective first—just minutes after the start of the attack. In their haste to get at the enemy, the light infantrymen had swarmed past their sappers, who were hacking a path through

drove the defenders—120 men of the Hessian Regiment von Bose—into the fort's interior. After a short fire-fight in the darkness, the Hessians surrendered. The Deux-Ponts column suffered severely in the assault, however, losing 46 killed and 68 wounded.

The moment the redoubts had been secured and the prisoners taken away, entrenching parties moved forward from the first parallel and set to work incorporating the captured works into the Allied second parallel. The British were not unaware of their new predicament: throughout the night they poured a devastating fire into the working parties. Not surprisingly, some of the worst Allied casualties of the siege were sustained by the soldiers along the second parallel during that terrible night of 14–15 October. Nevertheless, by daylight the second parallel had been very nearly completed, and heavy cannon were being trundled forward to new posi-

CORNWALLIS
SURRENDERS TO THE
ALLIED COMMAND.

the redoubt's abatis, and scrambled or crawled through the obstructions. Then, shouting 'Rush-on-boys' (an American substitute for the attack's watchword, which was 'Rochambeau'), they poured into the fort from three directions. A brief mêlée followed, but within a few minutes the British and German defenders were overwhelmed. Hamilton's men sustained 40 casualties.

The French were not quite so lucky. The men of the Deux-Ponts were held up by a 'strong and well preserved' abatis and had to stand with ordered arms for five minutes under a galling fire while their sappers hacked away at the obstacle. Once the way was clear, they too mounted the earthworks and

tions in the line.

At this juncture, Cornwallis began to despair. On the night of the 15th, he wrote to Clinton describing the status of the garrison and warning against a relief expedition:

'Sir: Last evening the enemy carried my two advanced redoubts by storm, and during the night have included these in their second parallel, which they are at present busy in perfecting. My situation has now become very critical. We dare not show a gun to their old batteries, and I expect that their new ones will open to-morrow morning, so that we shall soon be exposed to an assault in ruined works, in a bad position, and with weakened numbers. The

121

safety of the place is therefore so precarious that I can not recommend that the fleet and army should run great risk in endeavouring to save us.'

A breach of the interior defences was now inevitable. Soon, Cornwallis would be faced with a terrible decision—should he surrender his post or await a massacre in his undermanned trenches? There were, however, a few desperate measures which might at least postpone the inevitable capitulation. The first of these would involve a surprise attack on the second parallel. With a little luck a raiding party could slip into the Allied lines, spike the guns in the great batteries and return before a counter-attack could be mounted. Such a raid might undo all the progress the Allies had made in the past few days.

The sortie was made just before dawn on the 16th. A party of 350 men from the Guards and flank companies of the British army entered the Allied second parallel near American Battery No. 2, which had been constructed between the two captured British redoubts. By chance the British raiders stumbled into a portion of the line that was nearly deserted. Picking their way along the trenches, they bayonetted a few drowsy fusiliers of the Agenais Regiment and fell on the gunners of an American battery. After dispersing the artillerymen, the trench raiders spiked the guns of the battery. Then, as Count de Noailles led a contingent of French grenadiers toward them, they quietly slipped away.

This bold raid in fact accomplished little other than to add several dozen more men to the casualty lists of each army. The trench raiders had no proper tools either for spiking the guns or disabling the gun carriages. The bayonets they had jammed into the touch-holes of the cannon were drilled out within hours, and the following morning the same guns were rolled into battery for another day's work.

On the evening of the 16th Cornwallis attempted an escape—the only alternative still open to him short of surrender. The escape plan involved transferring the army (excepting the sick and the baggage) to Gloucester Point in boats and attempting a breakout to the north against Choisy's weak contingent.

Although only 16 boats were available for the operation, all went well until the weather abruptly changed. According to Cornwallis's report, 'A most violent storm of wind and rain . . . drove all of the boats, some of which had troops on board, down the river'. The failure of this plan and the desperate situation of the garrison at last forced Cornwallis to propose a surrender.

At 9 am on the morning of 17 October a British drummer scrambled to the top of the hornwork at the south-east apex of the British lines. There, not three hundred yards from the Allied batteries, he donned his drum and beat the *chamade*, the signal for a parley. In the fury of the bombardment he might have been missed, since no one could hear the drumbeat above the roar of the guns. Still, he stood his ground, manfully rapping out the plaintive beat. Finally, he was spotted and word was passed for the cannon to cease firing. As the guns fell silent a British officer mounted the parapet and, accompanied by the drummer boy, walked toward the American lines waving a white handkerchief. The siege had ended—four years exactly since the surrender of Burgoyne's army at Saratoga.

The details of the capitulation remained to be worked out. Both armies appointed commissioners to arrange terms, and on 18 October the Articles of Capitulation were drafted at the Moore House behind the first parallel. On the 19th the document was signed.

For the brave men of the British army there remained but one more trial. In outlining his terms to Cornwallis, Washington had specified that 'The same Honors will be granted to the Surrendering Army as were granted to the Garrison of Charles Town'. This meant that the British army was not to be granted the honours of war. At Charleston in 1780 Sir Henry Clinton had refused to grant the honours of war to General Benjamin Lincoln's Continentals. Instead, the American army had been required to march from the town with colours cased. Cornwallis had been second-in-command on that occasion, and most of the men in the Yorktown garrison had been present as onlookers. Now, Lincoln stood at Washington's side as commander of the American wing. Pride, not pettiness, demanded the imposition of harsh terms.

The last act of the Yorktown drama was played out in the afternoon of the 19th. At 2 pm the British and German regiments of Cornwallis's army, resplendent in newly issued uniforms, marched from their crumbling works toward the surrender field a mile or so away along the York–Hampton road. According to legend the long column was led by a band playing the melancholy English air, *The World Turn'd Upside Down*. 'Light Horse Harry' Lee, who witnessed this sad procession, recalled that 'Universal silence was observed amidst the vast concourse, and the utmost decency prevailed, exhibiting in demeanor an awful sense of the vicissitudes of human life, mingled with commiseration for the unhappy'.

And so the Siege of Yorktown, historically the greatest British defeat until Dunkirk, passed into history. Ironically, Sir Henry Clinton, whose incompetent leadership had combined with Cornwallis's impetuosity to produce this previously unthinkable disaster, was at that moment sailing to the garrison with a powerful army.

Cornwallis surrendered nearly 8,000 soldiers and seamen. Among the impedimenta of war taken were 144 cannon, 24 colours, numerous warships and transports, and the army's war chest of £2,113. 6. 0. British casualties during the siege were 156 killed, 326 wounded and 70 missing. The Allies lost 75 killed and 199 wounded.

The Siege of Yorktown, like the Battle of Saratoga, has justifiably been regarded as among the more decisive military events of history. The war, of course, continued for two years after the capitulation at Yorktown, but no significant military actions occurred during that period.

When Lord North, the brilliant but adipose British Prime Minister, heard the news of Cornwallis's defeat he is said to have exclaimed: 'Oh God! Oh God! It is all over. It is all over'. He might have been referring to his ministry, which survived only a few months more under tremendous Opposition pressure; but more likely he meant that Yorktown had ended British pretensions of crushing the American Revolution by military force. The American victory quite literally broke the back of the British war effort.

Article 10.th

The solemn Ratifications of the present Treaty expedited in good & due Form shall be exchanged between the contracting Parties in the Space of Six Months or sooner if possible to be computed from the Day of the Signature of the present Treaty. In Witness whereof we the undersigned their Ministers Plenipotentiary have in their Name and in Virtue of our Full Powers signed with our Hands the present Definitive Treaty, and caused the Seals of our Arms to be affixed thereto.

Done at Paris, this third Day of September, In the Year of our Lord one thousand seven hundred & Eighty three. —

D Hartley   John Adams   B Franklin   John Jay —

THE OFFICIAL MANUSCRIPT COPY
OF THE TREATY OF PARIS, SIGNED ON 3 SEPTEMBER 1783,
BY WHICH GREAT BRITAIN RECOGNIZED
THE INDEPENDENCE OF THE UNITED STATES.
THE TREATY WAS SIGNED FOR THE UNITED STATES
BY BENJAMIN FRANKLIN, JOHN ADAMS AND JOHN JAY,
AND BY DAVID HARTLEY FOR GREAT BRITAIN.
THEIR PERSONAL SEALS APPEAR BELOW
THEIR SIGNATURES.

INDEX

124

125

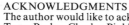

ACKNOWLEDGMENTS
The author would like to acknowledge the help of the following people: Terry Purke, Charles Pinkham and Kim Holien of the 3rd Virginia Regiment of the Continental Line, Brigade of the American Revolution; Bill Wigham of the Hèssian Regiment von Dittfurth B.A.R., and Thomas DeVoe of Morgan's Rifle Corps, B.A.R.

Roxby Press would like to express particular gratitude to The Library of Congress, Washington D.C., The National Army Museum, Chelsea and Lt.-Col. G. A. Shepherd, M.B.E., of R.M.A. Sandhurst.

They also acknowledge the courtesy of the following agencies and institutions for the illustrations in this volume: The Cooper Bridgeman Library, The Delaware Art Museum and Wilmington Society of Fine Arts, The Historical Society of Pennsylvania, The Mansell Collection, Mary Evans Picture Library, The National Portrait Gallery, London, Yale University Art Gallery.

Illustrations and maps for this volume were prepared and drawn by David Pocknell. Peter Gilder made the models and supervised the photographs which are by Ivor Innes.